Cover Photos: *Captain William J. Fetterman*
Margaret Sullivant Carrington
American Horse

Civilian, Military and Native American Portraits of Fort Phil Kearny

by members of the
Fort Phil Kearny/Bozeman Trail Association

Foreword
Catherine Curtiss

Introductions
Michael Massie
Joseph M. Marshall

Editorial Committee
Catherine Curtiss, Project Director
John D. McDermott
Mary Ellen McWilliams
Sonny Reisch

Published by
The Fort Phil Kearny/Bozeman Trail Association
528 Wagon Box Road
Banner, Wyoming 82832
1993

Additional Editing, Bibliography, Typography and Proofreading
CYNDE GEORGEN

Map
ROBERT C. WILSON

Cover Design
Michelle Gable
I.A.P., Inc.

Cover Photo Concept
Richard Schmidt

Printed in Wyoming
Pioneer Printing
Cheyenne, Wyoming

Second Printing 2001

ISBN 1-878856-14-6

Dedicated
to the memory of
Bozeman Trail Explorer

MARK D. BADGETT

As one of the original organizers and past President of the Fort Phil Kearny/Bozeman Trail Association, this book was his idea. It was also his idea to involve authors from the same diverse backgrounds and points of view as were represented by those people who were part of the Fort Phil Kearny story.

Primary funding for this publication was granted by the
HOMER A. AND MILDRED S. SCOTT FOUNDATION
Sheridan, Wyoming

with additional financial assistance from the
PETER KIEWIT FOUNDATION
Omaha, Nebraska

NICKERSON FAMILY FOUNDATION
MARK BADGETT MEMORIAL FUND
AND FORT PHIL KEARNY/BOZEMAN TRAIL ASSOCIATION
P.O. Box 5013
Sheridan, Wyoming 82801

Table of Contents

Foreword

The history of every country is born in the heart of a man or woman.
Willa Cather

The seeds for this book were planted by Mark Badgett, a lifelong Bozeman Trail enthusiast and researcher. Mark walked over 350 miles of the trail, delighting in the scenery and wildlife and pondering the impact of the Bozeman Trail era on both Euro and Native American lives. He commented one day, "You know, everyone was here." By that he meant fur trappers and traders, soldiers and their commanders, civilian contractors, women and children, government reconnaissance teams, emigrants on their way to the gold fields, and some of the leading Sioux, Cheyenne, Arapaho and Crow warriors, their bands and families. The Bozeman Trail era and Fort Phil Kearny touched the lives of an enormous number of people.

Mark's comments inspired many questions. Who were these people? Where did they come from and where did they go? How did the Trail and the Fort affect their lives? Did they ever again think of their time on the high plains of the Dakota Territory? How did the incursion of Euro Americans change the lives of Native Americans in their struggle to live on the lands granted to them by the Fort Laramie Treaty of 1851?

In order to pursue answers to the above questions, the Fort Phil Kearny/Bozeman Trail Association sent out a request, in the Association newsletter, asking interested members to write a biography on the life of someone who travelled the Trail, lived at the Fort, or lived in the villages along Powder and Tongue Rivers.

The response -- overwhelming and exciting -- came from Association members all over the United States and beyond, from people in all walks of life. The response mirrors the passion and curiosity Americans have with the part played by the American West in shaping the heritage, character, values and legacy of the United States. This legacy, though fascinating, can be disquieting because it involves the history of many people who were displaced and denied the rights we all cherish and value as citizens of the United States.

The project's intent was not one of judgement but one which could help promote an understanding of all viewpoints and lead to a more complete understanding of the part played by a diversity of people during the Bozeman Trail and Fort Phil Kearny era. We cannot change the past but we can, through understanding and awareness, work towards a more cooperative future.

The editorial committee was dedicated to ensuring that the writers of the biographies were able to express their own thoughts and opinions. Thus the committee gave wide reign to the writers. The editorial committee, consisting of Mary Ellen McWilliams, Sonny Reisch, Jack McDermott and myself, collectively reviewed each biography to check for historical accuracy, not viewpoint. Because our access to the references within each biography was limited, the committee was unable to check every footnote and reference, nor the complete accuracy of all historical information. Therefore, each author remains individually responsible for the accuracy of his or her biography.

The committee had great fun reviewing the biographies. In addition, we increased our own understanding of the impact of the Bozeman Trail era and Fort Phil Kearny on the lives of both Euro and Native Americans.

Our hope is that you as readers will be inspired to find a character in history who fascinates you and follow the path of his or her life. It is a wonderful adventure. In addition, we hope that if you find new information on any of the people included in this book, you will drop the Association a note. Understanding our past and finding all the documents and diaries is an enormous task and we invite you to participate in our adventure. History is not just for scholars, it is for all of us. History is the story of humanity and we are all part of that drama.

Catherine Curtiss, Project Director

A Time For Change

Dipping a gold pan into Grasshopper Creek accelerated the pace of change. For John White, the flakes of gold he retrieved from the streambed meant that searching for the big strike had ended and he could settle in the mountainous country of southwestern Montana. For the thousands of natives who had lived in this area for generations, the flood of newcomers who would descend on the area to strike it rich would change their lives forever.

During the last half of the nineteenth century, the West experienced the most dramatic changes in its history since the arrival of humans. Between 1850 and 1890, the American Indians who had lived on the land for at least 10,000 years were generally displaced by new peoples possessing different cultures and values. This transitional era precipitated diverse responses as each group struggled to adapt to new economies or environments. The Northern Plains region was not immune to these forces of change. Indeed, some of the most dramatic events in the nation's history unfolded in this arid region, with the brief two-year struggle for control of the land around Fort Phil Kearny symbolizing the efforts of two disparate cultures to control their destinies.

The geographic boundaries of the Northern Plains consist of the Yellowstone River on the north, the North Platte River on the south, the Big Horn Mountains to the west and the Black Hills to the east. Experts differ concerning the arrival of the first humans in the region. Based upon their oral traditions, many American Indians believe that they have always lived in this area. Conversely, most anthropologists, interpreting the physical remains, contend that humans first arrived approximately 10,000 years ago, although this date is constantly revised as older archaeological materials surface.

The inhabitants have depended upon the environment's natural resources to provide them with a living. When the region's climate grew significantly drier about eight thousand years ago, the natives converted from hunters stalking big game such as the wooly mammoth, to hunters and gatherers who utilized many plants and wildlife to forge a living. The dry, hot climate eventually forced most people to leave the plains to live in the mountains or in more moderate climes to the north.

The arrival of the Little Ice Age about five hundred years ago brought more moisture, cooler weather and many changes to the plains. A diverse ecosystem evolved with relatively lush vegetation and plentiful wildlife, including a rapidly-expanding population of bison which feasted with little competition on the tall grasses. Lured by this abundant supply of plants and animals, American Indians soon returned permanently, creating a lifestyle that efficiently exploited the environment's resources. While a few tribes chose a primarily agricultural existence, most embraced a culture that centered around the bison.

The Plains Indian culture evolved over the next four centuries. Because the buffalo spent most of the year in small groups, The Plains people did likewise, with tribes dividing into small groups, or bands, for all but two or three weeks of the year. These bands formed the foundation of human life on the plains. Each band was politically autonomous, selecting their leaders based upon hunting skills, bravery, service to the community and other abilities important to survival on the plains. In some bands, such as the Cheyenne, the people divided the decision-making among several individuals. If a leader failed to provide adequate guidance, his (or sometimes her) influence dwindled, or a family simply moved to another band with a leader more to its liking. Due to this democratic, decentralized political system, a Plains tribe never embraced one leader, although a few men temporarily exerted some symbolic or spiritual influence over several bands. Many of the leaders who later became well-known to Whites, such as Sitting Bull, Morning Star (Dull Knife), Crazy Horse, Red Cloud and Plenty Coups, were actually band leaders.

Religious or spiritual advisors usually received special status because their visions, foresight and knowledge enhanced the groups' ability to remain in balance with the environment. This equilibrium was crucial in a region that produced severe and sudden climatic changes that challenged the peoples' well-being. Through ceremonies, vision quests and oral traditions, medicine men did not attempt to forestall change but to anticipate it and provide advice in adjusting to it.

The family formed the core of the band's social life, with each member performing specific duties. A band was successful if it possessed plenty of horses, the people were good-natured, the children well-behaved and there was sufficient food to feed everyone, including the needy.

The vast landscape of the plains and the decentralized nature of the Plains Indian culture eroded tribal identities at times. To reinforce their shared heritage, the scattered bands of a tribe reunited for a period of two or three weeks each year, usually when the buffalo would briefly congregate to migrate or mate. Socializing and hunting culminated in a Sun Dance, a ceremony to reaffirm tribal identity and maintain the precious balance with nature and God.

When Euro-Americans arrived in North America, they entered a world of diverse civilizations that had dealt with change for millennia. For most natives living on the Northern Plains, seeing a White person for the first time elicited curiosity but not astonishment; the material culture of the newcomers had presaged their physical presence by decades. After temporarily expelling the Spaniards from New Mexico in 1680, the Pueblo Indians used the horses that the retreating foreigners left behind to enhance trade with the neighboring tribes. This significantly increased the size of the herds of many Southwestern bands. Within a few decades, the Shoshones in the Great Basin region of what is now Utah acquired a number of these critters and used their mastery in riding the horse to conquer their neighbors to the northeast, eventually expanding their territory through the western end of the Northern Plains to the Canadian border.

A federation of tribes led by the Blackfoot counter-attacked after purchasing guns from British traders. By the nineteenth century, the Shoshones had retreated south to western Wyoming while the Blackfoot, Crow and Assiniboine occupied much of the Northern Plains. Life remained in flux when the Lakota and Cheyenne, combining mastery of the horse and gun, expanded rapidly from the east to vie for control of the region. By staying in the Central Plains throughout much of this era, the Arapaho avoided most of these intertribal conflicts but eventually formed an alliance with the Cheyenne and Lakota.

The horse and gun modified the Plains Indian culture but did not change it. Instead, most bands incorporated these technologies into their daily lives, making hunting more efficient, travel easier and chance encounters with other tribes more likely. When Whites later arrived on the Northern Plains, they did not enter an empty wilderness but stumbled into a dynamic milieu of communities, economies and alliances.

In anticipation of the White settlement of the West, the federal government implemented its traditional Indian policy of removing natives from the paths of settlers to avoid conflicts. Initially, this consisted of eliciting promises from Plains tribes not to attack emigrants in exchange for annuities or recognition that a band controlled certain lands. By the 1860s, the reservation era had dawned in which the government would confine Indians to limited areas of the region and attempt to teach them Euro-American values. Most of the proponents of this policy envisioned that the acculturation process would culminate in the elimination of the reservations after the missionaries and agents had converted the natives from nomadic hunters to independent farmers. In addition, this policy also extinguished American Indian ownership of most of the West's natural resources.

The discovery of gold in California in 1848 tested this strategy for the first time. Thousands of Easterners rushed to the West coast either on ships or alongside wagons following the Oregon Trail. Emigrants had been using this overland path for a number of years to travel to Oregon and California for cheap farmland or to Utah for religious freedom. This trail closely followed the North Platte and Sweetwater rivers to its midway point at South Pass, Wyoming. From 1840-1860, approximately 300,000 emigrants travelled this route, most of them seeking their fortunes in the gold fields.

Worried that the sudden appearance of so many foreigners would precipitate conflicts with the natives, the federal government met with several Northern Plains bands in 1851 on Horse Creek in the Nebraska Territory, just downstream from an old fur trading center and the recently established military post of Fort Laramie. Like many other agreements between Whites and American Indians, the resulting treaty meant something different to each group. The United States thought that it had guaranteed the protection of the overland emigrants, won permission to establish military posts and assigned each tribe to large reservations in order to halt intertribal warfare. Guided by their distinct interests, each band interpreted the treaty somewhat differently, but they generally rejected the notion that a relatively powerless foreign government could restrict their movements or dictate their foreign policies. In addition, several bands declined to attend the discussions and thus were not bound by the accord. The credibility of the treaty was further eroded when the U.S. unilaterally changed the amount of the annuities that it promised to distribute to the participating tribes.

The failure of this initial effort at diplomacy did not result in American Indian attacks on the Oregon Trail emigrants. Instead, trade and cooperation characterized the relationship between White and Indian. When overland travel increased after the discovery of gold in California, conflicts arose but they usually occurred west of South Pass. However, the trail presented other problems for the residents of the plains, for the travellers inadvertently spread diseases that wreaked havoc on some villages. Their stock overgrazed the prairie adjacent to the route and the emigrants' desire for fresh meat resulted in the elimination of wildlife along the route. As a result of this damage, many Lakota, Cheyenne and Arapaho bands avoided the road.

The gold that lured emigrants through the North Platte River valley would eventually bring permanent settlers to the region. More than any other activity, gold and silver mining led to the White settlement of the West. Discoveries in the late 1850s at the Comstock Lode in Nevada and along the front range of the Central Rockies initiated four decades of continuous strikes throughout the Rocky Mountains. Towns were created overnight to service the itinerant prospectors. In just a few months, creeks were diverted, streambeds excavated, mines sunk, streets leveled, hundreds of buildings erected, wildlife eradicated and forests cleared in areas that had supported smaller Indian communities for centuries. These sudden environmental, economic and social changes were not confined to a few miles around the towns and mines. They spread for hundreds of miles because of the construction of trails that permitted the hauling of people and cargo to the isolated boomtowns.

John White's 1862 gold strike on Grasshopper Creek brought these sudden changes to the Northern Plains. Even though the resulting gold mining towns of Bannack and Virginia City existed on the periphery of this region, John Bozeman and John Jacobs' promotion of an emigrant route to the east of the Big Horn Mountains permitted this mining rush to touch the lives of the members of several tribes. To prospectors, a straight line was the best route to a mining strike, and there were no good direct routes to the Montana gold mines. Most miners took the Oregon Trail to Fort Hall, where they followed a long, winding path through the mountains of eastern Idaho and over the Continental Divide. Or they pushed their way up the Missouri River on boats before disembarking at Fort Benton to travel overland through broken country on a primitive road. In contrast, Bozeman and Jacobs' trail (which became known as the Bozeman Trail) provided a direct route over gently rolling plains from the Oregon Trail near the North Platte River to the gold mining camps.

The Arapaho, Cheyenne, Lakota and Crow, usually allies of the Whites, opposed the Bozeman Trail, not only because it disrupted the last tribal hunting grounds on the Northern Plains but because they possessed fresh memories of the disaster experienced near the Oregon Trail. A small group of Indian men conveyed their resentment during Bozeman and Jacobs' initial trip from Bannack to mark the trail in 1863 when the natives relieved them of most of their possessions and clothing.

Undaunted, Jacobs and Bozeman proceeded on their journey south to the North Platte River where they began their new guiding business by leading a group of emigrants back up the route that summer. At approximately the mid-point of the trail, near present-day Buffalo, several Cheyenne and Lakota explained to the party that the proposed road violated a treaty by crossing their hunting grounds and warned the emigrants that they would attack if the wagons proceeded up the trail. While most of the settlers heeded this advice and returned south, Bozeman and nine other men forged ahead by taking another passage to the west, over the Big Horn Mountains to the gold camps. Ignoring the warnings, Bozeman guided another wagon train over the route the next year, a journey that many other emigrant parties would repeat.

The growing tension between natives and intruders was exacerbated in 1865 when General Patrick Connor led a military expedition to the Northern Plains in reaction to recent fights between some Lakota and

Cheyenne bands and the army along the North Platte River. After establishing Fort Connor on the Powder River, Connor and his men attacked an Arapaho village on the Tongue River. Parts of this command nearly starved to death later that year while looking for more locals to battle. (The site of this engagement with the Arapahos is now called Connor Battlefield State Park.) The campaign accomplished little other than to steel the resolve of the tribes to maintain control of this region.

Hoping to avoid a war, the federal government invited many of the region's bands to Fort Laramie in 1866 to discuss a solution to the increasing violence. Unfortunately, the government failed to tell the Indians that it had already decided to construct forts on the Bozeman Trail. The arrival during the negotiations of Colonel Henry Carrington's Eighteenth Infantry, Second Battalion, shattered the Whites' credibility and precipitated the departure of several bands. Those that remained signed the treaty which permitted the army to fortify the trail. Congress never ratified this agreement.

The army constructed two military posts, Fort Phil Kearny and Fort C. F. Smith, and replaced the weary troops at Fort Connor, renamed Fort Reno. Carrington and his entourage settled at Fort Phil Kearny at the junction of Piney and Little Piney creeks, near present-day Story, Wyoming. Given the diversity of the occupants, the fort was a small town, with women, children, traders, farmers, mountain men, wood choppers, hay crews and mule skinners in the company of approximately seven hundred soldiers. Primarily due to military contracts, the post attracted many civilians, especially entrepreneurs who sought to fulfill the needs of the army. Businesses were created and farms were started. The erection of the fort resembled the founding of a gold town in that it resulted in the sudden establishment of a White community in the heart of Indian country. The post posed a more significant threat to the Indians' control of the area than the trail did.

The Lakota, Cheyenne and Arapaho were divided as to how to resolve this latest intrusion. This is not surprising, given the nature of the decentralized band system. Many of the leaders who had refused to sign the Fort Laramie treaty, such as Red Cloud and Man Afraid of His Horse, wanted to eradicate the settlement of foreigners while others, particularly Morning Star, advocated trade and negotiation. Some groups, including Sitting Bull's band, continued to avoid the Euro-Americans. With the continued presence of the United States Army, however, conflict was inevitable.

Several skirmishes transpired in the fall of 1866 before Crazy Horse and several other American Indians lured Captain William Fetterman's command into a trap, wiping out all of the seventy-nine soldiers and two civilians. Armed engagements continued for the next year and a half until the government decided to withdraw its forces from the trail, abandoning the posts in August of 1868.

The construction of the Union Pacific Railroad across southern Wyoming was proceeding quickly, and its transcontinental link with the Central Pacific Railroad the following year provided quick transportation to several trailheads leading to the Montana gold fields. The Bozeman Trail was no longer the most expeditious route. Just as importantly, the army simply could not continue to defend the trail and posts against a people who were determined to maintain their way of life.

The 1868 Fort Laramie treaty ended the war while sowing seeds for the next one. The Arapaho, Cheyenne and Lakota bands who signed the pact agreed to live near Indian agencies for a few months in order to collect annuities from the federal government, but were free to hunt and live on the Northern Plains for the remainder of the year. Several band leaders, including Sitting Bull, refused to participate in the talks. This treaty lasted until the discovery of gold in the Black Hills in 1874, when thousands of miners rushed to this most sacred of areas to the Cheyenne and Lakota. When the tribes refused to sell the Black Hills to the Whites, the army in 1876 sent three expeditions into the area to force the Cheyenne and Lakota onto smaller reservations. Even though a powerful force of warriors stopped one column and nearly annihilated another, led by Colonel George Custer, military defeats the following winter and the near-extinction of the buffalo at the hands of hide hunters and the railroad eventually forced the natives to accept reservations in the Dakotas and Montana.

In describing this volatile period on the Northern Plains, some historians and writers convey the impression that the outcome was inevitable; that technologically superior cultures naturally dominate and subdue more primitive ones. The only element of this era that was inescapable was change. There were many solutions to the sudden economic and social changes imposed upon the American Indians that would have left them with enough freedom and sufficient access to the region's natural resources in order for them to make their own adjustments during this transitional era.

Instead, the same forces that compelled them to move onto small reservations have plagued them over the past century. Because the federal government did not take its treaty obligations seriously, the tribes lost control of much of their remaining resources, either in further land cessions to Western states, loss of water rights to nearby developers, or cheap long-term leases of their land and minerals. They have also endured programs that mandated the acceptance of Euro-American values in place of their cultural traditions. Despite government policies which sought to acculturate and, at times, assimilate Native Americans, they did not go the way of the buffalo on the Northern Plains. By the 1960s, the American Indians had reasserted enough control over the reservations to achieve several legal and legislative victories in recapturing some of their economic, political and social rights. Even the buffalo has managed to reappear in some parts of the Northern Plains.

After the forced withdrawal of the Indians in 1876, White settlers slowly migrated into the region during the following decades, many of them using the Bozeman Trail. The establishment of Fort McKinney attracted farmers, ranchers and merchants who founded the town of Buffalo, Wyoming. Other communities were created, and while ranching formed the area's economic foundation, coal mining began to play an important role in the 1890s. Today,the Powder River area is the nation's top producer of coal.

The Northern Plains experienced significant changes in a brief thirty year period. In the place of small, semi-nomadic communities dependent upon the region's wildlife and plants, came larger, more permanent towns that rely upon technologies and global markets in exploiting the natural resources of the region.

The following biographies examine an important part of this transitional era by investigating the people and forces that created the brief history of Fort Phil Kearny. The authors, who have backgrounds and experiences as diverse as the occupants of the fort and Indian communities, explore many of the issues, ideas, and events that shaped this region's past, as well as much of Western history. As the biographies demonstrate, none of the historical figures were powerful enough to forestall or control change. It is how they dealt with change that influenced their futures and that of the Northern Plains.

MICHAEL MASSIE

ACCULTURATION & ASSIMILATION & NATIVE AMERICANS

A TREATISE

Acculturation and assimilation are freely applied terms in most discussions concerning the interaction between Native Americans and European Americans. Both are a part of the interaction of at least two diverse cultures. Beyond that generalization, they are two different social and intercultural phenomena. Acculturation and assimilation were both powerful forces in the interaction of Native Americans and European Americans. Assimilation was a stated policy of the United States government in its dealings with the various Native American tribes and cultures. It was a process which was applied and could be controlled. Acculturation, although it was (and sometimes still is) grandiosely touted as "policy," was a more natural and less controllable consequence of the interaction of two very diverse groups of people in North America.

To understand the difference between these two different social and intercultural phenomena, it is essential to know the basic definition of both. *Acculturation* is intercultural borrowing between diverse peoples, often resulting in new and blended patterns; and it is the process by which one acquires or becomes familiar with the culture of another society. *Assimilation* means simply to absorb, or to make similar.

Historically, both Native Americans and Europeans were acculturated as a consequence of their interaction. Acculturation does not necessarily require amicable interaction. Nor does it require that one of the interactive groups be technologically advanced or "superior" in any way. The basic and only requirement is that the interactive groups be different from one another. Contemporarily, acculturation is a significant aspect of the continuing interaction between Native Americans and Euro-Americans. It occurs with each succeeding generation, because acculturation could not erode or destroy the core aspects of Native American cultures.

Assimilation, on the other hand, was an intended and stated policy actively and intensely pursued by the United States government, with the support of Christian missionaries, to change Native Americans into productive, "civilized" citizens of American society. The basic intent of assimilation, as so applied, was to strip Native Americans of their inherent cultural traits, languages, values, traditions and customs. In short, to destroy one identity and replace it with another -- which was thought to be a better one.

For a period of time, Native Americans had no choices in the assimilative process. It was forced on us. Though assimilation is no longer obviously a stated or apparently enforced government policy, there are still many Euro-Americans who subscribe to the thesis that Native Americans are better off being assimilated into the dominant and therefore "superior" society. Therefore, acculturation and assimilation, as far as I am concerned, are both still significant forces in the lives of Native Americans. We are acculturated to life as it is now, since most of us choose to be a part of it. But we still resist assimilation.

Acculturation does not necessarily mean giving up or losing the core aspects of our cultures. It simply means knowing as much as possible about American society so that we can function within it the best we can -- and still be Native American. Many of us resist assimilation for the same reasons our ancestors did a few generations ago. We do not want to change. We see great value in ourselves as we are. We see a great value in our own cultures, and know that we are a part of the community of cultures which are a part of the entire human community. We resist assimilation because we know that we can make a better contribution to our society and the world, because we are stronger within the framework of our indigenous cultures.

JOSEPH M. MARSHALL

Chronology of Events 1851-1869

1851 The Fort Laramie Treaty recognizes the area between Powder River and the Big Horn mountains as "Crow Territory," but also recognizes the right of other tribes to hunt on and pass over the land.

1855 - 1865 Sioux and Cheyenne expand in force between Powder River and the Big Horns, pushing the Crow to the north.

1861 - 1865 The Civil War causes the U.S. Army to recall western forces for the war in the East.

1862 Gold is discovered in Montana.

1863 The Bozeman Trail is established as a shorter route to the gold fields of Montana; it is routed through the Northern Plains Indians' last and best hunting grounds.

1865 The Civil War ends. The U.S. Army turns its attention to the increasing hostilities between settlers, emigrants and Indian tribes in the West.

The Connor Expedition pushes up the Trail, attacking a non-hostile Arapaho village on Tongue River and driving many Arapaho into alliance with the Sioux and Cheyenne.

Fort Connor, later Fort Reno, is established along the Bozeman Trail in August.

Treaties signed at Fort Sully are claimed by the U.S. Government as having restored peace, though many Sioux leaders did not sign them and are unaware of a provision allowing the government to build roads and forts in the territory.

1866 Colonel Henry B. Carrington is ordered to garrison Fort Reno and build two more forts to protect emigrants along the Bozeman Trail.

Fort Phil Kearny is established on Piney Creek in July.

Fort C. F. Smith is established ninety miles north of Phil Kearny in August.

The Indians almost succeed in luring Carrington and Fetterman into a trap on December sixth.

The entire command of Captain William J. Fetterman is destroyed near Fort Phil Kearny by combined forces of the Sioux, Cheyenne and Arapaho on December twenty-first.

1867 Carrington is relieved of command of Fort Phil Kearny in January. Colonel Henry Wessells takes command and is later replaced by Colonel Johnathan Smith.

The Indians attack near Fort C. F. Smith in what is known as the Hayfield Fight on August first.

An Indian attack near Fort Phil Kearny is repulsed in what is known as the Wagon Box Fight on August second.

1868 The Treaty of 1868 calls for the abandonment of Forts Reno, Phil Kearny and C. F. Smith, and the Bozeman Trail by the Army. Indians burn Fort Phil Kearny after the soldiers leave.

1869 Completion of the transcontinental railroad makes the Bozeman Trail unnecessary for reaching the gold fields of Montana. Until the last major Indian Wars of 1876-77 (including the Battle of the Little Big Horn), the country is left to the Indians.

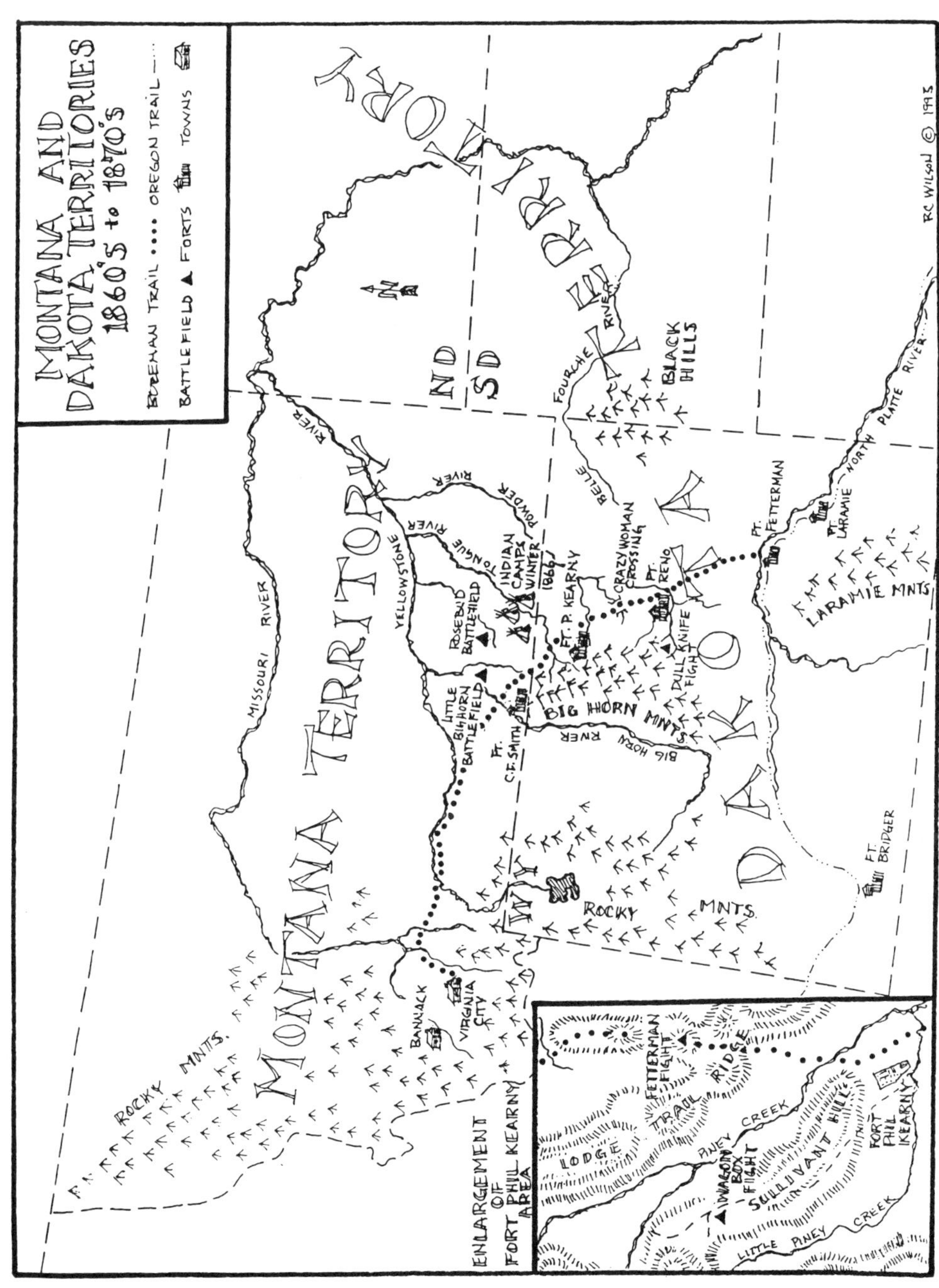
MONTANA AND DAKOTA TERRITORIES 1860's to 1870's
BOZEMAN TRAIL •••• OREGON TRAIL ——
BATTLEFIELD ▲ FORTS TOWNS
DAKOTA TERRITORY
MONTANA TERRITORY
ND
SD
WY
FOURCHE RIVER
BLACK HILLS
BELLE
POWDER RIVER
TONGUE RIVER
YELLOWSTONE
RIVER
MISSOURI RIVER
ROSEBUD BATTLEFIELD
INDIAN CAMPS WINTER 1866/7
FT. P. KEARNY
CRAZY WOMAN CROSSING
FT. RENO
FT. FETTERMAN
FT. LARAMIE
NORTH PLATTE RIVER
LARAMIE MNTS
DULL KNIFE FIGHT
BIG HORN MNTS
BIG HORN RIVER
LITTLE BIGHORN BATTLEFIELD
FT. C.F. SMITH
ROCKY MNTS
FT. BRIDGER
BANNACK
VIRGINIA CITY
ROCKY MNTS.
ENLARGEMENT OF FORT PHIL KEARNY AREA
FETTERMAN FIGHT
RIDGE
TRAIL
LODGE
PINEY CREEK
WAGON BOX FIGHT
SULLIVANT HILLS
FORT PHIL KEARNY
LITTLE PINEY CREEK
RC WILSON © 1993

JOHN BOZEMAN

John Marion Bozeman was born in Georgia in 1835. In 1860, he left a wife and three small daughters to go to the gold fields in Colorado, where he joined the Green Russell crowd of fellow Georgians in Georgia Gulch. However, all the better claims had been taken by the time he arrived, so in 1862 he went with the first party drawn to the newly discovered mines in what was to become Montana. He remained in the Deer Lodge Valley during the summer of 1862, but the work was arduous for little return. As soon as news came in January 1863 of rich discoveries on Grasshopper Creek he joined the rush to Bannack. But he apparently lost out again, and not securing a favorable location as well as tiring of the grinding drudgery, he lost interest in mining. In the spring of 1863 John Bozeman needed a new occupation -- and the rest is history.[1]

John Bozeman, John Jacobs, and Jacobs' half-blood daughter Emma, about eight years old, set out from Bannack in March 1863 to establish a shorter route to the gold fields from the Platte road, the main overland route to Idaho. They planned to locate a route to leave the Platte road somewhere west of Fort Laramie, go northwest along the eastern base of the Bighorn Mountains, cross the Bighorn River, follow up the Yellowstone, pass through the Bridger Mountains, and

---

[1]Merrill G. Burlingame, "John M. Bozeman, Montana Trailmaker," *Mississippi Valley Historical Review* 27 (March 1941):541-68; revised edition, 1971, has additional details and significant corrections; a second revised edition is widely available (Bozeman, Montana: Museum of the Rockies, 1983).

enter the Gallatin Valley. They left Bannack and traveled the route in reverse, apparently following Indian and trader trails much of the way. They were not heard from again, except for possibly being sighted once, until they arrived at Deer Creek station on the Platte road around the end of May.

Another party led by James Stuart left Bannack three weeks later to prospect for gold in the Yellowstone valley. On May eleventh, while traveling up the west bank of the Bighorn River, Stuart saw three riders leading three pack-horses coming down the opposite side of the river. When they were about opposite him, he called to them. They didn't return his call but kept on in the same direction at a faster pace. He and his men crossed the river and pursued them but could not catch them. In their trail however, they found a frying pan and a pack of cards. The encounter mystified Stuart, who could not figure out why the riders had not acknowledged him. He apparently did not recognize Bozeman or Jacobs, whom he knew well, nor did the riders recognize him. But in his note to his brother's journal when he edited it, Granville Stuart wrote in 1876 that the riders undoubtedly were Bozeman, Jacobs, and Jacobs' daughter.[2]

Two days later Bozeman's party encountered real trouble. They suddenly came upon a party of seventy-five mounted Indians, probably Sioux. Jacobs dropped his rifle and bullet pouch into the sagebrush before they saw him. The Indians took all their food and belongings and their horses, leaving them only three broken-down Indian ponies. After the Indians left, they retrieved the rifle and pouch, which was found to contain only five bullets. They went on but dared not stop to hunt, and they saw no game on their rapid trip southward. They arrived at Deer Creek in starving condition, around the end of May. They established a new camp near

---

[2]Granville Stuart, "The Yellowstone Expedition of 1863," *Contributions to the Montana Historical Society* 1 (1876):186-88.

Bissonette's trading post there and started recruiting emigrants to guide back to Montana on their new route.[3]

They spent a few weeks at Deer Creek gathering wagons, although relatively few emigrants that year were willing to take the risk of opening a new road through unknown country. Their train left on July sixth, but was stopped in the vicinity of present Buffalo, Wyoming, by a large party of Cheyennes. The Indians told them that if they went on they would kill all of them. After much discussion, it was decided they should turn back. However, Bozeman and nine companions on horseback went on to Montana. They went west and crossed the Bighorn Mountains, north through the Wind River Basin, through Pryor's Gap to the Yellowstone Valley, over a pass which one of the party named Bozeman Pass, and entered the Gallatin Valley where Bozeman is now. The rest of the 1863 train returned to the Platte road.[4]

In the spring of 1864, Bozeman returned to the Platte road and recruited a wagon train at Richard's Bridge, at present Evansville, Wyoming. That year he successfully led the first train to go over his route, which was largely over trails explored by Capt. F. W. Raynolds and Lt. H. E. Maynadier in 1859-1860. His train arrived in Virginia City at the end of July. On August ninth, Bozeman participated in the town meeting at which the new town of Bozeman was named after him. Two other large trains came over what has become known as the Bozeman Trail that summer, but Bozeman was never again to lead any emigrants over the route.

Bozeman probably would have led emigrants over the trail in 1865 as an employee of the newly organized Bozeman

---

[3]Oscar Collister, "Life of Oscar Collister, Wyoming Pioneer," *Annals of Wyoming* 7 (July and October 1930):370.

[4]John S. Gray, "Blazing the Bridger and Bozeman Trails," *Annals of Wyoming* 49 (Spring 1977):23-51.

to Fort Laramie Wagon Road Company, but the federal government banned all travel over it and launched a massive punitive campaign against the Indians in the Powder River country that summer. Bozeman may have been disappointed at losing the opportunity to guide emigrants over his new route, but he adapted in his usual versatile way by becoming an integral member of the growing community named for him. He remained in Bozeman and farmed, recorded land claims, recruited new businesses, and was elected probate judge.

When the prospects for a successful travel season in 1866 seemed assured, Bozeman was sent by the wagon road company to the Yellowstone crossing, where he set up a ferry operation. He set up the ferry about three miles east of Springdale, Montana, at the ford known as Bridger's Crossing. He was reported to be at the ferry from June until mid-September, when it was evidently abandoned on account of Indian troubles. Bozeman returned to his home in Bozeman to continue his other business interests.

Bozeman was about six feet tall with a ruddy complexion. Most observers described him as handsome, genial, kind and energetic. He was also known to be temperamental on occasion. He reportedly always wore a suit coat, even when traveling on the trail. Bozeman would have continued to scratch out a living, and we will never know if he would have gone on to become a successful local businessman or a forgotten unsuccessful one; but he was helped into legend by his untimely death at the hands of Indians on the very trail named for him.

In April 1867, John Bozeman and Tom Cover left Bozeman for Fort C. F. Smith to secure a flour contract for the new mill which Bozeman had attracted to his town. They spent the night of April seventeenth at Nelson Story's cattle camp near present Livingston, where Bozeman expressed his premonition to his longtime friend, W. S. McKinzie, that he would not come back from the trip alive.

Nevertheless, Bozeman and Cover continued on the next day. After traveling about ten miles, they stopped for a noon meal. They had just finished eating when they were approached by five Indians of the Piegan tribe of Blackfeet who were on foot, leading one pony. In the ensuing encounter Bozeman was killed, and Cover was wounded in the shoulder but escaped. Cover made his way back to Story's cattle camp, arriving in the early morning hours of April nineteenth.

Cover wrote his account of the incident -- in which he reported Bozeman was shot outright by the Indians and he barely escaped -- in a letter to Governor T. F. Meagher, May 4, 1867. All those involved in recovering Bozeman's body also reported that the culprits were Indians. Within weeks it was generally known that Bozeman's killers were Piegan renegades Mountain Chief and four of his sons and nephews. John Richard, Jr., a local mixed-blood businessman of the well-known Richard family, was with the first party to visit the scene. He subsequently traveled to Fort C. F. Smith to secure the flour contract for Cover, where on May sixth he described the incident to Lt. George Templeton. He also reported that the Blackfeet Indians who killed Bozeman were living with Crows, who were camped fifteen miles away.

As with most colorful Western figures who have died tragically, controversy about the circumstances of his death still lingers in Montana today. One of the leading figures in perpetuating questions about the incident was Nelson Story. Upon learning of Bozeman's death, Story accompanied several men to the site. Out of caution he sent a trusted employee, "Spanish Joe," ahead to check for Indian signs. Nelson later told his son T.B. that Joe found no signs of Indians, only suspicious evidence that indicated Cover had shot Bozeman and wounded himself to bolster his story. However, in many letters concerning the incident, Story always maintained that Indians killed Bozeman, and all the evidence to the contrary has been passed down as an oral tradition.

The truth about Bozeman's death will probably never be known.[5] But his death had the immediate effect of catalyst for the Montana Militia rampage, which was supposed to quell Indian depredations but only exacerbated the situation. The long-range effect was to immortalize his name. More important, the dramatic story of John Bozeman's life and death exemplifies the tenuous nature of our Western legends.

SUSAN BADGER DOYLE

---

[5]In addition to the lengthy discussion of Bozeman's death in Burlingame, "John M. Bozeman," 1983 ed., see also Dan L. Thrapp, *Vengeance! The Saga of Poor Tom Cover* (El Segundo, California: Upton & Sons, 1989), pp. 225-36; and John S. Gray, *Custer's Last Campaign, Mitch Boyer and the Little Bighorn Reconstructed* (Lincoln: University of Nebraska Press, 1991), pp. 56-58.

Jim Bridger

Jim Bridger was one of the best liked and most respected of the often heroic mountain men in the nineteenth century. He was liked for his humor, friendliness, and strength of character. He was respected for his honesty, extraordinary skill as a guide, and expert knowledge of western geography and Indians. He lived most of his life in the mountains and with Indians, had an indelible memory, and was considered to be the most skillful and reliable guide in the West. His three wives were Indian women: first a Flathead, second a Ute, and third a Snake woman. This life took its toll on him, however. Bridger was sixty-two in 1866 but by all reports looked, or at last seemed, much older.[1]

All who knew him agreed that he was talkative, companionable, and told unbelievable stories. Bridger did not always view others in the same light. He did not think much of the way military men operated or thought and consequently went off by himself a lot -- to scout and keep away from them -- when on a campaign. Less knowledgeable army men often thought him arrogant or over-confident, yet he was always right when he gave his considered opinion as to conditions, the route, or Indians. In contrast, he seemed to be quite sociable when off-duty and enjoyed "hanging out" and telling stories in camp or at a fort. Frances Grummond Carrington and Margaret Carrington wrote fondly about him in their memoirs.

---

[1]The best source on Bridger is J. Cecil Alter, *Jim Bridger* (Norman: University of Oklahoma Press, 1962); another excellent source is Stanley Vestal, *Jim Bridger, Mountain Man* (Lincoln: University of Nebraska Press, 1970); for his involvement with Fort Phil Kearny see Dee Brown, *Fort Phil Kearny,* reprinted as *The Fetterman Massacre* (Lincoln: University of Nebraska Press, 1973).

Bridger was more often called Old Gabe, Old Jim or Major Bridger by whites and Big Throat (for his enlarged goiter) by Indians. Maj. Gen. Grenville M. Dodge, who knew him well, described Bridger as "over six feet tall, spare, straight as an arrow, agile, rawboned and of powerful frame, eyes gray, hair brown and abundant even in old age, expression mild and manners agreeable."[2] What amazed and awed other mountain men, soldiers, and emigrants alike was his uncanny sense of direction and locality. He could go anywhere without a map or a compass. William Brackett said, "Bridger was a wonderful guide and a born topographer. The whole West and all the passes and labyrinths of the Rocky Mountains were mapped out in his mind."[3] It was this skill that made him the best known western guide through the 1860s.

Bridger began his career in the West when he answered William Ashley's ad in 1822 for one hundred young men to ascend the Missouri River, to be employed in the fur trade for one or two years. Bridger left St. Louis in April 1822, in the first of the two large keelboats in the expedition, commanded by Ashley's partner Andrew Henry. From then on his life on the frontier was a series of milestones. Bridger is credited with the discovery of the Great Salt Lake in 1824, since he was the first white trapper to report its existence and characteristics. In 1830, Bridger was one of five partners who organized the Rocky Mountain Fur Company, one of the most important firms in the mountains. Bridger entered into many other business arrangements in the next years, including the building of Fort Bridger with his partner Louis Vasquez in 1839-40.

---

[2]Grenville M. Dodge, "Biographical Sketch of James Bridger," *Annals of Wyoming* 33 (October 1961):174.

[3]William S. Brackett, "Bonneville and Bridger," *Contributions of the Montana Historical Society* 3 (1900):182.

Bridger's name is associated with virtually every aspect of the development of the Bozeman Trail. He explored the entire area it traversed in the decades before it was used by emigrants in the 1860s. In 1838, he and about seventy men wintered on the Powder River, near where the Bozeman Trail later crossed. His winter camp was near the Portuguese houses, just west of the ford where the old traders' trail crossed at the mouth of Salt Creek. In 1856-57, he guided Sir George Gore's British hunting expedition in the same area. In 1860-61, he was the chief guide for Capt. William F. Raynolds' expedition to explore the Yellowstone River drainage.

In 1864 he guided a large emigrant party over his route through the Wind River Basin west of the Bighorn Mountains at the same time John Bozeman led his party around the eastern base of the Bighorns. Bridger established the crossing at the Yellowstone that Bozeman used, although he used a different pass north of Bozeman's to the Gallatin Valley. In 1865 he was the chief guide for Gen. Patrick E. Connor, and he led the Powder River Expedition over a new cutoff from the North Platte and established the final route for the Bozeman Trail.

In March 1866, Bridger received orders to report to Col. Henry B. Carrington as guide for the Eighteenth Infantry expedition to the Powder River country. His salary was five dollars per day, which was raised to ten dollars per day by Carrington on June thirtieth at Fort Reno, after Cooke telegraphed him to discharge Bridger to curtail costs. Bridger was at Fort Phil Kearny until August second, when he was sent to accompany a large force of emigrants and survey the route to Virginia City for Carrington.[4] He went to Virginia City and was back at Fort C. F. Smith by the end of

---

[4]Bridger's survey is in Grace R. Hebard and E. A. Brininstool, *The Bozeman Trail,* 2 vols. (Cleveland: Arthur H. Clark, 1922), 1:119-21.

September.[5] On his return trip he reported that it took half a day to ride through the hostile Indian villages in the Tongue River Valley, and that fifteen hundred lodges of war parties were preparing to attack Forts C. F. Smith and Phil Kearny. Margaret Carrington credits his reports as having an important influence on her husband's military decisions.[6]

On October twenty-third, Bridger left Fort C. F. Smith for Fort Phil Kearny.[7] Captain Tenodor Ten Eyck recorded his arrival there on October twenty-sixth.[8] He remained at Fort Phil Kearny until November twenty-seventh, when he left at 4:00 a.m. for Fort C. F. Smith with Lieutenant Bingham.[9] According to Lt. George Templeton at Fort C. F. Smith, "The mail, escorted by Lieut. Bingham, 2d Cav...came up late in the evening in two days from Fort Phil Kearny... Bridger came along with the party and is to stop at this Post."[10] Thus, contrary to reports that Bridger was at Phil Kearny during the winter and spring of 1866-67, he was actually at Fort C. F. Smith, where he remained until June 1867.

It is important to note, however, that Bridger was at Fort Phil Kearny for the month of November 1866, and thus he was there when Lt. William Fetterman arrived November third. Colonel Carrington remembered years later that when

---

[5]George M. Templeton, Diary, 29 September 1866, Graff 4099, Newberry Library, Chicago, Illinois.

[6]Margaret I. Carrington, *Absaraka, Home of the Crows* (Lincoln: University of Nebraska Press, 1983), p. 133.

[7]Templeton, Diary, 23 October 1866.

[8]Tenodor Ten Eyck, Diary, 26 October 1866, MSS 82, Special Collections Library, University of Arizona, Tucson, Arizona.

[9]Ten Eyck, Diary, 27 November 1866.

[10]Templeton, Diary, 28 November 1866.

Fetterman boasted that he could take eighty men and go to Tongue River, Bridger replied, "Your men who fought down south are crazy! They don't know anything about fighting Indians."[11]

Bridger arrived back at Fort Phil Kearny on June 16, 1867. The new post commander, Col. John E. Smith, protested his presence, saying, "he is not needed here, one guide for this post is enough."[12] Nevertheless, Bridger remained there until Smith relieved him from duty on September twenty-third.[13] Bridger returned to his home near Kansas City, where he remained -- except for a brief stint helping move supplies from the Bozeman Trail forts in May and June 1868 -- until he died in 1881. Jim Bridger's contributions to our western heritage are inestimable, and his name lives on in American folklore, place names and legend.

SUSAN BADGER DOYLE

---

[11]Frances C. Carrington, *My Army Life and the Fort Phil Kearney Massacre* (Boulder, Colorado: Pruett Publishing Company, 1990), p. 253.

[12]Merrill J. Mattes, ed., *Indians, Infants and Infantry* (Denver: Old West Publishing Co., 1960; reprinted Lincoln: University of Nebraska Press, 1989), p. 134.

[13]Robert A. Murray, *Military Posts in the Powder River Country of Wyoming* (Buffalo, Wyoming: The Office, 1990), p. 98.

RED CLOUD
LEADER OF THE OGLALAS

Red Cloud was born in 1822 near the confluence of the Blue and Platte Rivers. There is considerable contradiction concerning Red Cloud's parentage. The two most ubiquitous accounts suggest that Red Cloud was named after his father or that his father was Lone Man, a Brule leader.[1] It is generally accepted among historians that Red Cloud's father was a leader of some significance. Most historical sources list Red Cloud's mother as Walks-As-She-Thinks, the sister of Chief Old Smoke. Red Cloud's father was killed at an early age and Red Cloud moved in with Chief Old Smoke's band. It is during this time that Red Cloud established himself as a leader among his people.

In his younger days he demonstrated the courage and bravery which was needed to become a hero among his people. Even though his father was a great leader, Red Cloud probably would have ascended to leadership because of the numerous brave deeds and the many coups counted in his lifetime. There are many stories about the viciousness he displayed in battle.

The following is a story that depicts Red Cloud's ferocious nature. During a battle with the Utes, Red Cloud rescued a drowning Ute warrior whose wounded horse dumped him in the middle of a stream. Upon reaching the shore, Red Cloud promptly scalped him.[2] Red Cloud's scalp shirt had over eighty scalp locks representing the numerous coups that he counted during his illustrious history as a

---

[1]James C. Olson, *Red Cloud and the Sioux Problem* (Lincoln: University of Nebraska Press, 1965), p. 16.

[2]Ibid., p. 19.

warrior. His scalp shirt was recently displayed as a featured exhibit in the Denver Art Museum and is permanently located at the Buffalo Bill Historical Center in Cody, Wyoming.

Red Cloud's Lakota name was Mahpiya Luta. There are several versions about how Red Cloud received his name. Many suggest that he took the name of his father when he died. Others suggest that Red Cloud was born in a year that a meteorite was seen moving across the sky and the light from the meteorite was so bright that it lit the sky and turned the clouds red. Nancy Red Cloud, the oldest living great-granddaughter of Chief Red Cloud, says that the origin of Red Cloud's name is a family secret.[3]

Red Cloud, one of the most renowned Sioux Chiefs, is most celebrated for his valiant leadership during the Northern Plains wars of the 1860s. He is the only American Indian leader to defeat the United States government in a war. His greatest coup was the defeat of the U.S. military, which resulted in the eventual abandonment of the western forts along the Bozeman Trail. Red Cloud, in his conversations with James H. Cook, stated that he led the forces that wiped out Fetterman in December of 1866.[4] The details of Red Cloud's involvement in the actual fight are unknown. Although his name appears on the monument, there is considerable speculation that Red Cloud was not in the area during the Fetterman Fight.

Red Cloud's involvement in the Wagon Box fight is well documented. It is clear that he was in command of the Sioux forces in the battle and that he gave the order to withdraw

---

[3]Interview with Nancy Red Cloud Horn Cloud, May 30, 1991.

[4]A number of historical sources suggest that Red Cloud was not present at the Fetterman Fight. In *Fifty Years on the Old Frontier* by James H. Cook, Red Cloud stated that he was present at the battle. There are no sources available to document whether Red Cloud actually participated in the battle.

rather than face continuing loss of life. Many believe that Red Cloud could have forced the battle and with high losses of life wiped out the small number of military men at the Wagon Box fight.

Red Cloud was recognized as a brilliant strategist in military operations for his part in this effective military campaign. However, Red Cloud's true genius was that of a negotiator and politician. His farsightedness is clearly evident in the provisions of the Treaty of 1868. Red Cloud's insistence on including the requirement that there be no future treaties with the Sioux unless it had prior consent from three-fourths of the males of the entire Sioux population was farsighted. It is the opinion of most Sioux people today that this provision was never fully consummated even though the U.S. government attempted by deceit on numerous occasions to satisfy this requirement.

There were two primary reasons why the U.S. government was never able to secure the necessary signatures on future documents. First, it was nearly impossible to locate three-fourths of the adult males, and second, because of the vacillating nature of the Sioux male and the political instability of that time in history, it was inconceivable to get three-fourths of the adult males to agree on a multifarious issue such as refashioning the Treaty of 1868. Red Cloud attempted to insure that the Treaty of 1868 could not change without maliciously violating this provision.

Chief Red Cloud died in 1909 in a house that was built for him by the United States Government. During his lifetime he was recognized as one of the great warrior chiefs of all time. Once he had agreed to peace and signed the Treaty of 1868 with the United States government, he kept his word and never fought the United States again on the battlefield. He did continue to fight for the rights of his people and the impact of his participation in the Treaty of 1868 is still being felt today. His body rests on the hilltop above the Red Cloud Indian School near Pine Ridge, South

Dakota. His warrior spirit can still be seen in the eyes of the Oglala Lakotas (Sioux) who have continued the struggle to recover lost land and force the United States government to honor the provisions of the Treaty of 1868. Chief Red Cloud is memorialized in Red Cloud and the Sioux Problem by James C. Olson, who describes Red Cloud as "one of the most celebrated members of his race, better known among both red men and white than almost any other Sioux."[5]

RICHARD WILLIAMS

[5]Olson, p. 15.

Col. Henry Beebe Carrington

Colonel Henry Beebe Carrington (1824-1912) was the commander of Fort Phil Kearny at the time of the Fetterman Massacre. Despite numerous humanitarian and scholarly contributions to society, he will continue to be remembered for Fetterman's pursual of Indian decoys over Lodge Trail Ridge and the deaths of eighty-one men on December 21, 1866.

He was born on March 2, 1824, in Wallingford, Connecticut, into an educated and patriotic family[1] (several relatives having served in the Revolutionary War) that included a sea captain and a Protestant minister. Despite an early interest in the military, a desired West Point education was not realized because of asthma and other respiratory concerns. Instead, Carrington studied at Yale (A.B., 1845; Law School, 1847). He then taught at The Irving Institute in Tarrytown, New York, and served as Washington Irving's secretary in 1846.

With a law degree, family property in Ohio, and promises of a healthier western Climate, Carrington moved to Columbus to practice law in 1848. His law partner until 1861 was William Dennison, later one of Ohio's Civil War governors. In 1851, he married Margaret Irwin McDowell Sullivant (author: *Absaraka: Home of the Crows).* Between 1852-1864, four of their six children died before the age of

---

[1]Carrington's boyhood home in Wallingford, Connecticut, is located on the campus of the Choate-Rosemary School and serves as a male dormitory. The Carrington family papers are located in the archives of the Sterling Memorial Library at Yale University, New Haven, Connecticut.

three; James Beebe Carrington (1860-1929) being the only child to reach adulthood.

Henry was an abolitionist and became friends with many important figures in state and national politics, including Salmon P. Chase, also a governor of Ohio and later Lincoln's Secretary of the Treasury. During 1854, Carrington directed the organization of the Republican party in Ohio, and in 1857 reorganized the Ohio State Militia and became the state adjutant general. In the election year of 1861, Carrington served as a bodyguard to President Lincoln through Indiana and Ohio enroute to Washington City from Springfield, Illinois. Carrington was appointed that same year as Colonel in the Regular Army of the United States, Eighteenth Regiment.

Governor Oliver P. Morton of Indiana was able to secure Carrington's services in 1862, and he continued his expertise of organizing, equipping, and transporting militia for the Union cause and was appointed as brigadier of volunteers. He was overall responsible for recruiting more than 200,000 volunteers from both states, but received minimal combat experience himself. At the same time, Carrington was very active in suppressing the organizations and individuals sympathetic to the Confederacy and unloyal to the Union, namely the Sons of Liberty and the Knights of the Golden Circle. The U.S. Supreme Court later ruled that Carrington acted illegally in many instances because neither Ohio nor Indiana had rebelled.

Carrington was mustered out of service after the War, but rejoined the Eighteenth Regiment in 1866 on active duty, and led the Second Battalion to garrison Fort Reno and create two new posts along the Bozeman Trail. The choice of Carrington as commander of the regiment was not greeted with enthusiasm by battle-hardened fellow officers, and his military actions were criticized throughout his tenure.

Enroute to the Powder River country from Fort Kearney,[2] Nebraska, the expedition reached Fort Laramie where the United States government was attempting to negotiate another treaty with the Sioux for the use of the Bozeman Trail. The Indians were indignant, to say the least, that the government had sent Carrington and his men to "guard" the Montana Road before a treaty had been agreed upon, and furious that Carrington's expedition reinforced their belief that they were being treated as idiots and savages. Oglala Sioux Chief Red Cloud acted outwardly hostile to Carrington and left before negotiations could be completed.

Carrington built Fort Phil Kearny between the Little and Big Pineys and established Fort C. F. Smith to the north before the year ended. Red Cloud and his Sioux, together with Cheyenne allies, constantly harassed travelers on the Bozeman Trail and especially the garrison at Fort Phil Kearny.

On December 21, 1866, Carrington, according to his own testimony, ordered Fetterman to "Support the wood train. Relieve it and report to me. Do not engage or pursue Indians at its expense. Under no circumstances pursue over the ridge, that is, Lodge Trail Ridge." Captain Fetterman pursued the Indians over the ridge and the overwhelming defeat at the hands of the Sioux, Cheyenne and Arapahoe destroyed any major military aspirations Carrington may have had. Previously, Carrington had been criticized for the lack of discipline and military training at Phil Kearny. His soldiers were outnumbered by Indians and poorly armed and supplied. The decision to transfer Carrington and move the Eighteenth Regiment's headquarters to Fort Caspar, reached prior to the fight, was immediately ordered.

Carrington served as post commander at Fort McPherson and Fort Sedgewick in Colorado after enduring blizzard

---

[2] Also spelled *Kearny*.

conditions enroute from Phil Kearny to Fort Caspar, and a pistol wound to the thigh while traveling to Fort Laramie.

Two formal investigations of the Fetterman disaster were conducted. The Sanborne Commission interviewed Carrington in March of 1867 at Fort McPherson and did not find him at fault. Unfortunately, Carrington's testimony was not made public until 1887, while unsupportive testimony was published by the Senate's Committee on Indian Affairs in 1867. A Military Court of Inquiry in the same year also did not censure Carrington.

Because of the leg wound and possibly also because of the controversies heard at the investigations, Carrington left active duty in 1870 to take a post teaching military science and mathematics at Wabash College in Crawfordsville, Indiana.

Mrs. Margaret Carrington died in 1870, and Carrington married the former Frances Courtney Grummond (author: *My Army Life*) in 1871. Frances was the widow of Lt. George Grummond, a cavalry commander killed with Fetterman. Henry and Frances parented three children: Eliza Jane (1874-1964), Henrietta (1874-1947) and Robert Chase (1872-1899). Henry also adopted William (Grummond) Carrington (1867-1897).

The Carringtons moved to Hyde Park, Massachusetts, a suburb of Boston, in 1878, where Henry worked as an author, Indian agent, and book salesman. He joined the Hyde Park Historical Society and was an active speaker for patriotic events. It was during these years that he wrote numerous military and historical books and periodicals. His *Battles of the American Revolution* (1876-1878) and *Washington the Soldier* (1899) are still considered important historical literary works because of his research in the military archives of Great Britain and France, and his personal battlefield surveys.

In 1889, Carrington directed a treaty with the Flathead Indians, and in 1891, assisted in their movement to the

Jocko Reservation in western Montana. In 1890, he directed a census of the Iroquois Nation of New York and the Cherokees of North Carolina. In 1908, Henry and Frances traveled to Sheridan, Wyoming, for a July Fourth dedication celebration and reunion that included ceremonies at the monument on Massacre Ridge and the former site of Fort Phil Kearny.

His involvement in the issuing of at least six editions of Margaret's *Absaraka, Home of the Crows* was indicative of Carrington's passion to be absolved of any blame for Fetterman's crossing of Lodge Trail Ridge.

Carrington died on October 26, 1912, at the age of eighty-eight and is buried in Fairview Cemetery, Hyde Park, Massachusetts.

During the 1908 visit to Sheridan, Wyoming, Carrington presented the Sheridan Public Library with a copy of *Wyoming Revisited, 1866*, a detailed account of his attempt to absolve himself of any blame for the deaths of Fetterman and the eighty others on the twenty-first of December nearly forty-two years earlier.

THEODORE L. MAGUDER

PIERRE "FRENCH PETE" GAZEAU

On October 1, 1859, Pierre Gazeau[1] applied to the Upper Platte Indian agent for a license to trade with the Sioux and Arapaho. After bonding, the license was approved on February 6, 1860. In early May of 1860, the firm of "Smith and Gazeau" purchased twenty-five pounds of sugar and coffee, seemingly in the Fort Smith area. Gazeau's partner, "Smith," must have been John Simpson Smith, an experienced trader around Fort Laramie and the Platte River.

According to the Federal Census of Nebraska Territory, 1860, Gazeau had been born in France in 1805 and had personal property estimated at five thousand dollars. His occupation was listed as trader, and at fifty-five years of age, was five years younger than his partner, John Simpson Smith.

When the Laramie County Commissioners met at Laport on January 8, 1866, they ordered that the judges and clerks who had served at the September 1865 county election be paid. Among those receiving their due were Pierre Gazeau and Henry Arrison. In Laport, there was a merchandise and liquor store owned by Henry Arrison.

As Col. Henry Carrington's soldiers of the Second Battalion, Eighteenth U.S. Infantry marched up the Bozeman Trail in June and July of 1866, a trading party headed by Pierre Gazeau and Henry Arrison preceded them.

About her meeting with French Pete on June 24, 1866, Henry Carrington's wife Margaret wrote,

---

[1]While Haymond spells the name "Gassoux," Baalon "Gassous," Henry Carrington "Gassaux," and Margaret Carrington "Louis [sic] Gazzoux," earlier records prefer Gazeau.

> Just before reaching the bason, where the Fort Reno road turns northward, following Sage Creek, and the northern Mormon road passes westward toward Salt Lake City, we found an extemporized shed of boards, where Louis Gazzons (French Pete), with his Sioux wife and half-breed children, were opening their merchandise to catch travel over the new route. Here the inevitable display of canned fruits, liquors, tobacco, beads, cutlery, crackers, and cheese were modistly conspicuous...[2]

Fort Phil Kearny's site was established on July 15, 1866, and in its vicinity the trading party of Gazeau, Arrison and their employees set up a new camp.

During Sunday, July sixteenth, "French Pete," as the Americans called Pierre, traded with the Cheyenne Indians, collecting numerous robes. That night, as the party sat smoking with the Cheyennes, Sioux Indians rode up and asked what had happened during the Cheyenne parley with Col. Henry B. Carrington at the fort that Sunday. When the Cheyennes reported that Carrington and the soldiers had no intention of going back down the Bozeman, the Sioux beat the Cheyennes and their chiefs about the back and face with bows. Blackhorse then warned "French Pete" to go quickly to the Cheyenne village, meantime sending a messenger to warn Carrington that the Sioux meant war. Gazeau did not act upon this advice.

It was on Monday, July 17, 1866, that Pierre's Sioux wife, Mary, became a widow and was found hiding in bushes with her five children. She and the children were discovered by Lt. Henry Haymond after he had seen the mayhem at "French Pete's" camp. Haymond later reported finding the dead bodies of four men, and another mortally wounded, under the wagons, and stated that "robes, fruit, and trading goods

---

[2]Margaret Carrington, *Ab-Sa-Ra-Ka: Home of the Crows, Being the Experiences of an Officer's Wife on the Plains* (Philadelphia: J. B. Lippincott, 1868), p. 87.

were scattered around."[3] He explicitly noted that no heads had been scalped.

Doctor Baalon described in detail the first civilian deaths in the vicinity of the new fort: Gazeau's body had one revolver shot above the right nipple, as well as a rifle shot in the same place, a rifle wound in the left lower back above the hipbone, an arrow wound in the right groin and another arrow below the nipple; Henry Arrison's body contained one revolver shot in the right side of his face, a revolver shot in his neck below the larynx, an arrow below the last false rib, another arrow in the left lower back at the level of the hipbone and an arrow in the left lower thigh; Thomas Burns, a teamster employee, was found with his throat cut, an arrow in his left groin, and an arrow in the back of his shoulder; an unidentified man was found with an arrow in the right side of his head behind the ear, an arrow in the right lower lobe of the lung, and two arrows in the left side of his back. Baalon did what he could for the dying man, Moss, whose throat had been cut, and who suffered revolver and rifle wounds in his right forearm and arrow and revolver wounds in his lower back.

The bodies of Gazeau, Dowaire, Moss and the unidentified man were buried by an army detail nearby the scene of death. The bodies of Henry Arrison, Gazeau's partner, and Thomas Burns were brought to Fort Phil Kearny, where they were the first to be interred in the newly established Fort Phil Kearny Cemetery.

Gazeau's twenty-two head of cattle and the two wagons with their remaining contents, were brought to the fort and turned over to John W. Hugus, in behalf of the widow and her estate. On November 8, 1867, a claim was received by the Indian Bureau, filed by James and Lois Green and Mary

---

[3]Henry Haymond, Letter, 20 July 1866, Fort Phil Kearny, Letters Received, Department of the Platte, File No. H-45-1866, Record Group 393, National Archives, Washington, D.C.

Gazeau, for the July 18, 1866, losses to the Sioux Indians. No definite action was taken.

On August 3, 1866, the Reverend William K. Thomas, who was a Methodist minister traveling with his eight-year-old son and an employee, passed by the hillside grave of "five men" on the left of the road. "As I passed by the grave I saw that the Wolves had made an opening to the inmates and had torn the flesh from the bodies and left their ribs exposed."[4]

FATHER BARRY HAGAN

---

[4]W. W. Thomas, Diary, 3 August 1866; the *Daily Leavenworth Times,* 20 October 1866, p. 1, c. 2, "From Helena, Montana," quotes a letter from C. M. S. Millard who found the remains of Rev. Thomas, his son, and their driver mangled by wolves after having been killed by Indians on 23 August 1866.

Perry A. Burgess
A Traveler to the "Land of Gold"

The Bozeman Trail was first a gold rush trail. The lure of gold in Idaho Territory, soon to be Montana Territory, was the reason for its existence. It was first used in 1864 as miners traveled over John Bozeman's shortcut to the newly discovered gold fields. The anticipated heavy traffic season of 1865 was abruptly halted by government order, and Gen. Patrick E. Connor's Powder River Campaign against the Sioux that summer led to the Bozeman Trail becoming strictly a military road. In 1866 more than a thousand emigrants poured over the route. Some preceded Col. Henry Carrington's troops, but the majority followed in his wake. After the close of the dangerous 1866 travel season, the trail was never again to be used as an emigrant road.

There are virtually no Bozeman Trail travel accounts left by miners. Perhaps the reason is that those who have left written accounts were more educated than those going to the mines tended to be. For whatever reason, most of the recorded travel accounts are from merchants or professionals who were going to the new territory to participate in the potential business opportunities offered by the burgeoning new territory. However, Perry A. Burgess, an 1866 emigrant, is representative of those emigrants who were lured by the gold fields. Like so many of his kind, he failed to strike it rich and was forced to make his living by any job he could get before leaving in discouragement.

Perry was literate enough to leave a diary of his journey over the Bozeman Trail in 1866. The original has been lost, but a transcription is now in the Western Historical Collection at the University of Colorado Library in Boulder. A version edited by Robert Athearn was published in 1950.[1] Not much is known of Perry's early life. He was born in 1843. He was twenty-three years old when he left his home in Lena, Illinois, employed by his uncles, Mansel and Lewis Cheney, and traveled with them and their families to Montana. Before leaving the settlements they picked up several more of his relatives. Perry was typical of most of the would-be miners: he was young, single, and traveled with a close-knit group of friends and relatives.

On May 14, 1866, the party left Plattesmouth and "started on our journey toward the land of gold." The group encountered no difficulties until July twenty-second, when they were traveling along the dry fork of the Powder River. His uncles Mansel and Lewis were riding ahead of Perry, who was with some boys driving the herd. The wagon train was well ahead of their small group. Perry saw nine Indians ride up to his uncles. They seemed to be friendly and were shaking hands when one of the Indians drew a pistol from under a blanket and shot Mansel, and he fell dead from his horse. The boys charged from where they were watching and drove off the Indians. They then caught up with the train, which returned to where Mansel was killed and found his body, stripped. The body was taken by the train and buried the next day about eight miles from Fort Reno. Several diarists remarked thereafter on the grave with its headboard marked "M. Chaney, killed by Indians July 22d, 1866."

Perry's train arrived at Fort Phil Kearny on July twenty-eighth and found a number of trains waiting to organize into one large train for safety. They left the fort on August second in a train made up of 110 wagons, 171 men, six women and five children. Seven miles from Fort Phil Kearny they passed the graves of "French Pete" and his men, who had recently been killed by Indians. Their graves had been so

---

[1]Perry A. Burgess, "From Illinois to Montana in 1866," ed. Robert G. Athearn, *Pacific Northwest Quarterly* 41 (January 1950):43-65.

shallow that they had been uncovered by animals, and the partly decomposed bodies were exposed. Some of the men in the party covered the graves again. The train continued on to the Gallatin Valley, where they arrived September first.

In Montana, Perry worked for his uncle Lewis Cheney and at odd jobs, including gold panning, for nearly two years. He returned to Illinois, by steamboat from Fort Benton, in July 1868. But typical of the restless, ever hopeful miner, he moved to Colorado in the 1870s to try his luck at placer mining. Again, he was not successful as a miner and had to find other work. He homesteaded in Routt County in 1875, where he was a founding settler of Steamboat Springs. He was listed as a miner in the 1880 Colorado census but was listed as a rancher in 1885. His uncle Lewis Cheney, who had the same gold fever and had even made a trip to the California gold rush in 1850, also went to Colorado in the 1870s. However, Lewis did strike it rich, in a sense, and became a wealthy banker. Perry Burgess never found his "land of gold," but he did find the nineteenth-century American Dream: a pioneering life in the West.

SUSAN BADGER DOYLE

DAVIS WILLSON
A BOZEMAN TRAIL EMIGRANT IN 1866

In many ways Davis Willson was a typical Bozeman Trail emigrant. He was young, single, and traveling with hometown friends and relatives to a new life in Montana. However, he stands apart in that he was educated and literate. His diary not only gives us a revealing glimpse of the Bozeman Trail experience, but also an understanding of the people and events he so observantly recorded.[1] His record is particularly valuable since he traveled over the trail during the peak of the 1866 season, in the wake of Col. Henry B. Carrington and the Eighteenth Infantry.

Davis began his journey on May 7, 1866, in Canton, New York. He traveled with nine young men, including his childhood friend Charlie Caldwell and his cousins, Charlie and Frank Rich. Despite the appearance that his group laughed and joked all the way to Montana, it is a serious and memorable story of friendships, of sharing good times and bad, of facing life-threatening danger, and of growing up.

Like the majority of travelers in 1866, Davis's group passed through Omaha. At Fort Laramie on July thirteenth, he and his companions joined up with Phillips and Company, a freighting outfit, whom he describes as "a hard set." This was undoubtedly the consequence of the military authorities cautioning travelers to stay close together and keep moving, in the anticipation of increased danger from Indian attacks after the breakup of the treaty conference.

Davis arrived at Fort Phil Kearny on August fifth. The train was stopped by soldiers two and a half miles from the

---

[1]Davis Willson, Diary, 1866, MSS File 1076, Special Collections Library, Montana State University, Bozeman, Montana.

post and was not allowed to camp nearer because their animals would eat grass needed for the army herds. The next day Davis exhibited his usual good-natured helpfulness and "made a report of number of men (their names and residence), of wagons, stock, guns, pistols, and ammunition in the train for the Commander of the Post." Captain Tenodor Ten Eyck, post commander at that time, recorded in his diary on August fifth that "about 150 citizen wagons came in within 2 miles of the fort & encamped. Report grave trouble with the Indians."[2]

Their train arrived at Fort Phil Kearny just as restrictions were being tightened. All trains that arrived at the end of July and in early August were ordered to wait until a large enough number collected to travel in safety. Carrington, Mountain District commander, seems to have been concerned that he had lost control over the flood of emigrants that was descending upon the new post and was aware that he had too few men to spare any as emigrant escorts. Davis's train evidently was deemed to be large enough, and it left on August seventh, accompanied by James Brannan, who was sent by Ten Eyck to arrest several deserters.

The train only made five miles the first day out of Fort Phil Kearny. Davis describes a most difficult ascent and descent of Fetterman ridge, in which the wheels were double-locked and the wagons slid down one at a time. Just past the fort, the train had to stop for nearly an hour and a half because trains ahead of them were having such a hard time crossing the Piney and beginning the ascent, and

> as we lay there the brass band at the fort commenced playing. Such sounds in such a scene! It gave me many strange feelings which I cannot describe. There was something in the wild sweet strains that filled and floated

---

[2]Tenodor Ten Eyck, Diaries, 1866-1867, MSS 82, Special Collections Library, University of Arizona, Tucson, Arizona.

> through the deep reechoing valley that spoke of home; yet so far distant and in so wild a place that it partook of the nature of the scenes around it. It was like looking through the "glass of time" into the dim Past, viewing with kindled emotions the forms & scenes that once enshrined and hallowed it, and yet the wild adventuresome Present all the while floating before dimming & blinding the vision.[3]

Eventually they moved on, and from his description, it seems Davis's train was one of the first to take the new cutoff to the Tongue which developed that summer. He called it one of the guide's cutoffs. They bore left at the base of Fetterman Ridge, crossed Peno Creek, and camped on Little Goose Creek. He added that "the country here is beautiful. Some of the loveliest vallies and streams I ever saw."

Davis settled in Bozeman, Montana, on his arrival. He lived there most of the rest of his life, becoming a prominent member of the community. Numerous articles in the Virginia City *Montana Post,* signed D. W., attest to his writing talent. He taught school for a time, served as registrar for the General Land Office in Bozeman for ten years, and fittingly, in 1889 was ordained as a Presbyterian minister.

SUSAN BADGER DOYLE

---

[3]Willson, Diary, 7 August 1866.

ANPETU OTANIN WIN & MNI AKU WIN
(APPEARING DAY & BRINGS BACK WATER)

Indian women of the pre-reservation era have had relatively little media exposure as far as their everyday existence was concerned. They have been portrayed either as uninhibited sexual creatures and drudges or romantic "princesses." None have ever truly examined the psychological and social barriers that existed within the female individual and, moreover, the importance of the whole group on her behavior and decisions.

We have some evidence for women's lives but only outstanding women. Two Lakota Sioux women of the nineteenth century were outstanding enough to provide insight into Lakota women's lives. Anpetu Otanin Win (Appearing Day) was the first wife of Spotted Tail, the most famous Brule leader. Their daughter, Mni Aku Win (Brings Back Water), became equally famous.

Though their lives were brief, the mother, Appearing Day, born about 1828, lived during the time when the Lakota Sioux first witnessed emigrants blazing a trail through their southern hunting grounds. This eventually became known as the Oregon Trail. Her daughter was a small child when Brigham Young led his group of Mormons along the Platte. Mother and daughter probably watched in fascination as the large numbers of white men and their families came and went along the Trail. Their Lakota Sioux men approached these wagon trains out of curiosity from time to time but were received with hostility.[1] These large numbers of people scattered the game which became alarmingly scarce. Then the sicknesses of cholera and smallpox appeared. Although Appearing Day and her small daughter were fortunately unscathed by the diseases, many camps of the Lakota Sioux and Cheyenne were not.

The scarcity of game and the disease epidemics caused great alarm among leaders of the camps. They knew the white man's invasion of their southern hunting grounds was the direct cause of their maladies. Hostility immediately arose towards these white men who were different from the traders and trappers with whom the Lakota Sioux were familiar.

The Fort Laramie Treaty of 1851, signed by the U.S. and the northern tribes including the Lakota Sioux and Cheyenne, was a result of the troubled relations between the white men and Indians along the Oregon Trail. Fort Laramie had become an Army post in 1849 and its traders served not only the Lakota Sioux, but the Oregon Trail travelers as well. Many of the Oglala and Brule Sioux continued to camp and live around the fort as they had since its creation in 1834. It was convenient for them as the annuities were distributed here.

After the arrival of the soldiers and the American immigrants, the Lakota Society somewhat changed its attitude toward intermarriage.[2] During the heyday of the fur trade, Lakota men willingly encouraged their daughters to marry the traders. These men joined Lakota families and brought prestige and wealth to their families. Many of the prominent Lakota had "white relatives." Wealthy fur traders were desirable, soldiers were not as acceptable to prominent

---

[1]George Hyde, *Red Cloud's Folk: A History of the Oglala Sioux Indians* (Norman: University of Oklahoma Press, 1930), p. 56.

[2]Ethel Lone Hill, Interview, 22 April 1992.

Lakota families. Perhaps this change was accelerated by the Lakota experiences with the ruthlessness of the soldiers and the immigrants which had led to open warfare in the 1850s and 1860s. In essence, the soldiers were the enemy.

Appearing Day grew up before this time of uncertainty, and her courtship and marriage were unaffected by all the turmoil.[3] She was the daughter of a chief and according to Lakota Sioux custom, her parents wanted her to marry a man of substance who could pay the price of many ponies. She defied tradition by adding another requirement: she would not marry a man unless she truly loved him.

There was much gossip among the people about a young beautiful woman who chose to remain unmarried even at the age of twenty. It was customary for young women to marry soon after menstruation and the performance of the Buffalo Ceremony.

Running Bear, a man much older than Appearing Day, was the man favored by her parents. He already had two wives and had a good standing within the band. But she had her sights on the young Spotted Tail although he was merely a warrior and by no means could be considered wealthy.

Because of Running Bear's strong desire to make Appearing Day his wife and the realization that his young competitor threatened his forthcoming marriage to her, he was compelled to confront Spotted Tail. When the rivals met, Running Bear threatened Spotted Tail with death if he did not give up Appearing Day. When Spotted Tail refused, the two were immediately caught up in a deadly struggle. By the time the people arrived to intervene, Running Bear was dead and Spotted Tail wounded.

Once again, Appearing Day defied tradition when she tended to Spotted Tail and nursed him back to health. The

---

[3]Marion E. Gridley, "Biography of Appearing Day," *American Indian Women* (New York: Hawthorne Books, 1974).

people all agreed that Spotted Tail had fairly won her. Appearing Day and Spotted Tail were married and lived happily along the Platte for a brief period. Because of his sincere love for her, he also defied tradition by remaining monogamous although he had become a rising leader.[4] Unfortunately, Appearing Day died sometime in the 1850s before Spotted Tail achieved chieftainship. After her death, he followed tradition by taking plural wives, but his beloved Appearing Day was never forgotten.

Appearing Day and Spotted Tail had a daughter. She was greatly cherished by her father maybe because she reminded him so much of her mother. They both seemed to have been beautiful, intelligent, determined and unconcerned with most traditions, but were loved and respected by their people.

Many writers and historians have struggled to accurately portray this daughter of Spotted Tail who was born in 1849, possibly somewhere on the Platte. Numerous poems and stories have surfaced often with romantic embellishments about this young Indian girl who frequently accompanied her father, Spotted Tail, to Fort Laramie. She has been given many different names by different people over the years, but the name used most frequently has been Mni Aku Win which when translated into English means Brings Back Water. This translation is slightly different from the original translation which was Brings Water. In order for the name to have been Brings Water it would have been Mni Au Win.

As a young girl, particularly after the death of her mother, Mni Aku Win accompanied her father on his brief trips to Fort Laramie in 1856-59, and again in 1864 for ten days.[5] It was during these trips that she received glimpses of another way of life. Many of the Lakota Sioux women who

---

[4]Ibid.

[5]Wilson D. Clough, "Mni Aku Win, Daughter of Spotted Tail," *Annals of Wyoming* 39 (1967):187-216.

lived around the fort willingly chose or were given in marriage to the U.S. military officers and soldiers. This they believed would give their families the prestige that it had given the families who gave their daughters to the traders and trappers of the past. Unfortunately, this was a different time and place.

The 1851 Treaty set the boundaries for their existence and guaranteed no more encroachments on their land. It was violated when gold was discovered in Montana, northwest of their territory and the shortest route was through the Powder River country. This route became the Bozeman Trail and it angered the Lakota Sioux and Cheyenne. Many bloody battles were fought along the Bozeman Trail in the 1860s. Even friendly bands joined the hostile bands to the north.

During this time, a legendary love story between Mni Aku Win and a white military officer began. There is evidence of a mutual physical attraction between Mni Aku Win and a young officer of Fort Laramie.[6] In one incident, he paraded in all his finery while she looked on.

Mni Aku Win was described as being of "modest demeanor and striking beauty."[7] She was "below medium height, with a face perfectly oval, illuminated by eyes black and flashing, with a small, straight nose, finely formed lips, and teeth white and perfect."[8]

The majority of historians concur that the young officer was Eugene Fitch Ware. He was born in Hartford, Connecticut, in 1841, served in the Fourth and Seventh Cavalry in the Civil War, became a second lieutenant in 1863, and was post adjutant at Fort Laramie from July 27 to August 31, 1864. He returned to Fort Laramie again briefly in October 1864

---

[6]Ibid., p. 197.

[7]Ibid., p. 202.

[8]Ibid., p. 203.

and again on April 4, 1865.[9] It was from his detailed written accounts of Mni Aku Win that many writers have constructed a legend.

At age twenty-three, Ware was said to have been the most popular and best looking man in the army at Fort Laramie. Although he despised his fellow officers and soldiers for marrying Indian women, his revised writings in 1911 indicated that he was the white captain whom Mni Aku Win loved.[10] He admittedly was the one who paraded for her during her ten day stay at Fort Laramie in 1864. Ware seemed to know the whereabouts of Mni Aku Win and her band after they had left Fort Laramie to join the hostile bands. He stated that at the time of her death in 1866 on the Powder River, she had not seen a white person since 1864.

The story was one of forbidden love for Mni Aku Win. She refused to marry any Lakota Sioux man and spoke determinably to other Lakota Sioux women of her ambition to marry a captain.[11] But in the eyes of the people, Spotted Tail could not allow his daughter to marry a white man, much less a military officer. It would have meant betrayal of his trust to the people. He along with Red Cloud, who were said to have been close friends, served as influential liaisons between the Lakota Sioux on the Powder River and the United States.

During the persistence of war with the U.S., Spotted Tail and his people lived on the Powder River along with Red Cloud and other hostile bands, moving back and forth on the Big Horn, Rosebud and Tongue Rivers.[12] It was on the

---

[9]Ibid., p. 195.

[10]Ibid., p. 201.

[11]Ibid., p. 198.

[12]James C. Olson, *Red Cloud and the Sioux Problem* (Lincoln and London: University of Nebraska Press, 1965), p. 30.

Powder River that Mni Aku Win became gravely ill and died in February 1866 at the age of seventeen. Some say she died of a broken heart while the more realistic story was that she succumbed to the hardships associated with living in the camps on the Powder River and possibly the severity of the winter.

Mni Aku Win secretly longed for a peaceful life which probably included marriage to the young officer. Before she died she made her father promise to make peace with the white men because of their superior power. Another wish was to be buried at Fort Laramie in the soldiers' cemetery which was carried out on March 8 or 9, 1866, in a spectacular ceremony.

Eugene Ware ended his account with this much-quoted passage:

> The daughter of Shan-tag-a-lisk was an individual of a type found in all lands, at all times, and among all peoples; she was misplaced. Her story is the story of the persistent melancholy of the human race; of kings born in hovels, and dying there; ...of beauty born where its gift is fatal; of mercy born among wolves, and fighting for life...There are those who are never in tune. They are not alone among the weak; they are the strong and the weak; they are the ambitious as well as the loving, the tender, the true, and the merciful.
>
> The daughter of Shan-tag-a-lisk wanted to find somebody to love worth loving. Her soul bled to death. Like an epidendrum, she was feeding upon the air.
>
> When wealth and civilization shall have brought to the Rocky Mountains the culture and population which in time shall come, the daughter of Shan-tag-a-lisk should not be forgotten; it may be said of her, in the words of Buddha: "Amid the brambles and rubbish thrown over into the road, a lily may grow."[13]

[13]Clough, "Mni Aku Win," p. 198-199.

Both Appearing Day and Mni Aku Win have provided valuable insights into the lives of exceptional Lakota Sioux women who lived during the times of encroachment and wars in the 1850s and 60s. They showed a self-determination within a strict Lakota society. They possessed a strong influence over the males, particularly those who loved them. After the death of Mni Aku Win, Spotted Tail strove for peace with the white men.

KAREN WHITE EYES

RIDGWAY GLOVER

Ridgway Glover arrived in Omaha, Nebraska, on May 14, 1866, and the following day registered at the Herndon House. A local paper stated he was from the Smithsonian Institution and worked with *Frank Leslie's Illustrated Weekly*, and that he planned on going to Fort Laramie to take pictures of Indians at the peace conference. In correspondence with the *Philadelphia Photographer* magazine, Glover said he reached Fort Laramie and there exposed some fifty negatives, many of which did not process successfully, and that he was planning on going to Virginia City, Montana Territory, and take scenes of the Rocky Mountains in winter.

Lieutenant George M. Templeton recorded in his diary on July fourteenth, as he camped near Bridger's Ferry on the North Platte River, that he was bringing along "a queer genius by the name of Glover...who wants to go to Col. Carrington's headquarters."

"Mr. Glover, though an eccentric and peculiar being, was generally respected by all who knew him"[1] was the comment of Pvt. Samuel S. Peters, Company H, Eighteenth U.S. Infantry. At Crazy Woman's Fork on July twentieth, Templeton's small party was attacked by Indians, and 1st Lt. Napoleon H. Daniels, Eighteenth U.S. Infantry, was killed. Glover wanted to seize the opportunity to take stereoscopic views of the circling warriors; this Templeton forbade.

Safely reaching Fort Phil Kearny on July twenty-fifth, Glover soon presented himself to Col. Henry B. Carrington,

---

[1]Elmo Scott Watson, "The Indian Wars and the Press, 1866-1867," *Journalism Quarterly* 17 (December 1940):305.

Post Commander, saying he was short of funds, but needed photographic chemicals to continue his picture-taking. Carrington employed him to work at the saw mill in the Pineys, commenting that the photographer struck him as a loner who must have met some great disappointment in life. Glover would occasionally drop by to visit Carrington and discuss, among other things, natural science. On one occasion Glover told Carrington that no Indian would ever hurt him. He made the same observation to Sgt. Frank Fessenden, Company G, Eighteenth U.S. Infantry, adding that he was immune from attack because the Indians would think he was a Mormon.

Glover soon formed the habit of leaving the fort without permission and hiking into the Big Horn Mountains nearby. Writing to the *Philadelphia Photographer,* Glover described the beauty he had found on a two-day hiking trip into the mountains: the geological formations, the trees and flowers, and particularly the many wild animals. Several days later he took a wood chopper, John Wilson, to hunt where he had seen plentiful game, but Wilson proved so noisy that Glover left him. A short while later the photographer came suddenly upon a huge grizzly bear who seemed spoiling for a fight. When Glover did not react the grizzly left, and Glover thankfully returned to the wood camp.

On Saturday, September 15, 1866, Ridgway Glover left the fort, alone and without permission. He was unarmed. On Sunday he was seen at the two wood camps and at each was warned not to go out alone because of the nearby presence of hostile Indians. On Monday, September seventeenth, his body was found, about daybreak, on the road from Fort Phil Kearny to the Pineys, one and a half or two miles from the fort.

Colonel Carrington wrote on that same September seventeenth that the body was found "...naked, scalped, and his back cleft with a tomahawk."[2] Chaplain David White, writing to *Frank Leslie's Illustrated Weekly* on September twentieth, said a rifle ball had passed near Glover's heart, killing him instantly, and that the body had been scalped. Sergeant Fessenden, who was among the first to find Glover's body, near dawn, gave an undated account saying, "They had clipped that long hair, taking the entire scalp. He was laying on his face, and the back was slit the entire length. Several arrows were sticking in the body."[3]

By inference, Fessenden indicated the corpse was naked. First Lieutenant William H. Bisbee found the body several hours later, and his January 1928 speech said, "I found him dead, scalped and badly mutilated, lying face downward across the roadway, a sign he had not been brave."[4]

Private Samuel S. Peters, who was not an eyewitness, wrote to *Frank Leslie's Illustrated Weekly* on September twentieth, from Fort Laramie, an account which had grown in the telling, saying the body had been disemboweled and a

---

[2]U.S. Congress. Senate. Executive Document 33, 50th Cong., 1st sess., 1889, p. 24.

[3]Grace Raymond Hebard and E. A. Brininstool, *The Bozeman Trail: Historical Accounts of the Blazing of the Overland Routes into the Northwest, and the Fights with Red Cloud's Warriors*, 2 vols. (Cleveland: Arthur H. Clark Co., 1922), 2:96.

[4]William H. Bisbee, Brigadier General, U.S. Army, "Items of Indian Service," from *Proceedings of the Annual Meeting and Dinner of the Order of the Indian Wars of the United States, 19 January 1928, in The Papers of the Order of Indian Wars,* comp. John M. Carroll (Fort Collins, Colorado: Old Army Press, 1975), p. 28.

fire put within the cavity, and that the head had been completely severed.[5]

Carrington wrote to Glover's brother in November that the body had been buried with suitable honors and that the only personal possessions Glover had left behind were a few letters, incomplete photographic equipment, and a blanket.

FATHER BARRY HAGAN

---

[5]Since Peters stated that Glover had been beheaded, it is difficult to know or to understand Fessenden's and Bisbee's remarks that he was found lying face downwards and with the implication that he was lying on his chest. How then could a fire have been lighted in the bowel area?

CHAPLAIN DAVID WHITE

The years of the Indian Wars brought men of various personalities and backgrounds to Fort Phil Kearny. One of the most "colorful" men was Chaplain David White, United States Army, known as the "Fighting Parson"[1] and described as "one who as far as looks went could hold his own with any of the young officers."[2]

David White was born May 18, 1818, in Bledsoe County, Tennessee. On September 21, 1842, he married Eliza Vance Davidson (Cumming), a widow with six children; seven more were born to Chaplain White and Eliza.

On August 18, 1862, he enlisted in the Army for a three year term with the 107th Illinois Infantry at Santa Anna, Illinois. He distinguished himself as a fierce fighting man in several military campaigns including the battles around Atlanta. White was honorably mustered out on June 21, 1865, and then on March 10, 1866, he received an appointment as Chaplain in the United States Army, with field and staff in the same regiment. His qualifications and background for the position are not entirely clear; however, it is known that he was a scholar of Latin and Hebrew and later, when appointed to Fort Phil Kearny, carried with him a copy of *Burton's Greek Grammar and Testament.* He is described in various newspaper accounts of the day as belonging to the

---

[1]"Camp Verde, Arizona Territory, February 1871-October 1872," *Southern Arizona Genealogical Society Bulletin* 3 (December 1967).

[2]Oliver Knight, "Frontier Army - Army Chaplains," Hagan Collection, Wyoming Room, Sheridan County Fulmer Public Library, Sheridan, Wyoming.

Methodist-Episcopal Church, while a more formal report described him as a methodist Clergyman.[3]

Chaplain White's first assignment was to Fort Riley, Kansas, but upon arrival he learned that the position was occupied. He was then sent to Fort Phil Kearny in the Dakota Territory and served there, except for a brief visit home, until its abandonment in August of 1868.

At Fort Reno, in July of 1866, Chaplain White joined a wagon train and detachment under the command of Lt. George Templeton to travel north to Fort Phil Kearny. On July twenty-first, on Crazy Woman Creek, the wagon train was attacked by Sioux.. White received a slight wound but continued to do battle and secured his reputation as the Fighting Parson:

> The ladies and some of the civilians began to pray rather loudly. The Chaplain, who used to be about as pious as a monk while in the post, suddenly seized a musket and said, "Ladies and gentlemen, there is a time for praying, and as we may gather from the Holy Writ, a time for fighting. God aids those who are willing to aid themselves. Now, stop praying and turn in to make some 'good Indians.'"[4]

White later volunteered to clear a ravine from which the Sioux had clear arrow range and, armed with an old fashioned pepper box, he declared "got two of the devils." He and Private Wallace then volunteered to "cut through" the Indians and ride back to Fort Reno for help. The besieged wagon train was rescued by a detachment under Captain Burrowes traveling south from Fort Phil Kearny to Fort Reno. Burrowes and Lieutenant Wands took over the

---

[3]*Arizona* (Prescott) *Weekly Miner*, 14 January 1871.

[4]John Finerty, *Warpath and Bivouac* (Norman: University of Oklahoma Press, 1961), pp. 309-406.

command when Lieutenant Templeton was injured and they decided to turn the wagon train around and head back to Fort Reno. At that moment, a detachment of infantry with Chaplain White and Private Wallace arrived from Fort Reno. It was not until the last week of July that the combined Wands and Burrowes wagon trains headed north for Fort Phil Kearny.[5]

Chaplain White finally received his official appointment as Post Chaplain on April 3, 1867, and accepted the Commission on July 17, 1867. As chaplain, he wore the uniform of the Army: on his shoulder straps were a shepherd's crook instead of the ranks usually noted. He also had the flag on his uniform.[6]

His presence at the fort was a comfort to the church-going people in situations of peace and peril and although he had no chapel in which to hold services, each new building was utilized for the service. Frances Carrington noted:

> [Chaplain White] was a devout Methodist, of good heart and excellent character in teaching the soldiers' children at the fort, for there were several, but very unsophisticated in general society matters.[7]

Colonel Carrington took careful pains to make the music at one of the Sunday services a special attraction for the men, arranging for a fine string band to accompany the several singers in a rendition of "Te Deum Laudamus." Frances Carrington remembered that a solemn Chaplain White

---

[5]Dee Brown, *Fort Phil Kearny, An American Saga* (Lincoln: University of Nebraska Press, 1961), pp. 84-90.

[6]Knight, "Frontier Army."

[7]Frances C. Carrington, *My Army Life* (Boulder, Colorado: Pruett Publishing Company, 1990), p. 102.

> asked the Colonel, "Isn't that a Catholic tune?" and upon answer by the Colonel, "Why, that is one of the oldest and most glorious hymns of the Church all over Christendom," he expressed surprise, but thought himself that "it seemed to be quite religious, but it was new to him."[8]

While stationed at the post, White devoted his time to conducting at least one service on the Sabbath, visiting the sick, organizing and teaching school to the children and Bible classes to the soldiers, along with the regular duties of marriages, baptisms and burials. It is thought that Chaplain White buried more victims of the Indian Wars than any other chaplain. In addition, chaplains were often expected to serve as librarians, gardeners, bakers, treasurers, and defense counsel at court martials. In fact, it was not uncommon for commanders to judge a chaplain's value to the army by how many non-chaplain duties he performed, and how well he did them.[9]

Chaplain White's family did not accompany him to assignments, but he was, despite absences, a devoted husband and wrote in his personal diary on April 2, 1866,

> Once again bade adieu to wife and children. I was deeply impressed with the possibility of its being a final parting. Oh God, preserve our health and permit us to meet in the flesh. Keep us from sin and grant us a happy meeting in heaven.[10]

---

[8]Ibid.

[9]Earl F. Stover, *Up From Handy Men: The United States Army Chaplaincy, 1865-1920,* volume 3 (Washington, D.C.: Office of Chief Chaplain, Department of the Army, 1977).

[10]David White Diary, Verde State Park, Camp Verde, Arizona.

In a later letter from Camp Verde, Arizona, he wrote,

> I had hoped to have a letter from home when I got here but it was a failure. Now, I want you to write yourself and not depend on the children. They do not know what to write as you do. It seem people (men) when they get far away from home forget the folks left behind. But to me, it makes them a thousand times more dear. Signed, My love to all, Yours till Death and Forever.[11]

In the summer of 1867, White requested a transfer from Fort Phil Kearny, as he had family at home in Santa Anna, Illinois. He was granted a leave in July of 1867, returning to the Fort on December tenth of that year.[12]

Chaplain White thought the hostile Indians were savages. Margaret Carrington recalled, "He thinks he did his duty; and the officers say that he thought it was just about the right thing to kill as many of the varmint as possible."[13]

White's feelings became more intense as he saw what he thought were the atrocities of Red Cloud's warriors. On December 21, 1866, Capt. William J. Fetterman's command was defeated and White had the task of overseeing a mass burial service.

His feelings about the Indians he considered as friendly were more compassionate. When nine Cheyenne arrived at the fort for provisions and permission to hunt in Tongue River valley, Carrington allowed them to camp on an island

---

[11]Letter from Chaplain David White to his wife, Fort Whipple, Arizona Territory, 19 February 1871. On file in the Wyoming Room, Sheridan County Fulmer Public Library Sheridan, Wyoming.

[12]David White Personnel File No. 2866, ACP 1872, Record of the Office of the Adjutant General, Record Group 98, National Archives, Washington, D.C.

[13]Margaret Irvin Carrington, *Absaraka, Home of the Crows* (Chicago: Lakeside Press, 1950), p. 142.

on Little Piney and gave them some bacon and coffee. This generosity did not sit well with the enlisted men and after rumor spread that these were the same Indians who had killed two men with the timber train, a group of soldiers began to talk of surrounding and killing the Cheyenne. Fortunately, Chaplain White was able to inform Colonel Carrington about the gravity of the situation in time for the Colonel to stop the soldiers from carrying out their plans.[14]

The Indians who came to the fort to trade and talk peace liked the Chaplain's prayers for them and held him in great esteem. When the Chaplain opened a Council meeting at the fort with a prayer, the Indians took him by the hand and placed him on a pile of twelve buffalo robes as a measure of their respect.[15]

He was well-received and well-liked at the fort, but his popularity declined during his last year and in later assignments, due to his vocal support of the temperance movement. His monthly reports to Washington showed concern for what he perceived as moral decay at the fort. He reported that the men and officers were drinking, gambling excessively and using profanity. He also requested that the trading post at the fort be closed on the Sabbath because he believed it caused the men to gather and drink. The request was denied as the civilians around the post needed to make purchases on the Sabbath when they were not farming. The result was that the officers and men were not allowed in the trading post during church service hours.

When Chaplain White served at Camp Verde five years later, he again was concerned with the condition of the troops. Once again he felt that excessive gambling, drinking, profanity and moral decay were evident. He reported this to

---

[14]Ibid., pp. 162-63.

[15]*Prescott Arizona Courier,* 8 April 1973, p. 10.

Washington which made him very unpopular with the commanding officers.

After serving at Fort Phil Kearny, Chaplain White served at nine different posts from 1868 to 1882. These included posts in Colorado (Fort Sedgewick), the territories of Wyoming (Camp Stambaugh, Fort Saunders) and Arizona (Camp Verde), Texas (Fort Eliot) and Kansas (forts Larned, Hayes and Leavenworth). While at Fort Leavenworth he requested a transfer in February of 1882 so he could minister to prisoners. Chaplain White retired from military life in 1886 and moved to Lawrence, Kansas, with his family.

During his retirement in Lawrence, he was involved with the University of Kansas and was considered an authority on Latin and Hebrew. Chaplain White was elected a Companion of the Military Order of the Loyal Legion of the United States on May 4, 1892, and Chaplain of the Kansas Commandry at the same time. He served until his death by apoplexy on October 28, 1901, at the age of eighty-three.[16]

His death was sad news to the town of Lawrence, attested to by the large crowd of friends present at his funeral and the many floral tributes.[17] As stated in the memorial,

> Post Chaplain David White was bold in the announcement of his faith in the Divinity of our Saviour, and was not discouraged by the sneers of the profane in preaching what he believed to be the Gospel.[18]

ANN KILPATRICK

---

[16]Military Order of the Loyal Legion of the United States, In Memorium, National Archives, Washington, D.C.

[17]David White Obituary, *Lawrence* (Kansas) *Daily Journal,* 28 October 1901, p. 4.

[18]Military Order of the Loyal Legion, *In Memorium.*

WILLIAM "BILL" DALEY

> It is given to but few men in this life to be part and parcel of the business, social, fraternal and political life of a great state during the time that its broad acres were the haunts of Indians and traversed by millions of wild animals and the few hardy pioneer settlers protected by a handful of federal troops.
>
> Yet this great transformation of a wilderness into a state of homes, ranches, schools, churches, populous cities and contented towns has all come to pass during the span of years covered by the life of William Daley since the day when he as a young man came to the boundless west, before the railroad, and far in advance of all the comforts and conveniences of our modern civilization.[1]

Said to have come West with cash capital of less than one dollar, Bill Daley became one of the most influential men of Wyoming. The son of Irish emigrants, William Daley, at twenty-two, had worked in shipbuilding yards in New Brunswick before signing on with a party traveling to the Rocky Mountains. On reaching Nebraska City, Daley entered the employ of a freighting outfit to Fort Mitchell. He then hired out to another freighting concern, that of A. C. Beckwith, Joe Sanders and Judge Kinney, taking sutler's supplies to Fort Phil Kearny.

On reaching the fort, Daley went to work for the government in his trade as carpenter, and in that capacity worked on the flagpole, having a part in its design, and taking part in the ceremonies and celebration upon the raising of that first flag on the last day of October 1866. The flagpole stood 124 feet high. The huge flag at its top was the

---

[1]"In Memorium," *Rawlins* (Wyoming) *Times,* December 1922.

first full garrison flag between the North Platte River and Montana. Margaret Carrington, in her journals, describes the entire ceremony and concludes,

> At the close of the prayer, the flag slowly rose to masthead, while national airs, the booming of cannon, and the sharp ring of presented arms paid it such tokens of respect as the occasion enjoined.[2]

On December 21, 1866, Bill Daley obtained a gun and prepared to accompany the Fetterman command. One of the officers refused to let him go, saying he should remain to work on the fort. In the aftermath of the tragic battle that day, he was one of the men assigned to blow up the powder magazine with women and children inside, if the fort were overrun by Indians.

In January of 1867, Daley was among those accompanying Colonel and Mrs. Carrington and Frances Grummond on their bitterly cold and arduous trip from Fort Phil Kearny to Fort McPherson, Nebraska. At Mud Spring, Daley was attacked by snow blindness which completely deprived him of his sight, temporarily, and which was accompanied by excruciating pain lasting for several days.

Daley worked on the rebuilding of Fort McPherson, and then went into business for himself delivering wood to the Union Pacific railroad. He was present at Promontory Point, Utah, in 1869 when the completion of the U.P. Railway was celebrated.

Bill Daley was in attendance at the Fort Phil Kearny reunion in 1908, forty-two years after the flag was first unfurled at Fort Phil Kearny. Also in attendance were General Carrington and his second wife Frances, Sam Gibson, Fred Newcomer and other Fort Phil Kearny

---

[2]Margaret Carrington, *Ab'Sa'Ra'Ka: Land of the Crows* (Lincoln: University of Nebraska Press, 1983), p. 156.

veterans. At that celebration, Daley was asked by Carrington to raise the flag to again fly over Fort Phil Kearny.

General Carrington gave him the flag flown on that occasion. This flag is now in the Wyoming State Museum, inscribed by Carrington with drawings by Daley. Never forgetful of his time at Fort Phil Kearny, Daley constructed a replica of the flagpole, which now stands on Carbon County Courthouse property in Rawlins.

Daley also financed the book, *My Army Life,* written shortly after the 1908 reunion by General Carrington's second wife, Frances Grummond Carrington, about her experiences at Fort Phil Kearny.

Through his long career, he had been involved in much of Wyoming's most dramatic history. As deputy sheriff for Carbon County, he was involved in the famous investigation of the hanging of Cattle Kate, of Johnson County War fame. He served in the Wyoming Territorial legislature from Carbon County at the time when the territory included the site of Fort Phil Kearny, and served on the committee which allotted the various state institutions to the towns of Wyoming.

He was instrumental in locating the state prison in Rawlins which at the time appeared a more lucrative source of income than the University, as the prison population was several hundred and growing and the University was only about a dozen students and faculty.

During the presidential campaign of 1900, Daley entertained Theodore Roosevelt and a party of fifty-two other prominent men of national and state reputation at his ranch. Several years later, as Roosevelt's guest in Washington, the President remarked to his wife, "This is the gentleman you have heard me speak of and at whose home in Wyoming I had the grandest dinner I ever sat down to."[3]

---

[3]*Daily* (Rawlins, Wyoming) *Times,* 17 August 1968.

On his death, at seventy-eight years, he had been accorded practically every honor of Masonry, in which brotherhood he held one of the highest ranks in the nation. He had built a desert claim into ranching interests of over sixty thousand acres, and had founded the First National Bank of Rawlins and later, the Rawlins State Bank.

Despite his success, Daley had the reputation, according to the *Rawlins Times,* of being the most kindly and approachable of men, ready to help wherever he was needed. He is one of those men and women who came to fight, work or seek for gold, and who stayed to write a large chapter in the history of Wyoming.

MARY ELLEN MCWILLIAMS, AUTHOR
BILL & CAROL DALEY, CONTRIBUTORS

NELSON STORY

By the time Nelson Story brought the first large herd of Texas longhorn cattle through the Bozeman Trail forts of Reno, Phil Kearny and C. F. Smith, leaving his mark on all three, he was already an established and successful resident of Virginia City, Montana Territory. He was twenty-eight years old and as for Fort Phil Kearny, he was just passing through.

As described by his grandson, Malcolm Story, he was

> a good shot, but no wild Bill Hickock. He was not a drinker, nor used tobacco, didn't swear, but if he were crossed unjustly and got riled, he was dangerous. He was 5'10" and 200 pounds. He demanded rigid compliance with his orders...otherwise someone was given their last pay check. He was a good roper, as was my dad and his older brother, Bud.[1]

Story was born in Ohio in 1836. He attended college but was prevented from graduating by the death of his father. He taught school briefly in Ohio, and was temporarily employed in the mercantile business in Illinois. According to Malcolm,

> by his mid-twenties he had already tried his hand at silver mining near Central City, Nevada; engaged in timbering in Kansas; and brought in the first wagon of goods ever taken to Blue River, near Breckenridge, Colorado. In 1860, Story, while hauling goods into Colorado, was stopped by Oteo Indians who stole all of the ox team but one steer.

---

[1]Malcolm Story to Mary Ellen McWilliams, 27 January 1986, Wyoming Room, Sheridan County Fulmer Public Library, Sheridan, Wyoming.

Story, by himself, hauled a wagon twenty miles with one sore-footed steer and a horse hitched by rope around the horn of a saddle.[2]

In March of 1853, Nelson Story and his wife Ellen started for East Bannack, soon to be in Montana Territory, traveling through Fort Bridger where they stayed for two weeks. They arrived at Bannack on June 4, 1863, just days before the discovery of gold at Alder Gulch. Story took fourteen pack animals to the present location of Virginia City and staked a claim of one hundred feet either side of the gulch.

He sold merchandise and mined gold, at one time working fifty men night and day, netting himself about fifty thousand dollars. In the spring of 1866, Story left Virginia City, Montana Territory, for the States with thousands of dollars worth of gold dust, exchanged it for cash and traveled to Fort Worth, Texas, with his money sewed into the lining of his jacket. At Fort Worth, he purchased about one thousand head of longhorn cows, hired a crew, and prepared to trail north.

On the way he was intercepted by Kansas ranchers, who objected to Texas cattle being brought through their country; this caused him to detour. At Leavenworth, he bought fifteen wagons, with merchandise to fill them, and, warned about Indian troubles along the Bozeman Trail, purchased the new Remington rolling stock rapid fire breechloading rifles for all his men.[3] On July tenth, he headed for Montana

---

[2]Peter Story to Mary Ellen McWilliams, 5 February 1991, Wyoming Room, Sheridan County Fulmer Public Library, Sheridan, Wyoming.

[3]Peter Story, 5 February 1991, and Harold L. Peterson, *The Remington Historical Treasury of American Guns* (New York: Thomas Nelson, n.d.), p. 168.

via Fort Laramie with his cattle herd, fifteen wagons of merchandise and twenty-seven men.

On the Dry Fork of the Powder River, his herd was raided by Sioux Indians. Two of his men were severely injured and about twenty head of cows were driven off. The wounded men were taken to Fort Reno, the first of the Bozeman Trail posts.

After seeing the wounded were cared for, and pitching camp, Story took some of his men and tracked the Indians about fifteen miles to their camp. Story's men surprised the Indians who were roasting one of the stolen beeves, and took back the stolen cattle.[4]

Story camped for almost a week near the post. Finally, determining his party was in more danger staying than in moving on, and seeing no solution in sight, he packed up and left in the middle of the night, in violation of Carrington's orders.

This enraged Carrington, who issued new and stringent regulations ordering all personnel of civilian trains, awaiting permits to travel, to be quartered within the stockade until given the go-ahead to travel north. In addition, he ordered that the stockade gates be locked at night and that all soldiers absent from quarters after tattoo be arrested and unless duly authorized, would be held to answer to charges before a garrison or general court-martial.[5]

Story suffered at least two more minor Indian attacks and a total of three men were killed by Indians on the trip north. Story traveled through Fort C. F. Smith, about ninety miles north of Fort Phil Kearny, and from there up the Bozeman Trail to a cow camp about thirty miles east of present-day

---

[4]Leeson, pp. 1163-1169. See T. R. Story notes in the margin.

[5]Dee Brown, *The Fetterman Massacre* (Lincoln, University of Nebraska Press, 1971), p. 138.

Livingston, Montana, arriving in early December. Here he left the cattle with a top hand and went on to Bozeman, where he built himself and his family a log home.

Story sold the steers and kept the heifers for breeding stock. He continued to ranch for many years, running his herd from Yellowstone Park to present-day Billings, Montana. He upgraded the herd with top quality bulls, and had U.S. contracts to supply the forts in the area. Story also trailed steers to the Union Pacific railroad in Cheyenne, Wyoming Territory, to ship east. During the brutal winter of 1885-86, he lost much of his herd.[6]

Story opened stores in Bozeman and Virginia City, selling nails at a dollar a pound, candles at seventy-five cents a pound and bacon at fifty cents a pound.

In April of 1867, John Bozeman and Thomas Cover, traveling to Fort C. F. Smith, camped at Story's cow camp on the Yellowstone. The next day, after resuming their journey, John Bozeman was killed, according to Cover, by attacking Indians. Story, also concerned for the danger of Indian raids to his cattle herd, immediately sent a trusted employee to investigate.[7]

Story then joined a group of men who went to bring Bozeman's body back for burial. It was decided, however, to bury him on the spot near where he fell. Story later arranged to have Bozeman's body moved to the cemetery in the town of Bozeman, and also paid for a monument in his honor.

---

[6]Malcolm Story, 27 January 1988.

[7]It was the popular conception at the time, according to Dr. Merrill Burlingame, that the initial investigation of the death of John Bozeman produced no evidence of Indian involvement. For more on the circumstances regarding the death of John Bozeman, see Story File, Sheridan County Fulmer Public Library; also, Merrill Burlingame, John M. Bozeman: Montana Trailmaker (Bozeman: Montana State University Museum of the Rockies, 1971), p. 323-44.

That same year, Story sold potatoes and turnips to the army at Fort C. F. Smith. These fresh vegetables kept the soldiers from suffering from the effects of scurvy, so tragic a problem at Fort Phil Kearny that same winter.

In 1868, with the abandonment of the Bozeman Trail posts, Nelson Story purchased, for about ten cents on the dollar, the remaining supplies left at Fort C. F. Smith. He resold them in stores in Helena and Bozeman.

He continued through his lifetime to involve himself in a variety of enterprises including the trailing of hundreds of head of mustang mares from California into Montana. He established a trading post on the Crow Indian reservation, established a bank, a flouring mill, and traded in real estate. He was also a member of the famous Montana "Vigilantes." He had a number of good Indian friends, especially among the Crow tribe, and including Chief Plenty Coups.

According to Malcolm Story, Nelson built a flour mill at Bozeman in 1883. It provided the largest consistent payroll in that area for the next forty-five years or so. He donated forty acres in Bozeman in 1893 to start the campus area for Montana State University and was a member of the first College Board that year.

In 1890, he extended his real estate holdings to business space in California, and by the time he died in 1926, his brother, Walter, managed the more than six hundred office rental units in downtown Los Angeles.

A metal sculpture of the man on his horse was dedicated by the City of Bozeman in 1984, and Story is buried in the cemetery there.

He and his wife Ellen (for whom the Ellen Theater in Bozeman was built and is named) had six children. Their descendants, into the fifth generation, still ranch in the Gallatin Valley near Bozeman, and two of his great-grand sons recently traveled the route of the legendary Story cattle drive of 1866, "probably the longest continuous overland drive ever made north from Texas."[8]

MARY ELLEN MCWILLIAMS

All personal biographical information not otherwise cited is from Leeson's Montana Personal History and Reminiscences *(House & Mill, 1885), pp. 1163-1169, with marginal notes by Thomas B. Story. See Fort Phil Kearny/Bozeman Trail collection, Wyoming Room, Sheridan County Fulmer Public Library, Sheridan, Wyoming.*

Special thanks to Malcolm and Peter Story and to Dr. Merrill Burlingame, all who read and corrected this biography. Also to Father Barry Hagan, C.S.C., who provided much source material, and to Charles Luxmoore, who researched the accounts of the rifles used.

Because, according to Dr. Merrill Burlingame, Professor Emeritus of History at Montana State University, the Story family has been careful through the years to present a "remarkably accurate account" of the events in the life of Nelson Story, I have used the family as authority in a number of instances where accounts differ.

---

[8]Brown, p. 134.

JOHN FITCH KINNEY

John Fitch Kinney was born on April 2, 1816, in New Haven, New York. He received irregular schooling in the area until about the age of sixteen, when he began teaching and started law studies. In 1836, he moved to Marysville, Ohio, where he continued to teach and studied law with Augustus Hall. In 1836, he was admitted to the Ohio bar and opened a practice. Two years later, in January of 1839, he married Hannah Dorothy Hall, sister of Augustus Hall, and the couple had seven children during the years 1839-1860.

In 1840, Kinney moved his practice to Mt. Vernon, Ohio, and in 1844, he moved again, joining the practice of his wife's father, Colonel Samuel Hall, in Lee County, Iowa. He settled in West Point, Iowa, leading an active political life as Secretary of the Iowa Legislative Council (1845-46). He was appointed Lee County Prosecuting Attorney (1846) and in 1847 was president of the Democratic party's State nominating convention.

In 1853, President Pierce named John Kinney to the post of Chief Justice of the Utah Supreme Court, an appointment he accepted because his wife was in poor health and he thought the Utah climate might help her. In the spring of 1854, the Kinneys set out for Utah and while enroute, his wife gave birth to a son named "Bill Nebraska," whom the Judge claimed was the first white child born in Nebraska Territory.[1]

In 1856, the Kinneys returned to West Point, Iowa, and in the spring of 1857, the Judge moved his family to Ne-

---

[1]John Fitch Kinney Papers, MS 619, Hall-Kinney Collection, Nebraska State Historical Society, Lincoln, Nebraska.

braska City, Nebraska. Kinney set up a law practice, involved himself in land speculation and promoted the town by persuading government freight contractors to make Nebraska City the starting point for their western routes. In 1860, he was reappointed Chief Justice of Utah Territory, holding that position until 1863, when a new administration in Utah replaced Kinney as Chief Justice. That fall he was elected as a Democratic delegate to the U.S. Congress for one term, and in 1865 he returned to Nebraska City and once again resumed his law practice and involved himself in real estate transactions.

Kinney was typical of the entrepreneurs and professionals who took advantage of the business opportunities on the western frontier. He had exhibited commercial tendencies when, as Chief Justice in Utah, he ran a store and boarding house on the side; he apparently continued to dabble in any business venture that presented itself throughout his long legal career.

In 1866, the Judge took advantage of the opportunities along the Bozeman Trail when he became, in effect, the sutler for Fort Phil Kearny. He apparently purchased operating rights in the business from Roger T. Beal, or his assignees. Beal held the appointment of sutler from August 1866 to July 1867.

The store that Kinney ran had high overhead costs, especially in the area of transportation. The greatest profits came from dealing with commissioned officers and with civilian and contractor employees. Civilian government employees received forty-five dollars a month for teamsters and the quartermaster and commissary clerks up to $135 a month. Civilian contractor employees received five dollars per day on up, according to the job, and could make a tidy sum collecting $128 a ton for prairie hay and $60 or more per cord for firewood. The soldier, however, was not very important to the store as a private made only $13 a month and the highest paid enlisted man received $34 a month.

Captain Ten Eyck noted in his diary that Judge Kinney, "would-be sutler," arrived at Fort Phil Kearny on August 7th.[2] Ten Eyck made frequent references to Kinney's activities at the post throughout the fall. Ten Eyck, like others at the post, always referred to Kinney as "Judge Kinney" since he was known to be a former territorial Supreme Court Justice.

The garrison's store became a social headquarters and a place for officers to drink champagne, wine, brandy and whiskey. During his brief time at the fort, Kinney took an active part in the social life of the post, particularly among the officers and their families. Ten Eyck's diary gives a few tantalizing glimpses of Kinney's life at the post, such as dining with friends and taking rides around the picket line. On September fourth, Judge Kinney visited the pinery with Doctor Horton, Lieutenant Wands and Captain Ten Eyck, where they were treated to a meal of elk meat. Two days later he accompanied Colonel Carrington, most of the officers, and their wives, on a picnic in the mountains.

Mrs. Carrington commented that Judge Kinney's catering seemed more like a banquet than a picnic, as he provided

> canned lobster, cove oysters, and salmon, jellies, pine-apples, tomatoes, sweet corn, peas, pickles, puddings, pies, domestic cake, from doughnuts and gingerbread up to plum cake and jelly cake.[3]

Margaret Carrington also mentions his reading a poem at the dedication flag raising ceremonies on the last day of October.

---

[2]Tenodor Ten Eyck, Diary 1866, MS 82, Special Collections Library, University of Arizona, Tucson, Arizona.

[3]Margaret Irwin Carrington, *Absaraka* (Lincoln: University of Nebraska Press, 1983), p. 142.

On September eighteenth, Judge Kinney and Captain Ten Eyck, the commander at the post, had to speak forcefully to the teamsters who were striking in order to persuade them to go back to work. According to Ten Eyck, they told them to go back to work or they would not be paid, and presumably the dispute was settled.[4]

Judge Kinney did not remain long at Fort Phil Kearny and on November nineteenth, he left with a large train, including the paymaster, to return to Nebraska.

Kinney did a great deal of business with the Indian Bureau once that Agency established an issue office and warehouse at Fort Phil Kearny, down along the creek. The agents negotiated with the tribes of the region to buy special presents for many influential Indians and had cash accounts at the trader's store for that purpose. This, and the fact that in February 1867 he was appointed commissioner to visit the warring Indian tribes, paid off for him; in the spring of 1867, Kinney was appointed by President Andrew Johnson as one of the Special Indian Commissioners to investigate the Fetterman Fight.

Kinney was sent by the commission to Fort Phil Kearny to meet with the Crow Indians. He arrived at the post on May thirty-first, and the council was held from June twenty-first to June twenty-fifth. Judge Kinney was the only member named to the commission to actually make the trip to the fort. On July 24, 1867, Kinney took the testimony of Captain Powell which was critical of Carrington, and which Kinney then forwarded to General Grant.[5]

---

[4]Ten Eyck, Diary 1866.

[5]Judge Kinney should not be considered an impartial investigator because he did not like Colonel Carrington. Carrington had previously denied a claim Kinney submitted for loss of sutler goods, which Kinney claimed were stolen by soldiers. For a full discussion of Powell's false testimony see: Michael Straight, "The Strange Testimony of Major Powell," *The Westerners,* New York Posse Brand Book, 1960, 7:4-8.

As soon as the investigation and his official duties of taking statements about the Fetterman fight were over, Kinney reverted to his old ways. He applied for and was granted permission to trade with the troops and citizens at the sutler's store as he had the fall before. Hinting at a previous problem, General Order No. 45, dated July 1, 1867, states that he was allowed to trade, "with express condition that no intoxicating liquors of any kind shall either be kept or sold." Kinney did not remain at the fort very long, and by October he was in Washington D.C. to write his final report.

Judge Kinney was the only commissioner who expressed the idea that the best way to deal with the recalcitrant Indians was for the army to defeat them and to place the peaceful Crow on a separate reservation.

The Judge returned to his law practice in Nebraska City, which was interrupted by one last governmental assignment as agent of the Yankton Sioux, from December 11, 1884 to January 1889. In 1889, he moved to San Diego, California, where his wife Hannah died in 1895. Kinney remarried in 1899 and moved to Salt Lake City, Utah, where he died on August 16, 1902.

ROBERT A. MURRAY

John Bratt

Bullwhackers, the frontier freighters, were the backbone of the Western fort systems, and without their continuous deliveries, neither the military nor the frontier towns would have survived. Descriptions of bullwhackers range from "a driver of oxen in teams from five to eight yokes usually attached to two canvas-covered wagons...the term was as familiar as that of 'chauffeur' today"[1] to "bullwhackers were a picturesque group of men who were patient, tolerant, and self-reliant; they offered a brave front in time of danger and appeared immune to distance."[2]

Flannel shirts, pants, broad brimmed hats, heavy boots, and a belt that carried a revolver, knife and cartridges were the clothing commonly worn by the bullwhackers on the trail. The whips gave the bullwhackers their name because they continuously used them to train and encourage the oxen to pull the heavy loads. The whip had a three foot stock and twelve feet of lash with poppers on the end. When brand new the whip included extra buckskin to repair the lash and to make new poppers. The bullwhackers' skills included wagon circling and shoeing oxen, and they were expected to repair yokes and bows, fix wheels, tighten tires, wedge boxes, and care for their own possessions, all while keeping an eye on their beasts, the weather and the Indians.

John Bratt was not a typical freighter. He was born on August 9, 1842, in the town of Leek, Staffordshire, England,

---

[1]William Francis Hooker, *The Bullwhacker, Adventures of a Frontier Freighter* (Lincoln: University of Nebraska Press, 1988), p. 1.

[2]Nolie Mumey, *Wyoming Bullwhacker, Episodes in the Life of James Milton Sherrod* (Denver: Range Press, 1976), p. 15.

the son of a minister. Bratt was well-educated and a moral man. However, his penchant for mischief discouraged the idea of having John follow in his father's footsteps; instead he was apprenticed to a merchant. A keen sense of adventure led John to America where he worked hard and shrewdly, raised a fortune and lost it. He attended Lincoln's funeral, worked on a levee gang, and traveled from New York to Chicago, to New Orleans and to St. Louis, where he arrived in the spring of 1866.

In April of that year, John began his western adventures as a bullwhacker. John's education and morality, however, set him apart from the other bullwhackers and he formed an immediate judgement, which seemed to stay with him throughout his tenure:

> I began to get acquainted with my fellow bullwhackers. A few good men, some medium, and others very bad. Lack of enforcement of law and order seemed to add to their meanness. The men ranged in years from 20 to 45, and as I seemed to be the only one in this crowd of about 33 men who did not drink, swear, play card, smoke or chew tobacco, I was soon put down for a "goody-goody" or a fool.[3]

On May 15, 1866, Bratt joined a wagon train loaded with six thousand pounds of staples headed for the Dakota Territories to supply the forts being established along the Bozeman Trail. The lead cattle were trained, but the rest were mostly wild. It was the bullwhackers' job to harness and train the oxen during the first days on the road. The train traveled but one mile the first day, and it took about two weeks to train the cattle well enough to make them steady workers.

---

[3]John Bratt, *Trail of Yesterday* (Chicago: University Press, 1921) p. 52.

Bratt is almost comical when he describes the first time he swears at his steers. About sixty miles into the journey one of the oxen stepped on his foot, and he said, "Damn you!" There was much celebration amongst the other men who cheered him. But Bratt "was just as busy in the opposite direction, quietly asking God to forgive me and asking Him to keep me from it in the future."[4]

After crossing the North Platte River at Fort Caspar, Bratt reports friendly visits with the Cheyenne Indians, during which he himself became friendly with Dull Knife when he gave him an extra plate of food. Dull Knife had come to the camp to retrieve a stolen buckskin. The wagon train boss, Captain Bass, at first hid and then to avoid a confrontation, gave the Cheyenne army provisions. Bass was later dismissed for giving away the supplies.

When Dull Knife left the camp he shook hands with Bratt and warned him to watch out for the more ferocious Arapaho. The Arapahos did indeed attack as the wagon train was crossing a dry fork of the Platte northwest of Fort Caspar. The men were successful in their defense, and the whole incident made them more cautious travelers.

During their stop at Fort Reno, on Powder River, Bratt suffered a severe overdose of alcohol, administered when

> half a dozen bullwhackers seized me that night, threw me down and forced down my throat between a pint and a quart of the worst old road ranch whiskey that I ever smelled. The result was that I had to be hauled in the wagon for over a week.[5]

The perpetrators showed their remorse and were, of course, forgiven.

---

[4]Ibid., p. 54.

[5]Ibid., p. 80.

Near the Powder River crossing, the wagon train ran into a herd of five thousand buffalo, traveling in a flatiron shape and moving to the southwest. The ox-trains had to be divided in two to allow the buffalo to pass. The herd "was led by a large male, the cows, calves and yearlings on the inside, protected on the flanks by dry cows, heifers and males of two years and over, thus displaying a wonderful instinct in protecting their young."[6]

The wagon train arrived at Fort Phil Kearny in mid-September of 1866, in the midst of Red Cloud's war. Colonel Carrington, the commander at the Fort, ordered that the supply wagon train camp near the fort, along Piney Creek. It took three days to unload all the supplies.

Bratt remained at Fort Phil Kearny until early November 1866. During this time he worked for Carter and Coe, who had both wood and hay contracts at the Fort. All teams of hay and wood cutters entering and leaving the Fort were under military escort. Bratt's first trip to the hayfield was at night, leaving the Fort about 8:00 p.m., and arriving at the hay camp late at night. At daybreak he was given instructions on loading the wagons and on defense, in case of an Indian attack. There was a breastworks in the middle of the hayfield where all the haymakers, mowers, rakers, and teamsters with their teams were to take cover when the Indians "swooped down on them, which was often three to four times a day."[7]

In spite of these defensive measures, men were killed every day. Mister Carter hired a group of men called "mountaineers" or "Bailey's Bunch." Bratt describes the mountaineers as a group of about fifty mounted men who protected the camps and teams day and night. They were

---

[6]Ibid., p. 81.

[7]Ibid., p. 89.

paid five dollars a day and were supervised by Captain Bailey, who was a strict disciplinarian but highly respected. Bratt writes, "they did not know what fear was and were always ready to fight Indians." Bratt naturally adds, "I came across only one who did not drink, chew tobacco and swear."[8]

The bullwhackers, wood choppers, mule skinners, mountaineers and other civilian workers camped just outside the Fort where they enjoyed evening campfires and much gambling took place. In the event of an Indian attack these men were under the supervision of Captain Bailey, and each man was given a location and job to do when there was an Indian attack on the Fort.

Bratt describes one night when Indians attempted to set the grass and brush on fire and the night herders barely made it safely inside the Fort. About 4:00 a.m., a soldier standing guard at the corner of the stockade screamed for help because he thought some Indians were trying to rope him. His imagination had gotten the best of him; the civilians were alarmed and guarding the camp near his position on the stockade.

It was soon after this encounter that Bratt had a flash of intuition of impending disaster, and he decided to abandon the log shack that he and two other men were building on Piney Creek and return to Fort Mitchell. "To my Guardian Angel alone I attribute this timely warning."[9] Bratt was probably in Nebraska, near Fort Mitchell, when he learned of the Fetterman disaster.

John Bratt concluded his life as a cattleman, businessman, and mayor of North Platte, Nebraska. His moralistic attitude is a major theme throughout his autobiography, but in spite of his diatribes, his descriptions of the work and daily life are

---

[8]Ibid., p. 91.

[9]Ibid., p. 102.

a rare treasure and provide a unique picture of civilian life along the Bozeman Trail and at Fort Phil Kearny. John Bratt died in North Platte, Nebraska, on June 15, 1918, after a brief illness.

PATTY MYERS

HORATIO SYDNEY BINGHAM

Horatio Sydney Bingham was the son of farmers recently immigrated from Ireland. Born April 3, 1838, Bingham spent his early years on the family farm in Vermont. His family later moved to Winona, Minnesota.

On April 29, 1861, Bingham enlisted as a private in the First Minnesota Infantry. Horatio fought at the First Battle of Bull Run and in the Peninsula Campaign, attaining the rank of sergeant. Sergeant Bingham was wounded at the Battle of Antietam and was honorably discharged from service in November of 1862.[1]

Horatio returned home to Winona but did not stay long. In January 1863, Bingham was given the commission of captain, commanding Company L, Second Minnesota Cavalry.[2] He spent much of his time in administrative positions, while his unit pursued Sioux Indians involved in the 1862 Minnesota Uprising. Captain Bingham served as recruiting officer for his unit, as Acting Ordnance Officer for Minnesota, and as Chief of Cavalry for Minnesota. In addition, he served on the staff of General Pope.[3]

Bingham was mustered out of volunteer service in April of 1866. However, on April sixteenth, he received the commission of second lieutenant, Second United States

---

[1]Information on Bingham's early life acquired from letter from David Bingham to Kevin O'Dell, 8 April 1989.

[2]Muster Roll, Company L, Second Minnesota Cavalry, 4 January 1864.

[3]Letter from H. S. Bingham to Lieutenant J. T. Morrison, 1 March 1865.

Cavalry.[4] Lieutenant Bingham took command of Company C and was assigned to Fort Phil Kearny. Company C and three other officers, including Captain Fetterman, arrived at their new post on November 3, 1866. Bingham and his company quickly went to work relieving wood trains and escorting mail and supplies. On December third, Bingham and twenty-four of his men returned to Fort Phil Kearny after delivering mail to Fort C. F. Smith in a record seven days.[5]

On the morning of December 6, 1866, the fort's wood train came under attack. Two relief parties were placed in the field. One was commanded by Col. Henry Carrington and the other by Fetterman, with Bingham and thirty cavalrymen accompanying. The inexperienced officers and men quickly became confused and drawn away into small groups. One such group contained Bingham, Lt. George Grummond (who disobediently left Carrington's command), two sergeants and two privates. Bingham pursued a party of warriors who were merely decoys. The small party became surrounded. The five men rode for an opening towards a bluff.[6] Bingham fell back to the rear of the fleeing party and upon exhausting his pistol ammunition, fought his pursuers with his saber. Sergeant Bowers was pulled off his horse and mortally wounded by a tomahawk to the head. The united Carrington/Fetterman party quickly met up with the desperate Grummond party. Upon seeing the condition of Sergeant Bowers, Carrington sent for an ambulance from the fort.[7] He then proceeded to search for Bingham. His naked body was

---

[4]Letter from H. S. Bingham to General Thomas, 19 April 1866.

[5]Dee Brown, *Fetterman Massacre* (Lincoln: University of Nebraska Press, 1962), pp. 158-59.

[6]Order of the Indian Wars 1 (Fall 1980):9-11.

[7]Ibid.

found bent over a stump, scalped three times, and pierced with several arrows.[8]

Shortly after returning to the post, Sergeant Bowers died. Three days later, he and Lieutenant Bingham were buried. At the time of his death, Horatio Sydney Bingham was a mere twenty-eight years old.

KEVIN O'DELL

[8]Ibid.

Tasunka Witko
(Crazy Horse)

The legend of Tasunka Witko, the Oglala Lakota warrior and leader, will live as long as anyone keeps alive, in memory, the turbulent history of the High Plains from the mid- to late nineteenth century. Many names, both Indian and White, emerged from that era called the "Indian Wars" to occupy a place in history, and to live on in our imaginations.

We have managed to elevate some of those historic figures to superhuman levels. Tasunka Witko among them. It is well to perpetuate a legend, but not at the price of forgetting that the legend was a man, a human being...a real person. In the case of Tasunka Witko, however, it is easy to mix reality with legend.

I first heard of Tasunka Witko when I was a small boy. My maternal grandfather spoke of him often. However, my grandfather rarely gave a physical description of the great warrior. More often, he spoke of this or that battle, and Tasunka Witko's role in it. Rarely did he actually speak the great warrior's name. He simply referred to him as *Oglala zuya-wicasa ohitike wan he.* That courageous Oglala warrior.

In the summer of 1950 I was five. I accompanied my grandfather as he dragged logs with a team of horses. At a crossing on the Little White River (in south-central South Dakota), he paused to comment on the battle on the Greasy Grass River in 1876. "That river was like this one," he told me. "It was a day like this, when that courageous Oglala warrior led other warriors against Yellow Hair. Yellow and all his soldiers were killed that day."

Some three hundred miles and seventy-three years from the Battle of the Little Big Horn, my grandfather spoke of it as if it had been just yesterday and over the next hill. This is how I came to know Tasunka Witko; from my grandfather's words, from his vivid storytelling, and from the tone of respect in his voice whenever he spoke of that *courageous Oglala warrior.* I feel the same kinship, the same respect my grandfather felt. So much, that there were moments when I fully expected the great warrior to come riding up a draw, or up to my campfire. There are times when I still do.

He was born in the Black Hills, probably in the early 1840s. His father was Oglala and his mother a Sicangu (some say the sister of the Sicangu leader, Spotted Tail). At the age of seventeen or eighteen, he was given the name of Tasunka Witko by his father. It was an honorable name, long in the family and passed from father to son. That tradition ended with Tasunka Witko of legend, for he had no son.

The precise translation of *Tasunka Witko* is *his crazy horse*. The phrase *crazy horse* is translated into Lakota as *sunkawakan witko.* As we can see, the purveyors of legend have left us with a slight, but indelible, mistranslation from Lakota to English.

Tasunka Witko has been called and portrayed as a ruthless savage, a bloodthirsty warrior, and the son of a white man. He was none of those. He was, most certainly, a product of his environment and of the times and circumstances into which he was born and had to live.

The Lakota, or Western Sioux, of the 1840s were several generations into the horse culture. They were a strong, proud people living close to the Earth. Nomadic hunter/warriors who numbered far more than their Nakota and Dakota relatives living east of the Mnisose (Missouri River).

The territory of the Lakota was vast. It encompassed all of what is now western South Dakota, northwestern Nebraska, most of eastern Wyoming to the Shining Mountains (Big Horns), and up into a small portion of southeastern Montana. They fought with the Crow, the Snakes, the Pawnee, and the Blackfeet. They allied themselves with the Cheyenne and Arapaho.

The Lakota way of life was one in which the hunter/warrior was revered. Survival, life itself, depended on the strength, skills, and ability of the hunter/warrior -- the provider and protector. Into this world, Tasunka Witko was born.

More than likely, a toy bow was hung near his cradle-board to show him the way of his coming manhood. And as soon as he was able to walk, his training to be a hunter/warrior began. He learned the many physical skills necessary to his calling: tracking, weapons construction and use, "wilderness" survival, and horsemanship, to name a few. He learned that being a hunter/warrior was a way to gain status among his people. But he also learned that a hunter/warrior had a lifelong obligation to the people, ending only with death.

Guided by tradition, schooled by a formidable warrior, and tempered by fights against old Lakota enemies (such as the Crows and the Snakes), young Tasunka Witko emerged as a significant leader while still a relatively young man. It is said of him that, by his late teens, he had won more war honors than most warriors did in a lifetime. He was chosen as a Shirtwearer when barely in his twenties, a position he held until his death.

Tasunka Witko was born into a world already firmly inhabited by White people. As a boy he witnessed the Grattan Fight.

After a White immigrant's cow had wandered into a Lakota camp and was killed, an old Lakota leader attempted to pay the cow's owner much more than the animal was worth. But to no avail. This bad situation was intensified by a young cavalry officer who had bragged that with a handful of men he could ride through the entire Lakota nation. This officer, Lieutenant Grattan, attempted to arrest the Lakota warrior who had killed and butchered the cow. Further complications arose when an interpreter deliberately ridiculed the Lakota. The result was immediate tragedy for Grattan and his men. Grattan's entire command of thirty soldiers were wiped out by the Lakota.

This incident taught the future Lakota war leader that the White man's attitude toward the Lakota was not good. The authority assumed and exercised by the Whites over the Lakota, simply because they were White, was unacceptable to the young Oglala Lakota. The Grattan incident influenced his thinking anytime he had to deal with the White man.

Tasunka Witko won a strong following with his early exploits as a warrior. But he also made enemies among his own people; a notoriety he enhanced by trying to steal another man's wife. Although a Lakota woman was free to leave a husband if she so chose, Tasunka Witko's rival was a weak man who could not live with his wife's decision; he shot Tasunka Witko in the face with a revolver and took back his wife.

The ill-fated attempt to finally win the woman he had loved since boyhood shows clearly that, after all, Tasunka Witko was a man. He did a very human thing. But his status as a warrior and a leader has overshadowed, in our minds, any weaknesses he may have had as a man.

The ultimate personal fate of this particular Oglala was unalterably entwined with that of his people. Because of his reputation, and his influence over his fellow warriors, he was feared by the U.S. Army. To defeat Tasunka Witko would be to defeat the Lakota. The Army was well aware of the role he had in significant engagements, such as the Fetterman Fight in 1866.

The Fetterman Fight may well not have occurred when and how it did had it not been for the leadership exhibited by Tasunka Witko. Previous attempts to lure the soldiers out of Fort Phil Kearny had failed because of over-exuberance on the part of a few young, inexperienced warriors who opened fire prematurely. But not so on December 21, 1866. Tasunka Witko led a small group of Lakota and Sahiyela (Cheyenne) warriors who were selected to act as decoys. Their task was to lure the soldiers into a trap. The soldiers, under the command of Captain Fetterman, were leery. But Tasunka Witko and his decoys, riding well within the soldiers' rifle range and hurling insults and threats, were able to lead Fetterman's command into the trap. Tasunka Witko put himself directly in harm's way on several different occasions, knowing there was no substitute for leadership by example. The result was the complete annihilation of Fetterman's command.

Because of such actions, Tasunka Witko's reputation among his own people was greater than the notoriety he may have achieved among his enemies. He never lacked for followers whenever he rode against an enemy, Indian or White.

There were other great victories in which Tasunka Witko had significant roles, such as the Battles of the Rosebud and the Greasy Grass, both in 1876. During the Battle of the Rosebud the Lakota and Sahiyela defeated a larger, combined force of soldiers and Snakes (Shoshoni) under the command of Gen. George Crook. Eight days later, the Lakota and Sahiyela responded to a direct attack on their encampment on the Greasy Grass River (Little Big Horn River) by the Seventh Cavalry under the command of Lt. Col. George Custer. In three hard-fought engagements over two days, the Lakota and Cheyenne defeated their attackers, killing about half of the soldiers; including five entire companies under the direct command of George Custer. Tasunka Witko was the primary warrior leader in both of these major battles.

The Battles of the Rosebud and the Greasy Grass were the last major engagements the Lakota would win. Thereafter, they fought primarily defensive actions as the Army stepped up the campaigns against them. And when the great war leader's own camp was attacked, many Lakota felt that the end had come. Finally, to insure the survival of his own people, Tasunka Witko surrendered.

It is important to emphasize that Tasunka Witko did not surrender as a direct result of being defeated on the field of battle. Neither did he surrender to save his own life. He probably envisioned his own death in some battle. His belief in what a warrior's death should be. But perhaps he knew, or hoped, that there were other ways to win and ultimately survive. A warrior could fight and die. But the women, children, and the old ones would suffer if there were no more warriors to protect them. For that reason Tasunka Witko put aside his warrior pride and surrendered.

Though the "Indian Wars" for the Lakota were essentially over by 1877, Tasunka Witko's rivals continued to be envious of the place he had in the hearts and minds of his own people. In September of 1877, Tasunka Witko died at Fort Robinson, Nebraska, killed by a bayonet and the envy of little men.

I have haunted the mountains of his birth. I have seen the place where he died. I have walked the trails where he led warriors into battle, and often into victory. In those places I can feel the presence of old warriors. And there are times when I pause at the bend of a river, in a wooded glade, or on a prairie meadow...fully expecting to see that courageous warrior come riding into view. Such is his place in legend and in the hearts of men, even today.

JOSEPH M. MARSHALL

CAPT. WILLIAM JUDD FETTERMAN

Born in April 1835 in Cheshire, Connecticut, William Judd Fetterman was the son of George Fetterman, an 1827 graduate of West Point, and Ann Marie Judd of New London.

Little is known of William Fetterman's early life. His mother died shortly after his birth, and the elder Fetterman died in 1844 when the boy was nine. Young Fetterman then became the ward of his uncle on his mother's side, Henry Bethel Judd, an officer who had served with distinction during the Mexican War. Thus Fetterman grew to manhood in a military family, and his one great ambition was to continue that tradition. When eighteen years old, Fetterman submitted an application to West Point, but was unsuccessful in securing an appointment.

On May 14, 1861, Fetterman received a commission as a first lieutenant in the newly established Eighteenth U.S. Infantry. He was promoted to captain on October 25, 1861, taking charge of Company A of the Second Battalion on November twenty-eighth. In April and May of 1862, Fetterman participated in the Siege of Corinth, Mississippi, and on the last day of the year, his regiment met the enemy at Stones River, Tennessee. Holding the center as part of General L. H. Rousseau's Division, the Eighteenth lost nearly three hundred men -- or nearly half its strength -- in an hour of fighting. At the end of the war, Fetterman received a brevet of major for "great gallantry and good conduct" exhibited during this engagement.

In the spring of 1864, Fetterman commanded Company A in the famous Atlanta Campaign of William Tecumseh Sherman. At New Hope, Georgia, on May twenty-seventh, he led the Second Battalion into battle, and he continued to command through the fighting at Kenesaw Mountain, the Smyrna Church, and Peach Tree Creek. In the Siege of Atlanta from July 21 to August 19, 1864, he functioned as Acting Assistant Adjutant General of the Fourteenth Corps.

The Battle of Jonesboro on September first was the Eighteenth Infantry's major contribution to the winning of the Atlanta campaign. Here the regiment overran the Confederates' first line of defense. Receiving the brevet of lieutenant colonel for great gallantry and good conduct for his service at Atlanta and Jonesboro, Fetterman remained as AAAG for the Fourteenth Corps until the close of the war. He received his orders to report to Fort Phil Kearny on September 1, 1866.

Certainly Fetterman had an impressive Civil War record. Twice breveted for gallantry and moving from company to battalion commander, the young officer had earned an enviable reputation. According to Fox's *Regimental Losses*, his regiment had suffered more casualties than any other in the regular army, and with the exceptions of the battles of Chickamauga and Chattanooga, he had been through it all.

William Fetterman, the much-lauded Civil War commander, reached Fort Phil Kearny on November third. On November fifth, after only forty-eight hours on the job, he requested and received permission from Col. Henry Carrington to set an ambush for the Sioux by using hobbled mules as bait. The Sioux, however, embarrassed the secreted detachment by capturing another cattle herd a mile away. A second important incident occurred on November seventh when Fetterman started out to visit the pinery with three other officers. As they entered a ravine, they were suddenly fired upon from about fifty paces by fifteen to twenty rifles in two volleys. None were hit. After a relief party arrived, the group returned without incident. The lack of accuracy no doubt re-enforced Fetterman's depreciatory view of the

Indians' skill with arms and, being made a fool of by the Sioux earlier, undoubtedly fired his resolve.

Fetterman soon voiced his opinion that the Sioux were not to be respected as a fighting force. According to Margaret Carrington, the officer declared that with a company of regulars he could whip a thousand Indians and with a regiment, could defeat the whole array of warring tribes. In consequence, Fetterman requested a detachment of fifty mounted soldiers and fifty civilians for the purpose of chastising the Sioux in their camps on Tongue River. Carrington's refusal apparently strengthened Fetterman's resolve to take any opportunity to engage the foe in sustained battle.

Fetterman had his first chance for real combat on December sixth. About 1:00 p.m., the Sioux attacked the wood cutting party. Carrington decided to attempt to intercept the Indians when they retreated over Lodge Trail Ridge, which was their custom when reinforcements arrived. Carrington sent Fetterman and 2nd Lt. Horatio S. Bingham with thirty of the cavalry to relieve the wood party and assembled twenty-one mounted infantrymen under Lt. George Grummond to attempt the cut off.

When Fetterman reached the scene, he found a party of ten under siege by one hundred Sioux and gave chase, following them five miles into rough, ravine-filled country. Near a fork of Peno Creek, other Sioux poured out of ravines, nearly encircling the party. Fetterman brought the column to a halt, but, unexpectedly, Lieutenant Bingham and three-fourths of the cavalry bolted, riding through Indian lines back down the road to Fort Phil Kearny. Only the arrival of Carrington's column saved the day, but not before Bingham and Sgt. Gideon R. Bowers were killed and one sergeant and four privates wounded. Fetterman's first sustained encounter with the Indians had hardly been a success. According to Carrington, Fetterman and Brown were soon plotting to find a way to meet the Sioux and their allies in force.

The story of December 21, 1866, is easily told. An hour after the wood train left, word was received that it was under attack. Citing his seniority, Fetterman requested the command, which eventually numbered eighty men, among them Capt. Frederick Brown and Lt. George Grummond. Carrington gave his assent, but ordered Fetterman not to pursue the Indians out of sight of the post. However, following decoys, Fetterman pushed over Lodge Trail Ridge and down the other side into an ambush. There, troops fell to a force estimated at 1,500 to 2,000 warriors. The Sioux warrior American Horse clubbed Fetterman from his horse and finished him with a knife, cutting his throat clear to the cervical spine. A party sent to investigate the sound of heavy firing reached the scene too late, as the victorious Indian force moved away to the northeast.

Burial of the officers took place on December twenty-fourth, with Fetterman and Brown placed in one grave. In retrospect, Fetterman's extensive Civil War experience did not prepare him for battle on the plains, where the plan was never to stand but to strike quickly and depart rapidly. Fetterman's arrogance and reckless courage were a fatal mix in guerilla warfare on the plains.

JOHN D. MCDERMOTT

Blue Feather & Na Do Nun Ha (Arthur Brady & Wife)

My grandfather, Blue Feather, was born in 1834 and lived to be 104 years old. He and my grandmother, Na Do Nun Ha, survived the Sand Creek Massacre; he fought at Fetterman Ridge, and was there to watch Little Wolf finally burn down the Buffalo Creek Fort (Fort Phil Kearny). He and my grandmother were among the Cheyennes to return from Oklahoma with Little Wolf and Dull Knife in what became the Northern Cheyennes' own "Trail of Tears" in 1878.

He was my history teacher and I learned many things from this great man. My father died when I was a child and my mother and us children went to live with my grandparents on Muddy Creek near Busby, Montana. My grandfather died when I was fifteen. He rode horseback from his home, near Busby, to Lame Deer when he was over 100 years old.

Many old men and women would camp with my grandparents and I was an errand boy during this time. I listened to the war stories from these old warriors. They always welcomed me to their fire.

My grandfather and grandmother were with Black Kettle when they camped at Sand Creek in 1864. It was understood that his was a peaceful camp and that the military would respect the American flag, and a white truce flag the Chiefs had been given when at Fort Lyon for peace talks.

Although these flags and assurances were given, my grandfather felt they were not necessarily true, and he had moved a tripod that held his weapons, rope and bridle closer to the entrance of his lodge. During the dark of the morning, soldiers firing into camp woke my grandfather and he ran out and missed the tripod, but recovered from panic, and ran back to grab his bridle and rope. The firing into camp stampeded the horse herds and they circled and stampeded through camp.

My grandfather ran and intercepted the horses and threw his rope at them as they ran by. Luckily he caught one horse that belonged to the family herd and recognized this animal as one that was used to drag tepee poles and had never been broken to ride. He quickly threw a buffalo robe on the horse as it jumped around, and put my grandmother on this horse and let the animal go. The horse ran after the herd. The herd followed riders who had caught horses and escaped during the firing.

My grandparents lived in the camp on Tongue River the winter of 1866. The winter camp life of the warriors was to be in constant readiness to defend their camps. The horses were always near the lodges at night. Horses were tied in the front of the lodge so that they could be mounted on a moment's notice.

They were watching the Buffalo Creek Fort [Fort Phil Kearny]. The Sioux and Arapahoe tribes were camping with them, and camps stretched some distance up the Tongue River and adjoining streams. A camp this large would afford the people protection and concentrate efforts to attack the Buffalo Creek Fort at every opportunity.

Food and horses were needed throughout the winter to carry out the battle with the soldiers. To support such a large camp, much buffalo meat was needed. Hunting parties were busy bringing buffalo meat by pack horses from various distances along the Tongue River.

During the arrow making around the winter fire it was learned that the medicine men had guaranteed victory over the soldiers and that the medicine man had given one hundred soldiers to the warriors. This news went from one warrior society to the next. All of the warriors cried, "Thank you, thank you." They knew that sometime that winter they would kill all the soldiers in the field.

Protection of the camp was the most important duty, and one of the warrior societies would remain in camp to guard it against enemy attack. Hunting and caring for the horse herds was the second most important duty and was carried out by another of the warrior societies. The remaining were assigned attack duty at the Buffalo Creek Fort.

It was many miles of hard riding in the winter to attack the fort. Horses would become tired. Many small dome-like shelters were made in the bush bottoms to hold the warriors while the horses ate and rested to and from the camps. The shelters became covered with snow and were hard to locate. A dome shelter held five people and a small fire could be made to cook and warm themselves. They were made between the camp on the Tongue River and the Buffalo Creek Fort. Many were constructed that winter as the carrying of the dead and wounded would be a constant duty.

The dead were never left on the battlefield but were taken some distance for burial. Wounded were returned to camp where the doctoring took place by the medicine men. Snow blindness and frostbite were the most common winter health problems. These would be cured by the medicine men in camp. Many medicine men could cure snow blindness and frozen feet instantly.

My grandfather and grandmother were with Dull knife and Little Wolf when they were sent to Oklahoma. They stayed with Little Wolf when the tribe split on the return from Oklahoma. They spent the winter on Lost Chokecherry Creek in Nebraska, starting north again the following spring. They would return north to their homeland even though twelve thousand troops tried to stop them.

The things I tell my students now (at Dull Knife College) are going to be needed. The elders won't be around any more. The same happened to me. I always thought my grandfather would be there forever and I did not have to ask him questions. It is a crazy feeling when the answers are up to you.

BILL TALL BULL

George Washington Grummond

Born in Michigan in 1834, George Washington Grummond was destined for a life of controversy, violence, and tragedy. In society, he was considered genial, and those who knew him casually held him in high esteem. But Grummond proved to have an uncontrollable temper, brought to the fore when drinking, and, on occasion, his rages threatened his own life and those with whom he came in contact. Death in the Fetterman Disaster of December 21, 1866, ended his short, turbulent career.

Grummond came from a long line of merchant sailors who traced their lineage back to salmon fishermen in County Aberdeen, Scotland. The family migrated to Michigan from western New York in about 1810. George's older brother, Stephen Benedict Grummond, became a successful businessman, running a steamship line and operating one of the largest fleet of tugs on the Great Lakes. Young Grummond worked as a sailor in his early years. On February 22, 1855, he married Delia Elizabeth Shannon in Buffalo, New York. Born to the union were two children, George Welnot (November 9, 1859) and Mary Evangeline Amelia (June 26, 1863).

When the Civil War broke out, Grummond left his family to join Company A of the First Michigan Volunteer Infantry as its first sergeant, later receiving a commission as a captain. On March 9, 1863, he joined the reorganized fourteenth Michigan as a major and in six weeks earned promotion to lieutenant colonel. Grummond led his troops in several bloody conflicts, including the Battle of Bentonville, North Carolina, on March 19, 1865, where his regiment particularly distinguished itself. When the colonel of the fourteenth received orders to rejoin his command in the regular army on June 23, 1865, Grummond took charge. He was mustered out on July eighteenth.

On the surface, Grummond's record appeared noteworthy. In writing a recommendation for him, his commander, Col. Henry Mizner, stated that the veteran campaigner was the most proficient officer in his command, leading his men into action rather than driving them, and displaying conspicuous gallantry during the Battle of Bentonville. However, a closer look reveals a series of transgressions that prophesied a stormy future.

Grummond committed a series of brutal acts, while intoxicated, which earned him the hatred of his junior officers. On August 17, 1864, eight of those officers petitioned the Assistant Adjutant General of the Department of the Cumberland, requesting an investigation to determine whether Grummond was fit to command. The letter detailed numerous offenses committed between August 22, 1863, and July 6, 1864. Among them were repeated drunkenness on duty in the presence of the enemy, shooting at a fellow officer who was in the process of complying with an order, pistol whipping a sergeant, brutally beating a private, and shooting in the breast an unarmed, aged civilian whom he then denied medical attention.

At midnight on June 26, 1864, in a drunken rage, he had ordered his men to storm the heights at Kenesaw Mountain, Georgia. Only a ruse by Cpl. Patrick Walsh of Company B deterred him from this suicidal act. Climbing above him, Walsh pelted the officer with gravel, convincing his by-that-time not-too-perceptive commander that the little stones were enemy bullets.

As a result of his subordinates' petition, Grummond appeared before a general court martial, which found him guilty of threatening to shoot a junior officer and of shooting an unarmed civilian. His punishment was a public reprimand.

Another individual unappreciative of Grummond's behavior during the Civil War was his wife, Delia, who sued him for divorce. Grounds were that he had "grossly, wantonly, and cruelly refused and neglected to provide" suitable maintenance for his family in absentia. The divorce was final on August 23, 1865, and the court ordered him to pay two thousand dollars alimony within one year, a staggering sum in those times, which may help to explain some of his future actions, such as borrowing money from enlisted men in his company while at Fort Phil Kearny.

In the meantime, Grummond had repeated marital vows a second time without reference to his first marriage. On August 3, 1865, he had taken Frances P. Courtney for his second wife, the ceremony being performed at her home in Franklin, Tennessee, where the officer had apparently met her in November of 1864. Applying for a commission in the regular army following the war, Grummond received appointment to the Eighteenth Infantry as a second lieutenant. The Grummonds reached Fort Phil Kearny on October 6, 1866; Frances just having become pregnant.

Grummond continued his impetuous ways during his first major encounter with the Sioux on December sixth. In an attempt to deal decisively with Indians raiding the wood train, Colonel Carrington sent Captain Fetterman, with mounted infantry, and part of Lieutenant Bingham's Second Cavalry in pursuit. Carrington and Grummond, with a detachment of twenty-five to thirty men, moved north across Piney Creek, hoping to cut off the warriors' path of retreat. The scheme worked to the extent that Carrington's force met the raiders as planned. As the fighting began, Grummond suddenly left the command, disappearing around a hill, apparently going to the aid of Bingham, who for some unknown reason had bolted Fetterman's detachment and was nearly surrounded. Carrington later stated that he had sent Grummond an order by messenger to "keep with me and obey orders or return to the post," but the orderly was not able to get through. The eventual arrival of the combined Carrington-Fetterman force saved Grummond from certain death, but the men were too late to save Bingham, who had been dispatched.

In his next foray, Grummond was not as lucky. On December 21, 1866, he volunteered to lead the mounted infantry during Fetterman's relief of the wood train. Disobeying Carrington's specific orders not to follow the raiders over Lodge Trail Ridge, Fetterman gave chase, and in the ambush that followed, all troops died. Grummond's body lay about 40 rods north of the point of rocks where most perished, suggesting that he was one of the first killed in the advance or fell in covering the retreat.

In January of 1867, Frances left Fort Phil Kearny with her husband's body, and returned to Franklin, Tennessee. George Grummond was then buried in the Haven Rest Cemetery (Plot 33). Frances gave birth to a son, William Wands Grummond, on April 15, 1867, four months after Grummond's death.

Frances learned upon her return to Franklin that her husband had been previously married. Grummond's first wife, Delia Grummond, read in the newspapers about the Fetterman Disaster and put in a claim for the body. Matters were further complicated when both women applied for Grummond's pension, and officials discovered that the officer had wed Frances before his divorce from Delia was final, making him a bigamist for twenty days. After due deliberation, the Pension Bureau ruled that both marriages were legitimate. The second was valid because the laws of Dakota Territory recognized cohabitation for twelve months as a binding union, and the couple had lived together for a year following August twenty-third.

After the death of Margaret Carrington in 1870, Frances began a correspondence with Colonel Carrington which resulted in courtship and marriage on April 3, 1871. Carrington later adopted Frances' son, William.

In retrospect, George Grummond appears to be one of those who possessed great courage but lacked discipline in human affairs and whose life and death reflected an inability to strike a balance between passion and responsibility.

JOHN D. MCDERMOTT

For a short sketch of Grummond and his checkered career, see John D. McDermott, "Introduction," in Frances Carrington, My Army Life *(Boulder, Colorado: Pruett Publishing Company, 1990), pp. xxci-xxix; information on the Grummond family was provided by descendant, John B. Horton, Warren, Michigan, in letters of 6 December 1991 and 11 February 1992; see also "George W. Grummond," Pension File 23, Records of the Veterans' Administration, Record Group 15, Washington, D.C.; "Obituary,"* Army Navy Journal, *12 January 1867, p. 335; Margaret Carrington,* Absaraka, Home of the Crows, *ed. by Milo Milton Quaife (Chicago: The Lakeside Press, R. R. Donnelley & Sons Co., 1950); testimony of Henry B. Carrington, "Records of the Special Commission to Investigate the Fetterman Massacre and the State of Indian Affairs, 1867," Records of the Bureau of Indian Affairs, Record Group 75, National Archives, Washington, D.C.*

FRANCES C. GRUMMOND CARRINGTON

Frances Courtney, the third and youngest daughter of well-to-do tradesman Robert Courtney and Eliza Haines Courtney, grew up in Franklin, Tennessee. She was well-educated in local schools, as were her two sisters and two brothers. Her mother was a member of one of Franklin's original families. Her father, a Virginia native, died two years prior to the Civil War, which divided the Courtney family. Eliza Courtney, her daughters Frances and Octie and son John, were staunch Union supporters, while son William and daughter Jennie, who was married to a Confederate officer, sided with the Confederacy.

Franklin shifted between Rebel and Union occupation until it was taken by Federal forces, who improved fortifications at Fort Granger. That post was, for a time, under the command of Lieutenant George Washington Grummond of the Fourteenth Infantry.

On November 30, 1864, Franklin was the scene of one of the Civil War's bloodiest battles. The Courtneys sought shelter in their cellar while the sounds of battle raged overhead and shells burst in their yard. Six hours of Rebel charges into fortified Union positions resulted in massive casualties.

To the people of Franklin were left the horrifying sights and sounds of the dead and dying and the care of the wounded. Many opened their homes to the wounded Rebels, while Union wounded were carried to a nearby church, which was soon full. Eliza Courtney, Frances, Octie, and John took Union wounded into their home and into the other two houses the family owned. For over two weeks they nursed and fed the wounded from their own food stores.

After the War, Frances and her family were recognized for their efforts to care for and raise funds for the Union wounded. Frances was invited to attend the Chicago Sanitary Fair as a guest of Gen. George Henry Thomas, who cited her services during the war as deserving the gratitude of the nation. Shortly after her return to Franklin, she married Lt. George Grummond. Her brother William, who had only a few months before faced Grummond from across Rebel lines, signed the marriage bond.

With the post-war reorganization of the Army, Grummond opted to remain in the military, becoming a member of the Eighteenth U.S. Infantry. After being sent to first eastern and then southern assignments, Grummond was ordered in 1866 to join the Second battalion at Fort Phil Kearny, then under the command of Col. Henry Carrington.

On September 17, 1866, Lt. Grummond and his wife Frances, then pregnant, arrived at the fort. Frances became a favorite of the garrison's female contingent and a friend to the commanding officer's family. Readily admitting a deficiency in culinary talent, Frances accepted life in a tent and army food with good humor.

On December 6, 1866, Grummond's narrow escape from a Sioux ambush brought home the dangers of their new life. When her husband insisted on riding out with his men on December 21, 1866, despite the urging of his friend Alexander Wands to think of his family and remain, Frances could not have foreseen how that decision to seek the glory of war would turn her world upside down. In a matter of hours, she was a widow.

In the terrifying weeks between her husband's death and the relief column's arrival from Fort Laramie, Frances, in the eyes of the U.S. Army had no status; an officer's housing, upon his death, passed to his replacement. By taking Frances into their own household, the Carringtons protected her from the possibility of being thrust out into the cold -- then more than 30 degrees below zero.

When Colonel Carrington received orders to report to Fort Caspar, Frances prepared to accompany his party, selling her household goods to others at the Fort. It is perhaps due to the fond regard she engendered that her auctioned goods brought more than twice their value.

On January 23, 1867, in the teeth of a howling snowstorm, with temperatures reaching forty below, Frances began the long and dangerous trip back to her Tennessee home in a canvas-topped ambulance, cared for by Lieutenant Wands and the Carringtons.

Just outside of Fort Caspar the party was attacked by Indians, but Carrington's quick order to close up the wagons insured their later safe arrival at the fort. New orders then required Carrington and his party to report to Fort McPherson, the new headquarters of the Eighteenth Infantry. Backtracking to Sage Creek, they were again attacked. Carrington was wounded in the thigh by the discharge of a faulty revolver. The train continued on to Fort Laramie and at Bridger's Ferry, Frances met her brother William who was awaiting her arrival.

In March of 1867, after another seven weeks of travel, Frances arrived in Franklin, Tennessee, and on April fourteenth, she gave birth to son William Wands Grummond. Her husband, whose body had accompanied her on the long trek east, was revealed a bigamist and the father of two other children. Grummond's divorce from his first wife had not been final until three weeks after his marriage to Frances. What a staggering blow this must have been to Frances. Brother William acted as her representative while government officials tried to untangle the complications of Lt. Grummond's deceits. The laws of Dakota Territory recognized common-law marriages of over a year's standing and Frances was finally recognized as the legal wife at the time of Grummond's death.

In 1868, when Frances visited her sister Octie in Cincinnati, she discovered Margaret Carrington's book, *Ab-Sa-Ra-*

Ka, and learned that the Carringtons resided in Crawfordsville, Indiana, where the Colonel taught military science at Wabash College. However, she apparently did not renew contact with the Colonel until after she read the news of Margaret's death. An exchange of letters was followed by the marriage of Colonel Carrington and Frances Grummond on April 3, 1871. Willie Wands Grummond was adopted by Colonel Carrington after the marriage.

Upon taking up residence in Carrington's home in Illinois, Frances settled into the role of faculty wife. Carrington continued to teach, was active in the Republican Party, and traveled frequently to lecture on his frontier experiences and research his *Battles of the American Revolution.*

Frances and Henry had three children: Robert Chase, born in 1872; Henrietta, born in 1874; and Eliza Jane, also born in 1874.

Frances' social conscience manifested itself throughout her life. She and Henry both spoke on behalf of the Indians and the need to understand their culture and way of life, and they were both active in the GAR and their church. Frances was Henry's most loyal supporter, even during the years the military community shunned him and his efforts to vindicate himself for the December twenty-first tragedy. Frances and Henry testified on behalf of Ten Eyck's widow in her pension rights hearing. Finally, after twenty years of suppression and the persistence of the Carringtons, Henry Carrington's official report on the Fetterman tragedy was released by order of General Sherman.

In 1908, the citizens of Sheridan, Wyoming, invited the Carringtons (Frances then 63; Henry, 84) to attend a July fourth celebration and dedication of a new monument erected to honor those who lost their lives on December 21, 1866. The Carringtons endured a long train trip and then a carriage ride over the mountains to return to a scene which must have never been far from their thoughts in the intervening forty years.

In 1908, Frances attempted to publish her Civil War experiences, but was discouraged on the grounds that reminiscences were flooding the market. She was, however, encouraged to write about her life at Fort Phil Kearny, which resulted in *My Army Life and the Fort Kearny Massacre.*

Within a year of the publication of *Army Life*, Frances was terminally ill. The ultimate cause of her death on October 17, 1911, was probably tuberculosis. Colonel Carrington died on October 26, 1912. They are both buried in Fairview Cemetery in Hyde Park, Massachusetts.

DEANNA UMBACH KORDIK

FREDERICK HALLAM BROWN

Born in New York, apparently in 1831, Frederick Hallam Brown was the son of Mathew and Mary Ann Brown. The elder Brown became a successful businessman in Toledo, Ohio. Young Brown showed a special aptitude for commerce, and when he enlisted in the Eighteenth U.S. Infantry shortly after the beginning of the Civil War, his experience earned him assignment as a quartermaster sergeant.

The army quickly recognized his ability by promoting him to second lieutenant on October 30, 1861, and five days later appointing him Regimental Quartermaster. Promoted to first lieutenant on March 24, 1862, he took command of Company G of the Second Battalion on December 4, 1863. His first company assignment was to guard the National Cemetery then being established at Chattanooga, Tennessee.

By the end of the Civil War, Brown had participated as company commander or regimental quartermaster in dozens of important battles in Georgia, including the Battle of Kenesaw Mountain, June 12-July 3. On September 1, 1864, Brown was breveted captain for great gallantry and good conduct during the Atlanta campaign, and in September and October of 1864, he temporarily commanded the Second Battalion. From September 15 to October 26, 1865, Brown was on regimental recruiting service, but in November 1865, he joined his regiment at Fort Kearney, Nebraska, where it was preparing to move to the Dakota Territory in the Spring.

What can we say about Frederick Brown on the eve of his departure to Indian Country? Like his friend, William Judd Fetterman, Brown had served with distinction during the Civil War in a regiment that took heavy losses in pivotal campaigns. Also like Fetterman, he possessed social skills that made him a desirable companion. "Kind-hearted" were words often used to describe him, and the *Toledo Blade* called him "a kind and genial gentleman." It is also true that he was something of a character. While at Fort Kearney, Nebraska, one of his chief pleasures was to fill his half of an officers' quarters with Pawnee Indians, feed them, and persuade them to perform various dances into the wee hours. Because of premature balding, his friends called him "Baldy Brown," while the Sioux more imaginatively referred to him as "The Man With Two Faces."

In April 1866, Brown was appointed Chief Quartermaster of the Mountain District, Department of the Platte, soon to be headquartered at Fort Phil Kearny, and on May thirty-first, earned the rank of captain. As the quartermaster of the newly established frontier post, Brown was in charge of the protection of army stock and in this role had carte blanche to organize and pursue Indian raiders. It was apparently this aspect of his work that he found most interesting or at least it was that part of his duty that kept him most occupied. At any rate, his overall performance as quartermaster did not bring him plaudits from high command. For example, Gen. William Hazen reported on October 16, 1866, that he had found the property at Fort Reno utterly uncared for and the affairs of Capt. Brown at Fort Phil Kearny hardly better.

Brown did experience occasional success in his constant struggle to keep army stock out of the hands of marauders. On September twenty-third, Indians drove off twenty-four head of cattle. Brown and twenty-three men pursued, and during a sharp fight at close quarters, they killed thirteen Indians, apparently wounded many others, and they recaptured the stock. Brown was said to have planned to write a history of this affair for publication. According to Col. Carrington, Brown's repeated dashes, and especially his success on September twenty-third, had inspired the officer with reckless daring in the pursuit of the Sioux.

About this time, Brown received a copy of a September sixth order telling him to report to his company at Fort

Laramie, but he did not immediately comply. Consequently, on November twenty-fifth, that post's commander complained to the Assistant Adjutant General of the Department of the Platte that Brown had not yet arrived and should have been in residence by at least November tenth. The fact was that Brown wanted one more chance to even the score.

A refusal by Carrington of Brown and Fetterman's request for fifty mounted men and fifty civilians to attack the Tongue River camps had apparently caused the two to plot a foray when the opportunity presented itself. That Brown was prepared for one last fight there is no doubt. On the night of December twentieth, he made a call on the Carringtons with spurs fastened in the button hole of his coat, leggings wrapped and two revolvers at his belt, stating that he was ready by day and night and would have one scalp before leaving for Laramie.

The events of December twenty-first are well-known. Captain Fetterman, disobeying orders, led eighty men, one of whom was Frederick Brown, across Lodge Trail Ridge into an ambush from which none survived. According to Colonel Carrington, the unassigned Brown went out without his consent or knowledge. Whatever his status or motivation, the Sioux reported to the Crows that The Man With Two Faces died a very brave man. It is quite probable that Brown took his own life at the very end. Surgeon Samuel Horton reported that while Brown's body had been horribly mutilated, there was a hole in the left temple made by a small pistol ball which had probably caused his death.

In his eulogy, Colonel Carrington said that Brown's failing was that he had underestimated his foe. The judgement seems fair. Frederick Hallam Brown's remains now rest in Custer Battlefield National Cemetery, Crow Agency, Montana.

JOHN D. MCDERMOTT

ADOLPH METZGER

A bugle is an unlikely symbol for heroism. Yet the story of Adolph Metzger's heroism during the final minutes of the Fetterman Battle is tightly linked to the instrument he carried into battle on December 21, 1866. How Metzger came to be on that windswept ridge is an intriguing mixture of fact and mystery.

Adolph Metzger was born in southern Germany during the late 1830s. In 1848, he joined the tide of Germans emigrating to the United States, eventually finding his way to Pennsylvania.

On May 29, 1855, Metzger began his military career and was mustered into the Fifth United States Infantry. On his enlistment papers, he gave his age as twenty-one. His physical description was five feet five inches tall, dark complected, with blue eyes and brown hair.

During his five year enlistment, Metzger served as a private in campaigns against Indians in Kansas and the southwest, and with Lt. Col. Phillip St. George Cook's 1857 expedition against Mormons in Utah. On May 33, 1860, he was mustered out at Hatch's Ranch, New Mexico Territory.

After about three months of civilian life, Metzger reenlisted at Newport, Kentucky, for another five year stint, this time in the First U.S. Infantry. He stated he was single and twenty-four years old. (This is one of the mysteries of Metzger: he had only aged three years during a five year period.)

Without explanation in his personnel records, and before the expiration of his enlistment in the First Infantry, Adolph Metzger enlisted in the Second U.S. Cavalry for three years, beginning July 12, 1864. This enlistment, which took place near Light House Landing, Virginia, shows further discrepancies in the Metzger story. The signature is still the same bold, large, well-formed script, but his height is now five feet eight inches, and his age is twenty-five, aging him only one year after almost four years! (One explanation for these discrepancies might be that Metzger was only in his mid-teens at the time of his first enlistment, based on his parents' marriage date of September 1837. The change in height could be explained by physical maturing, although the age problem might indicate he intentionally or unintentionally altered the facts each time, for whatever reason.)

On August 2, 1864, Adolph Metzger married Fredericka Cooper in Philadelphia. Although there is no documentation in Metzger's records of his specific military activities during the last year of the Civil War, units of the Second Cavalry were involved in actions against Confederate guerrillas in Maryland and Virginia until after the Petersburg campaign near the end of the war.

After returning to Pennsylvania for a time, Metzger rejoined the Second Cavalry. Even though the war was over, he had two years of service left for this 1864 enlistment.

On November 3, 1866, Bugler Adolph Metzger and Company C, Second U.S. Cavalry, arrived at Fort Phil Kearny. He had eight months of military duty to fulfill before discharge.

Metzger and the other troopers soon experienced the frustrations of fighting an elusive foe, joining in the often pell-mell pursuits of Indian raiding parties that characterized the garrison's response to attack. On December sixth, part of Company C participated in the series of skirmishes that would eventually lead to the deaths of Lieutenant Bingham and Sergeant Bowers. Metzger was with Carrington during the last part of the action, attempting to communicate the colonel's commands to the scattered soldiers, and fighting with the intensity of an experienced combat veteran. In contrast to the actions of many of his comrades, Metzger had followed his colonel's orders without question.

After the near disaster of December sixth, Carrington ordered Captain Powell to drill Metzger's C Company in basic horsemanship and firing weapons. On December nineteenth, their drilling was interrupted to relieve the wood train. Carrington's orders to only relieve the train, and not chase Indians, were followed without incident.

According to Ten Eyck's diary, December twenty-first was cloudy with an appearance of snow after a week of bright days. In spite of the weather, Indians again attacked the wood train. Adolph Metzger of C Company was ordered out as bugler, with Lieutenant Grummond taking out the cavalry while Fetterman took the infantry. It was to be Metzger's last assignment. But the manner in which he carried it out would live on long after his passing.

With no surviving witnesses from U.S. forces to describe the battle, only the evidence of the battlefield and the stories of the battle told by the Indian participants to contemporaries remain to tell us of the action.

Ralph K. Andrist, in *The Long Death,* quoted Indian accounts that the cavalry panicked at Grummond's death and retreated, trying to join the infantry on higher ground. It is not unreasonable to presume that Sergeant Metzger was with veteran cavalrymen near Grummond, as the bugler's duty was to signal his officer's commands. Once that officer had fallen, his place was with the next in the chain of command. Those officers would be Brown and Fetterman.

All the men in Company C that day were privates, most of them raw recruits, except for Metzger, a Sgt. James Baker, a pair of corporals (James Kelly and Thomas F. Honigan) and an artificer, John McCarty, who were no doubt the veterans spoken of.

As the body of Brown's horse was found near the civilians' position, Metzger may have drawn him up on his own horse and fallen back to join Fetterman's group on what is now Monument Hill. Surrounded, the survivors fought on through a hail of arrows, until the circling Indians closed in. As they fought in a small area, bodies often fell atop each other as each man was struck down.

Thomas E. H. Lewis, one of those in the Ten Eyck rescue party, states that the only living thing on the field was a badly wounded gray horse, Dapple Dave, which may have been Metzger's mount, since John Guthrie identifies the horse as belonging to Company C, Second Cavalry. It had long been the practice in that unit to mount buglers on white or gray horses, for it made it easier to locate the commanding officer in battle.

William Murphy, one of those retrieving the bodies, states in the July 30, 1928, *Winners of the West*, that all the bodies were stripped, scalped and mutilated save two, who were not scalped, but "the Indians had drawn a buffalo bag over their heads."[1]

While J. W. Vaughn, in *Indian Fights: New Facts on Seven Encounters*,[2] places Metzger's body near those of Wheatley and Fisher, he cited no evidence for that conclusion. John Guthrie, a member of the party sent out with Ten Eyck to recover the bodies, places the body of a bugler he named Footer atop the bodies of Brown and Fetterman, indicating his death occurred after theirs. Since Carrington lists only one bugler, Metzger, among the slain, Guthrie's Footer may have been Metzger, because of Indian reports given shortly after the battle.

Guthrie's account in *Annals of Wyoming* identifies a second unmutilated body as being that of Sergeant Baker, whose scalp was intact, "but his little finger was cut off for

---

[1]William Murphy, "The Forgotten Battalion," *Winners of the West*, 30 July 1928, p. 6.

[2]J. W. Vaughan, *Indian Fights: New Facts on Seven Encounters* (Norman: University of Oklahoma Press, 1966).

a gold ring."[3] This seems to validate Murphy's account of two bodies offered respect by the Indians. Lewis, Murphy and Guthrie were eye-witnesses to the scene -- one which no number of years could erase.

The *Sheridan Post* of April 22, 1923, quoting from the *Phil Kearny Scout* (a post newspaper), spoke of Sioux warriors describing to Crow scouts at Fort C. F. Smith their account of the battle. Reporting that the soldiers fought well, they expressly mentioned their admiration of the bugler. "He actually beat them over the head and rallied them together."[4] Mitch Boyer (Michael Bouyer), a soldier at Fort C. F. Smith who often carried dispatches to Bozeman and would scout and die with Custer ten years later, also quoted this same story from Indian sources he knew personally as truthful in testimony to the Sanborn Commission investigating the disaster in 1867.

William Daley, in a letter to the Wyoming Historical Society, stated, "One bugler had 60 arrows in him. The Indians told at Ft. Laramie that he had killed 15 Indians."[5] The *St. Louis Republican* correspondent stated, "Indians are quoted on the bravery of the bugler as saying he killed several by beating them over the head with his bugle."[6] For that nearly incredible feat, Metzger's body was spared the mutilation which befell his comrades-in-arms.

---

[3]John Guthrie, "Fetterman Massacre," *Annals of Wyoming* 9 (October 1932):714-718.

[4]*Sheridan* (Wyoming) *Post,* 22 April 1923, from Wyoming State Historical Research Publication Division, WPA Project 1475.

[5]William Daley, Letter to Wyoming Historical Society, H 85-14, Peter McLeod Manuscript, p. 6.

[6]Elmo Scott Watson, "The Bravery of Our Bugler is Much Spoken Of," *Old Travois Trails* 1 (1941):139.

Publisher/writer Balch accompanied Major Gordon to the battle site in 1867, where Gordon stated, "one boy was seen to knock two Indians down with his bugle before he was run thru with an Indian lance."[7]

In *Warpath and Bivouac*, John Finerty quotes Red Cloud's people as saying, "They attempted to take this brave bugler alive, but he killed so many of the warriors that he had to be finished."[8]

In *The Great Sioux Nation*, Hans claimed that it was rare that an Indian did not scalp his victim. A person slain and not annihilated by scalping, Hans stated, becomes the warrior's servant in the "Happy Hunting Grounds." The scalp of a man who was known to be a remarkably brave man was seldom disturbed after death. General Carrington, in his book, *The Indian Question*, further stated that "an enemy who is respected for his courage would be permitted to find paradise,"[9] according to his conversations with the Sioux.

While modern historians have differed over the site of Metzger's death, descriptions by those who first saw the battlefield must hold the most weight. But no confusion remains on one singular event of the battle that day. Undaunted in the face of overwhelming odds, Adolph Metzger fought to the death, armed at the last with only his bugle. The accounts of his death by foemen as well as comrades speak volumes as to his devotion to duty and his personal courage. His body was interred at Fort Phil Kearny until

---

[7]Henry Davenport Northrop, *Indian Horrors or Massacres by the Red Men* (Philadelphia: n.d.), p. 36.

[8]John F. Finerty, *Warpath and Bivouac* (Chicago: A. M. Donoghue, 1880), p. 80.

[9]Henry Beebe Carrington, *The Indian Question* (Boston: DeWolfe and Fiske, 1909), p. 17.

1888, when those of the fallen were exhumed and reburied at the Custer Battlefield National Cemetery near Crow Agency in Montana.

DEANNA UMBACH KORDIK

AMERICAN HORSE
(WASECHUN-TASHUNKA)
THE MAN WHO KILLED FETTERMAN

Warrior, chief, scribe, traveler, philosopher and orator all describe American Horse, a complex and influential leader of the Oglala Sioux. He began his adult life a warrior but rapidly became an outspoken progressive, guiding his people through the transition from nomadism to reservation life. He journeyed to several cities while with Buffalo Bill's Wild West show, was a frequent visitor to the nation's capitol as an Oglala representative and was party to nearly all the significant events affecting the Oglalas from mid-century to his death at Pine Ridge on December 16, 1908.

American Horse, son of Sitting Bear, was born in the Spring of 1840.[1] His birth name was Cannot Walk *(Manis-*

---

[1]Bureau of Ethnology, "Pictographs of North American Indians," in *Fourth Annual Report* (Washington, D.C.: Government Printing Office, 1886), p. 140. Some historians have suggested that an elder American Horse, who was killed in the Battle of Slim Buttes in 1876, was either the father or uncle of the younger American Horse. However, He Dog, in his recollection of the Slim Buttes Battle, stated that the elder American Horse was a Sans Arc, while it is well known that the younger American Horse was a member of the True-Oglala band. Some Indians believe that the elder American Horse has been misnamed by white historians and that his true name was Iron Shield. The American Horse Winter Count is unequivocal on the lineage. The entry for 1840-41 states that "Sitting-Bear, American Horse's father, and others, stole two hundred horses from the Flat Heads...." American Horse himself stated that "there was never an American Horse killed." See Eli S. Ricker interview with American Horse, 1906, Ricker MSS, Nebraska State Historical Society, Tablet No. 16, p. 25. Had American Horse known of an elder American Horse, he would not have made this statement.

hee).[2] In 1858 at the age of eighteen, he received his adult name. Eli S. Ricker recorded the event, told him by American Horse, as follows: "He got a big Army horse and rode it in battle and killed men and from this received his name of American Horse."[3] A few years later (1865 or 1866) American Horse was involved in his first known depredation against whites when he rode with Red Cloud in an attack on a wagon train near the present location of Casper, Wyoming.[4]

American Horse chose the bitter-cold winter day of December 21, 1866, as the pictographic event to record in his Winter Counts for the 1866-67 year. It was the day "they killed one hundred men at Fort Phil Kearny."[5] American Horse stated that he and nine other Sioux warriors, acting as decoys, led Captain Fetterman and his command into a trap set on a barren ridge overlooking Peno Creek. Captain Fetterman, Captain Brown and others were making a last stand among some large boulders, as American Horse circled back into the battle. Ricker recorded American Horse's description of Fetterman's last moments as follows:

> American Horse himself ran his horse at full speed directly on to Colonel Fetterman, knocking him down! He then jumped down upon him and killed the Colonel with his knife.[6]

---

[2]Ricker, p. 28.

[3]Ibid., p. 26.

[4]Ibid., p. 30.

[5]Bureau of Ethnology, p. 144.

[6]Ricker, p. 20.

Although some writers contend that Fetterman and Brown shot each other, American Horse's version was confirmed by Red Cloud[7] and is supported by the post surgeon's report of the massacre. The report shows a bullet hole in Captain Brown's left temple, but is silent regarding any gunshot wounds to Fetterman's head. Rather, it states:

> Col. Fetterman's body showed his thorax to have been cut crosswise with a knife, deep into the viscera; his throat and entire neck were cut to the cervical spine, all around. I believe that mutilation caused his death.[8]

Additional evidence suggests American Horse first hit Fetterman with a war club. American Horse's war club, labeled the "Fetterman Disaster Club," is currently on display in Gering, Nebrasa.[9]

1868 is known as the Year of Peace in the Powder River country. For the Powder River Sioux, the dynamic shifted from fighting whites to treating with the government and engaging in a host of negotiations, bickerings, and discussions about the meaning of the treaties. American Horse was involved in most of these events and continued to gain prominence as a leader.

Addressing the Foster Commission at Pine Ridge in June of 1888, American Horse delivered the greatest Indian oratorical performance of record. He spoke for three days, carefully dissected the impending treaty, and persisted with

---

[7]James H. Cook, *Fifty Years on the Old Frontier* (Norman: University of Oklahoma Press, 1957), p. 198.

[8]Samuel Horton, Post Surgeon, Statement, in "Special Commission to Investigate the Fetterman Fight," Bureau of Indian Affairs, Record Group 75, National Archives, Washington, D.C.

[9]The war club resides in the archives of the Agate Fossil Beds National Monument in Gering, Nebraska, catalog no. AGFO 355.

his questions until all its provisions were clearly explained. In a disagreement over the location of the southern boundary of the reservation, he brought up the issue nine different times, each time using a different tactic. At one point during the discussions, Commissioner Foster said, "I have been very pleased with the speech of American Horse. I am sure that if he had the education of a white man he would sit in the Great Council of the Nation."[10]

American Horse was also very interested in the severalty option in the treaty. He requested that plots be staked out to illustrate acreages, asked questions about the tax consequences, and noted that the acreages were considerably more generous than others he had observed. It was the severalty issue, more than any other, that separated him from his brethren. While most were apprehensive of, if not down right hostile to, abandoning communal property, American Horse whole-heartedly embraced the idea of private property ownership. In a speech delivered at the Commissioner's farewell ceremony he said, "When I am laying on my death bed, if you do not defeat this bill, I will have the satisfaction of knowing that I can leave a piece of land to my children..."[11] Besides No Flesh, American Horse was the only significant Oglala leader to sign the treaty.

Unfortunately, following the treaty, the beef ration was halved. The cause was government mismanagement but many of the Indians blamed American Horse for their hunger. Out of desperation, the Indians sought salvation through a Christ-like Messiah who promised true believers a bounty of food, resurrection of deceased relatives, and revival of the buffalo culture. Belief was manifested by the frenzied ghost dance which swept the reservation like wild fire.

---

[10]U.S. Congress. Senate. Executive Document 5, 51st Cong., 1st sess., p. 91.

[11]Ibid., p. 113.

Little, a prominent ghost dancer, used the issue of a meager beef distribution to enflame the Indians. Agent Royer, new to the job and fearing for his life, ordered the Indian police to arrest Little. The police rushed out and were quickly surrounded by a mob of angry ghost dancers brandishing rifles, knives and clubs. American Horse, despite his waning popularity, pushed between the ghost dancers and the police and challenged the dancers with these words:

> Stop! Think! What are you planning to do? Kill these men of your own race? Then what? Kill all these helpless white men, women and children. And then what? What will these *brave* words and *brave* deeds lead to in the end? How long could you hold out? Your country is surrounded by railroads. Thousands of white soldiers could be here within days. What ammunition have you? What provisions have you? What will become of your families? This is child's madness! Think my brothers, think! Let no Sioux shed the blood of a brother Sioux![12]

A moment later Jack Red Cloud jumped into the fray and thrust a cocked revolver in American Horse's face shouting, "This is the one who betrayed us! Here is the man who sold us out! Here is the one who brought on this trouble by selling our land to the whites!"[13] American Horse simply turned his back and walked away. Relying solely on his power of persuasion he had single handedly saved the lives of several Sioux policemen. There is no doubt that the courage that once fired the young warrior was still strong in his heart.

The painful but short-lived ghost dance punctuated the end of the wraggling over the reservation system. There

---

[12]David H. Miller, *Ghost Dance* (New York: Duell, Sloan and Pearce, 1959), p. 130.

[13]Ibid.

would be more trips to Washington and more commission meetings, but nothing compared with the two previous decades. In his waning years American Horse frequently visited the ranch of his white friend, James H. Cook, and appeared as an attraction in such events as the Pioneer Days in Cheyenne, Wyoming, as he continued to try to bridge the gap between Whites and Indians. In a time of retrenchment, this was American Horse's legacy: he looked to the future, embraced change, and helped his brethren adapt to a new way of life.

ELBERT D. BELISH

Tenodor Ten Eyck

Tenodor Ten Eyck was born on August 5, 1819, in Freehold, New Jersey, and educated as an engineer and surveyor. In the 1840s, he was living in Pontiac, Michigan, and sometime about 1845 he married Mary Hascall. A year later Mary had a son, Thomas, and she died. On May 25, 1847, Tenodor married Mary's sister Martha.[1]

By 1860, the growing family - including Thomas (age fourteen), Mary (twelve), Alice (eleven), Minnie (ten) and Fannie (three) - had moved to Green Bay, Wisconsin. Budget Ryan, a servant from Ireland, also lived with the family.[2]

On June 4, 1860, Ten Eyck left Green Bay to try his luck in the gold fields near Denver, Colorado. After an unsuccessful summer and early fall prospecting with the Wisconsin Mining Company, he returned home, arriving on November twenty-first.

The following year he was employed by the State of Wisconsin as a civil engineer. When the Civil War began, he enrolled as a private and was assigned to the Twelfth Regiment, Wisconsin Volunteer Infantry. He served with that regiment until February 1862, when he was promoted to captain in the Eighteenth U.S. Infantry. He was given command of H Company, Second Battalion and ordered to a detachment

---

[1]Martha Ten Eyck Pension Records, Certificate #601912, National Archives, Washington, D.C.

[2]When Tenodor Ten Eyck was away from home he wrote many, many letters to his wife, the former Martha Hascall, and family. He mentions Alice, Minnie, Fanny and Birtie, his daughters, frequently. He also had a brother, Jim, and a sister, Sarah, but mentions them only once by name.

near Huntsville, Alabama, where he was captured. He was later paroled and then sent to Camp Wallace near Columbus, Ohio. His exchange became effective in January 1863; he reported for duty at Camp Thomas, Ohio, and then was placed in command of a post on the Nashville & Ohio Railroad.

On September 20, 1863, Ten Eyck was captured on the battlefield of Chickamauga and sent to Libby Prison near Richmond, Virginia.

While in Libby Prison, Ten Eyck became very ill and his wife Martha petitioned to have him released. Martha was granted an audience with President Lincoln and after relating her story of Ten Eyck's serious illness and his debilitating condition due to dysentery, the President exclaimed, "I gave that order to Senator Howe and Senator Ten Eyck months ago!" He then took a large sheet of paper, wrote on it and before handing it to her stated, "Take this to General Hancock. I think he can arrange this for you." Ten Eyck was paroled on December 9, 1864, and ordered to report for duty in thirty days.

His imprisonment during the Civil War totalled one year and ten months.

Much of 1865 was spent as a commander of Company H, Second Battalion with duty at Camp Carrington, Ohio, Evansville, Indiana, and Camp Thomas, Ohio, where he served as a mustering and disbursing officer. During this period he was selected to serve as a Guard of Honor when President Lincoln's body lay in State for one day in Indianapolis, Indiana.

In November, he and his company were sent to Fort Kearney, Nebraska, and he was stationed at Camp Cottonwood where he was appointed to a number of administrative boards.[3]

---

[3]In his 1865 diary on December ninth, Ten Eyck noted that "he left Dick (my negro boy)" on the march from Leavenworth, Kansas, to Fort

He marched westward with the Eighteenth Infantry, commanded by Col. Henry B. Carrington, from Fort Kearney on May 19, 1866, arriving at Fort Laramie twenty-one days later. From Fort Laramie they traveled to Fort Reno at which time Ten Eyck was designated post commander for a new fort to be constructed yet farther north.

The column then continued in a northwesterly direction, arriving on Piney Creek on Friday, July thirteenth. After scouting the area, it was decided to build the new fort on the plateau between the forks of Piney Creek. Thirteen days later, the new post was named Fort Philip Kearny by order of General St. George Crooke.

Ten Eyck supervised the first phase of the construction of the fort in his role as post commander. Several civilians and soldiers had been killed by Indians even though Cheyenne chiefs and their attendants had visited the command proposing peaceable intentions and were given safe-conduct papers and some provisions by Colonel Carrington. During this time conflict began to arise between Colonel Carrington and Ten Eyck, and Carrington relieved Ten Eyck as post commander, assuming the role himself.

Soon afterward, Ten Eyck was arrested by Colonel Carrington for "a mistake made at Dress Parade," which lasted for six days, and he then resumed command of his company. This was Ten Eyck's first serious problem as a result of his known habit of drinking heavily.

Adding to the frustrations of construction and internal command problems were the constant threats and actuality

---

Kearny, Nebraska. Early in the spring of 1866 he hired another servant, Susan Fitsgerald, known as "Black Susan." She accompanied him throughout his military career in the West and when he went to Chicago in 1868, she then continued on to her home in Tennessee, and Ten Eyck took her sixteen year old son with him and provided him with room and board while he attended school there.

of Indian attacks, which continued throughout the fall of 1866.

In his diary, Ten Eyck wrote about his part in the Fetterman Disaster of December 21, 1866:

> Ordered to take 36 men and reinforce Fetterman, and came in sight of enemy at 4 for reinforcements and artillery, then moved forward on the high ground. Enemy was scattered over about 1 1/4 miles on road. As I advanced those nearest left (say about 100) when we discovered the dead bodies of the whole of Fetterman's men laying on a knowl [sic] stripped naked and terribly mutilated.[4]

About half the slain men were loaded into three wagons and one ambulance and the bodies were taken to the fort. Colonel Carrington returned to the scene with Captain Ten Eyck and eighty men the next day and transported the remaining bodies "who were butchered on that fatal day" back to the post. Two men were sent by Colonel Carrington to Fort Laramie the evening of the twenty-first with a request for help.[5]

Ten Eyck noted in his diary that the weather for December twenty-first was "cloudy with appearance of snow." The

---

[4]Tenodor Ten Eyck, Diaries, 1860-1871. MS, Special Collections, University of Arizona, Tucson, Arizona. (Partial transcripts located in Wyoming Room, Sheridan County Fulmer Public Library, Sheridan, Wyoming).

[5]Carrington and Ten Eyck were blamed by some for the Fetterman Disaster and there was great effort and time spent (some twenty years) in rebutting these accusations. Colonel Carrington's address to the audience at the dedication ceremonies for the monument erected at the Fetterman battle site on 3 July 1908, is a forceful recitation of the events occurring nearly forty-two years earlier, absolving himself and Ten Eyck of any fault in the disaster. Fetterman had clearly disobeyed orders and Carrington possessed many written statements from witnesses to prove it.

next day was "pleasant" and December twenty-third was "cold and melancholy with the duty of preparing the dead for burial and digging graves." The bodies of Captains Fetterman and Brown and Lieutenant Grummond were buried on December twenty-fourth at 1:00 p.m. "without any services or military honors." Ten Eyck was shocked at this proceeding, "but noted it appeared necessary in the opinion of Col. Carrington, Brev. Maj. Powell and others." It began snowing on Christmas day, reaching about five inches on the level by December twenty-sixth when the remainder of the men were buried.

Although Ten Eyck was ordered to leave Fort Phil Kearny and go with Colonel Carrington to Fort Caspar, his new commander, General Wessells, requested that he remain at the Fort as commander of Company H. After General Wessells' arrival, a notice was posted for "Daily Drilling" and target practice for the first time at the post, although Dress Parade had been held on an irregular basis.

After turning H Company over to Lt. E. R. P. Shurly, Ten Eyck left Fort Phil Kearny on July 9, 1867, for Fort Laramie, with Companies C, E, B, and G, Eighteenth Infantry. He was soon sent to Fort Sanders, then on to Fort Bridger where he received notification of a brevet rank of major for his service in the Civil War. Shortly after arriving at Fort Bridger he was ordered to leave for Fort Fetterman. He arrived at Fort Fetterman on September fourteenth and three days later was placed under arrest for drunkenness by the commanding officer, Col. M. E. Dye. Ten Eyck was confined to his quarters and three days later requested a personal interview with Dye, which was refused. Dye however dropped the charges when Ten Eyck sent him a written statement promising to take the pledge of temperance.

On October fourteenth he was again placed under arrest for drunkenness by Colonel Dye, relieved of all duties and ordered to report to Fort Laramie to attend his General

Court Martial, which began January 6, 1868.[6] He was charged with "conduct unbecoming an officer and a gentleman" and specifically, for being drunk on September seventeenth and October fourteenth. He was allowed to prepare a written defense for himself, based primarily on the fact that written charges were never submitted by Dye. Ten Eyck then returned to Fort Fetterman where he was restricted to an area within a two mile radius of the post for nearly three months.

On February eighteenth, the court found him guilty and sentenced him to be dismissed from the army. As a result of Ten Eyck's zealous defense, the ruling was soon overturned on the request of Gen. W. T. Grant and he was released from arrest.[7]

Late in May he left Fort Fetterman with Headquarters and F Companies for Fort Laramie and then continued on to Fort Sedgewick, where Colonel Carrington was in command. He requested leave of absence which was later changed to sick leave after he became ill and was confined to his home for a period of several weeks.

Ten Eyck was honorably mustered out of the service on January 1, 1871, and during that year served as an engineer for the U.S. Government in Green Bay, Wisconsin.

Major Tenodor Ten Eyck died at his residence, 5704 Madison Avenue, Chicago, Illinois, on February 27, 1905, at the age of eighty-five, following a stroke.

JEAN KIMBLE, AUTHOR
SUSAN BADGER DOYLE, CONTRIBUTOR

---

[6]Tenodor Ten Eyck, Records of the Judge Advocate General, Court-Martial Case Files, Box 1451, Case 0.0.2772, Record Group 153, National Archives, Washington, D.C.

[7]An article appeared in the *Army Navy Journal,* 2 May 1868, which elaborated on the startling turn of events in Ten Eyck's court martial.

James Pierson Beckwourth

The slave son of a slave mother and a free white father, James Pierson Beckwourth was born in Virginia, probably in 1800. His father took him to St. Charles, Missouri, in 1810, and manumitted him in 1824. Apprenticed at the age of fourteen to a St. Louis blacksmith, his efforts in this job, as well as his work in the Galena, Illinois, lead mines five years later, were components of a contemporary's description of Beckwourth as physically powerful, lean, and standing six feet tall. Having had about four years of formal education, he spoke French, in addition to his native English, and would later become proficient in several Indian languages.

He was among those accompanying William Ashley through South Pass, Wyoming, in the autumn of 1824 and the winter of 1824-25, perhaps saving Ashley's life three times in several weeks. He attended his first rendezvous with the fur trader in 1825 at Henry's Fork of Green River, near present day McKinnon, Wyoming. Beckwourth returned to St. Louis in January 1826, from the Republican River, to obtain horses for Jedediah Smith. In the spring of 1826 he was in Cache Valley, Utah (he was the first to use this name). There he took as a servant the Indian widow of a Canadian fur trader who had died in the valley. He attended the 1826 rendezvous, near today's Hyrum, Utah, where General Ashley decided to return permanently to St. Louis. After Ashley's departure, peace came to the Flat Head and Blackfeet Indians and Beckwourth set up a trading post in a village of the latter. There he acquired two Blackfeet wives, daughters of the chief.

In the winter of 1826-27, Beckwourth trapped with Thomas Fitzpatrick along the Portneuf and Bear Rivers, attending the rendezvous of 1827 at the south end of Bear Lake, Utah. Later in 1827, he accompanied William Sublette to the upper Snake River Valley in Idaho, where the trappers wintered. Still in Idaho in the spring of 1828, the party was attacked by Blackfeet Indians. At the rendezvous of 1828, again on Bear Lake, Beckwourth was again attacked by Blackfeet. At this rendezvous, Caleb Greenwood, spinning a yarn, told the Crow Indians that Beckwourth was really a Crow Indian, son of "Big Bowl," and that he had been captured as a boy and carried off by the Cheyennes. When Beckwourth and Robert Campbell, both working for the firm of Smith, Jackson and Sublette, were trapping in the winter of 1828-29 in the Powder River area of Wyoming, home of the Crows, Beckwourth realized that among these Indians he might prosper more financially than among the fur companies. In early 1829 he signed a promissory note for sums owed to Smith, Jackson and Sublette, and went to live with the Crows, quickly learning their language and customs. Beckwourth claimed to have had ten Crow wives during this period. In 1833 he was hired by Kenneth McKenzie of Fort Union, North Dakota, to work as an agent for the American Fur Company among the Crows, and to help in the construction of Fort Cass, near the boundaries of today's Yellowstone and Treasure counties of Montana.

An encounter with an old trapping companion, Thomas "Peg-Leg" Smith, led Beckwourth to leave the Crows and go with Smith to California in 1835. In the vicinity of Los Angeles, the sixty Indians who had accompanied them involved them in the stealing of a huge horse herd. Beckwourth wintered near the Great Salt Lake in 1835-36.

Sometime during 1837, a rumor was spread that Beckwourth was responsible for the great smallpox epidemic among the Indians of the Missouri. Leaving St. Louis in April, he returned to the Crows for some months, during which time he met the artist Alfred Jacob Miller, who did a painting of Beckwourth among his friends, along the Oregon Trail. In the autumn Beckwourth went, as a civilian employee of the U.S. Army, to the Florida Everglades in the First Seminole War.

Working along the Santa Fe Trail in 1838, he was in charge of Fort Vasquez, Colorado, working for Andrew Sublette. After the sale of this company, he temporarily worked for Bent, St. Vrain & Co., then opened a store in Taos, New Mexico, in 1840. It was in Taos that he married Louisa Sandoval, with whom he traveled to today's Pueblo, Colorado, to set up a trading post. Leaving his wife and baby daughter in 1844, he went to California to trade and became involved in the 1845 California Revolution against Mexico, at the battle of Cahuenga. He next became involved in an expansive "round-up" of horses in California, which he ran off to Colorado. Upon his return to Pueblo he found his wife had remarried, so continuing on to Santa Fe, he opened a saloon and hotel.

Beckwourth returned to California in 1848, engaging in various businesses connected to the gold rush. In 1850 he discovered Beckwourth Pass in the Sierra Nevadas and operated a ranch and hotel in a valley near the pass at the present town of Beckwourth, California.

In October 1854 he met Thomas D. Bonner, to whom he dictated his adventures. *The Life and Adventures of James P. Beckwourth, Mountaineer, Scout, and Pioneer, and Chief of the Crow Nation of Indians* appeared in two printings, in the United States and England, in 1856. Another printing was brought out in the United States in 1858, and a French translation appeared in 1860. Beckwourth himself never received a cent in royalties from these editions.

Few of the more than three thousand men engaged in the fur trade in the United States and Canada had the opportunity that Bonner made available to Beckwourth for autobiographical recounting. The book's repute for veracity has varied greatly over the years. Hubert Howe Bancroft said, "...nor can the slightest faith be put in his statements."[1] Wright Howes stated, "Highly colored, but basically authentic narrative..."[2] Gordon Dodds wrote, "Now research indicates that Beckwourth's basic narrative is true... Although Beckwourth recounted his *Adventures* in the vein of a raconteur determined to amuse his fellow trappers..."[3] Richard M. Clokey opined, "Beckwourth...provided in his autobiography an unmatched description of the Ashley style of leadership in the wilderness."[4]

After his eight years in California, Beckwourth next traveled to St. Louis, and in November of 1859 went to Denver, again working for Louis Vasquez. It was in Denver he married Miss Elizabeth Lettbetter, by whom he had a short-lived daughter. He sold his Denver property in July of 1864 and was soon living with a Crow woman named Sue. He played a role in the Sand Creek Massacre, and gave testimony during the 1865 investigation of this tragedy. In 1865-66, he went up to the Green River area with four other

---

[1]Henry R. Wagner and Charles L. Camp, *The Plains and the Rockies: A Critical Bibliography of Exploration, Adventure and Travel in the American West, 1800-1865* (San Francisco: John Howell Books, 1982), p. 514.

[2]Wright Howes, *U.S. IANA (1650-1950), A Selective Bibliography in Which are Described 11,620 Uncommon and Significant Books Relating to the Continental Portion of the United States* (New York: R. R. Bowker for Newberry Library, 1962), p. 65.

[3]Gordon Dodds, *The Reader's Encyclopedia of the American West*, ed. Howard P. Lamar (New York: Thomas Y. Crowell Company, 1977), p. 86.

[4]Richard M. Clokey, *William H. Ashley, Enterprise and Politics in the Trans-Mississippi West* (Norman: University of Oklahoma Press, 1972), p. 145.

trappers. Beckwourth was the only one to return alive, three being killed by Indians and the fourth drowned. In 1866, Beckwourth, then at Fort Laramie in Wyoming, went to work for the army sent to guard the Bozeman Trail.

The date of Beckwourth's arrival and his specific duties at Fort Phil Kearny were not recorded. Col. Henry B. Carrington hired him as an assistant guide and interpreter for the Bozeman Trail post. Beckwourth arrived at Fort C. F. Smith on the evening of September 1, 1866, in advance of the inspection party of Col. William B. Hazen. The diary of 1st Lt. George M. Templeton is the main source for Beckwourth's activities at this post.

It was on September thirteenth that Templeton and four armed soldiers went across the river with Beckwourth to talk with an Indian party that Beckwourth had thought were Crows, but who were in reality Sioux. These Indians, shortly after leaving Templeton and Beckwourth, killed a miner. Beckwourth, in the Indian tradition, made medicine on September seventeenth, and the following day told Templeton that something bad was going to happen.

On the night of September twenty-ninth, accompanied by Pvt. James W. Thompson of Company D, Eighteenth U.S. Infantry, age nineteen, Beckwourth left the fort, riding towards Clark's Fork and the Crow encampment. He told Thompson he was not feeling well and soon began suffering from a nosebleed. Upon their arrival at the Crow camp, Beckwourth was made comfortable in the great, red-hued lodge of Chief Iron Bull, where he died on an unspecified date in October of 1866. Another version of his death stated that when Beckwourth became ill, Thompson -- leaving sufficient wood and water by his companion -- rode ahead to the Crow camp and, knowing no Crow, by means of sign language induced some of the Indians to return with him to the place where he had left Beckwourth. When they reached this place, they found Beckwourth dead.

Colonel Carrington, who had sent Jim Beckwourth on the mission to assess how much support the army could expect from the Crows in the war against the Sioux, said, "Beckwith died in their village without giving me the result of his visit."[5]

FATHER BARRY HAGAN

---

[5]U.S. Congress. Senate. Executive Document No. 33, 50th Cong., 1st sess., 1887, p. 30.

JOHN "PORTUGEE" PHILLIPS

As the man credited for carrying the news of the Fetterman Disaster through hostile Indian country 236 miles from Fort Phil Kearny to Fort Laramie, John "Portugee" Phillips has long been celebrated in histories, novels and poems as Wyoming's frontier hero. While time has diminished his achievement, as fact has replaced fiction, he remains a man worthy of respect and admiration, exemplifying pioneer qualities of self-sacrifice and endurance.

John Phillips was born Manuel Philipe Cardoso on April 8, 1832, the fourth of nine children of Filipe and Maria Cardoso. Born near the town of Terra, on the island of Pico in the Azores, he entered life as a citizen of Portugal. At the age of eighteen, he left the Azores aboard a whaling vessel bound for California, where the youth intended to pan for gold.

For the next fifteen years, he followed the lure of yellow metal in California, Oregon, and Idaho, reaching the Montana fields in 1865. In the spring of 1866, he joined a party of miners headed for the Pryor and Big Horn Mountains, prospecting until the first snows of late summer. Arriving with forty-two of his compatriots at Fort Phil Kearny on September fourteenth, he apparently worked as a water carrier for a civilian contractor.

Following the annihilation of Capt. William J. Fetterman and his command on December twenty-first, Phillips volunteered to ride to the telegraph office at Horseshoe Station on the North Platte with Col. Henry B. Carrington's dispatches, about 190 miles in subzero weather. While the general story is that he rode alone on this perilous mission, Phillips was in fact accompanied by one Daniel Dixon to Fort Reno and by others along the way, including Robert Bailey. The pay for the service was three hundred dollars apiece for Phillips and Dixon, which they received in January of 1867.

In a reminiscence, Carrington stated that Phillips chose one of his horses for the ride. Jack Wallace, a contractor's employee, reported the name of the animal as "Dandy," a blue grass horse, black with three stocking feet. Wallace also stated that Carrington gave Phillips a Spencer repeating rifle and one hundred rounds of ammunition, which the scout strapped to his ankles, the weight keeping his feet firmly in the stirrups. The first stop was Fort Reno, which the couriers reached in the early hours of December twenty-third. There they received an additional message from Lt. Col. Henry Wessels to carry to Col. Innis Palmer at Fort Laramie, thus extending their obligation.

According to the telegrapher at Horseshoe Station, Phillips, Dixon, and Robert Bailey arrived about 10 a.m. on December twenty-fifth, when the dispatches were wired to the headquarters of the Department of the Platte in Omaha, and to Washington, D.C. To deliver the message from Wessells to Palmer, Phillips went on to Fort Laramie, arriving at 11 p.m., where a full dress dance was in progress. The appearance of the huge form of Phillips, garbed in a buffalo overcoat, pants, gauntlets, and cap, quieted the festivities, and his message caused preparations for a rescue party, delayed in departing by deep snows until January sixth. In addition to receiving his pay, Phillips was given the best horse in Company F of the Second Cavalry.

Although Phillips did not ride alone, he was certainly of the stuff from which heroes are made. When carrying mail back to Fort Phil Kearny from Fort Laramie in mid-April 1867, he at one point found himself surrounded by fifteen Sioux in war paint. With humorous self-deprecation, he wrote in a report to his superiors that he had escaped, but noted that "without aid of my faithful horse, and good revolver, [I] would have lost my hair, the part of my body I feel most anxious about on the prairies."[1]

Phillips continued to work as a mail courier for the government, but when the army abandoned Fort Phil Kearny, he moved to Elk Mountain, west of the present day city of Laramie. There he supplied ties to the Union Pacific Railroad, then being constructed across southern Wyoming. In the decade that followed, he made his living by contracting with the army to furnish supplies and transportation at Fort Laramie and Fort Fetterman. On December 16, 1870, in Cheyenne, Phillips married Hattie Buck, a native of Crownpoint, Indiana, then twenty-eight years old. The couple had several children, one of whom was appropriately named Paul Revere Phillips.

About the time of his marriage, Phillips established a ranch on Chugwater Creek as a base for his contracting activities. The ranch also accommodated travelers and served as headquarters for a small stock raising venture. In 1876, he built a hotel on the property, as travel had increased with the Black Hills gold rush. One acquaintance describes him as having a fine dairy herd and growing water-cresses with diverted river water.

In 1878, he sold his ranch holdings and moved to Cheyenne, arriving on October eighteenth. There Phillips remained until his death from nephritis on November 18, 1883. He is buried in Lakeview Cemetery. Hattie Phillips died in 1936 in a Los Angeles nursing home at the age of ninety-four.

During a visit to Milwaukee, Phillips attended a parade in honor of General Grant, who was running for the presidency. Upon seeing the scout in the crowd, Grant stopped the procession and insisted that Phillips ride with him in his

---

[1]Letter from Phillips to Quartermaster George B. Dandy, Fort Laramie, 16 May 1867, Letters Received, Records of the Mountain District, Record Group 393, National Archives, Washington, D.C.

buggy. Although of humble origins and not particularly successful in life, Phillips was a national figure then and today he remains a symbol of courage and devotion to duty.

JOHN D. MCDERMOTT

DAVID STUART GORDON

David Stuart Gordon was born in Franklin County, Pennsylvania, on May 23, 1832. In 1857, Gordon moved to Leavenworth, Kansas, where he engaged himself in business. When the Civil War broke out Gordon went to Washington and joined a company, known as the Frontier Guard, organized to protect the capital and President Lincoln. The company was quartered in the East room of the White House. Gordon then received a commission as second lieutenant, Second Dragoons and reported for duty with the Second Cavalry. Gordon was taken prisoner at the first Battle of Bull Run and held a Confederate prisoner for thirteen months[1] and cited for "gallant and meritorious service" in the Gettysburg campaign.[2]

When the Civil War ended, Gordon served in the Frontier army in Kansas and at Fort Lyons, Colorado Territory, and in October 1866, was posted to Fort Laramie, Dakota Territory.

In April of 1908, Gen. Alfred E. Bates wrote to then-retired Brig. Gen. David S. Gordon asking him to give a synopsis of the January 1867 march from Fort Laramie to Fort Phil Kearny. The following account of that march is taken from Gordon's reply to General Bates.[3]

---

[1]*New York Times* Obituary, 29 January 1930.

[2]*Who Was Who* (Chicago: A. N. Marquis Co., 1942), 1:470.

[3]David S. Gordon (General), U.S. Army, Oakland, California, to Gen. Alfred E. Bates, Colorado Building, Washington D.C., 2 March 1908. Fort Phil Kearny/Bozeman Trail Association vertical file: David S. Gordon, Wyoming Room, Sheridan County Fulmer Public Library, Sheridan, Wyoming.

On Christmas night 1866, Lt. David Stuart Gordon was attending the full dress garrison dance at Fort Laramie. Everyone was

> superlatively happy enjoying the dance, not withstanding the snow was from ten to fifteen inches deep on the level and the thermometer indicated twenty-five degrees below zero, when a huge form dressed in buffalo overcoat, pants, gauntlets and cap, accompanied by an orderly, desired to see the Commanding officer...the dress of the man, and at this hour, looking for the Commanding officer, made a deep impression upon the officers and others...as he could scarcely be designated for an animal or a man.

Upon being summoned by Gen. Ennis Palmer, Commander at Fort Laramie, Gordon learned that the man was Portuguee Phillips, and he was delivering a dispatch from Col. Henry B. Carrington which told of the Fetterman disaster:

> Six companies of the 18th under Major Van Vost, and two of the troops of the 2nd Cavalry, commanded by myself were ordered to get in readiness and march to the relief of the garrison...the snow was so deep and the thermometer indicated twenty-five degrees below zero...

Because of the inclement weather, the infantry under Major Van Vost was not able to leave for Fort Phil Kearny until New Years' day. Gordon continues:

> Rumors were currently afloat that the garrison [Fort Laramie] might be attacked [and] on account of these reports, I was held with my command of cavalry forty-eight hours longer after the Infantry left...
>
> After making every preparation for the comfort of the men on account of the severity of the weather and getting ready the necessary transportation of the camp and garrison equipage and forage of the animals, I commenced my march of 250 miles over a road entirely obliterated by

> snow and some places drifted from three to six feet deep. On account of the drifts, I was compelled to countermarch the command by file and plunge a cut thru the drift by the horses, and many places had to shovel out to get the wagon thru, as well as the men on foot.
>
> [We] overtook the infantry command the second day out [January 5th] and both commands were marched together...the command stopping at Fort Reno on the Powder River. Here, Col. W. Wessels, of the 18th U.S. Infantry joined the command and marched with it, as he had orders to relieve Col. H. B. Carrington at Fort Phil Kearny on his arrival.

Because of the severity of the weather and the deep snow the men were forced to chop holes in the ice and water the horses from buckets. According to Gordon,

> Our long forage gave out after being on the road ten days and the mules being cold and hungry for hay, as they had been accustomed to in the post, became as restless as bears and many of them broke their halters and halter-chains, and not satisfied with gnawing off the tongues of some of the wagons and wagon boxes, they took a square meal of the manes and tails of their mates...
>
> With not a few frozen ears, noses, fingers, toes, and one man frozen to death, we reached [the] unfortunate garrison on the 16th of January...
>
> We found the fort poorly supplied, nothing in the way of delicacies or canned goods of any description, except the Government rations, consisting of sugar, coffee, bacon, hard tack and flour; no potatoes or canned meat, and the worst of all, no wood to burn but green cottonwood branches...and not a pound of forage for the animals... consequently we were obliged to turn out the animals and let them forage for themselves...
>
> Because of the lack of vegetables the hospital was crowded to its limits by men down on their backs with scurvy, and no special remedy available other than drugs to prevent the entire garrison being afflicted. It was a

> pitiful sight to see some of these poor soldiers so emaciated and weak and afflicted to the extent that their teeth were ready to drop out of their mouths...
>
> After consideration, the Commanding Officer thought best to send Capt. James T. Peale, commanding Troop L, 2nd Cavalry, back to Fort Laramie with the cavalry horses. He made the march all right, but reached there without the animals, 150 horses all having perished from cold and no grazing, evidence of which march, their carcasses, could be seen for many years after.

The command at Fort Phil Kearny had no knowledge of the conditions at Fort C. F. Smith. A reconnaissance expedition under Captain Gordon was made to evaluate the conditions along the Big Horn Road on January 22, 1867. After traveling about five miles and encountering fifteen foot drifts, the expedition was forced to turn back. Gordon, in his report wrote, "any command which would attempt to go beyond this point in the present state of weather and conditions of road would be attended with failure and disaster."[4] A second attempt under the command of Captain Van Vost and Gordon was made a week later, on January twenty-ninth, and it too resulted in failure. Contact with Fort C. F. Smith was not made until early February when Sergeants Grant and Graham successfully reached the post.

In November 1867, Lieutenant Gordon was a member of the Second Cavalry companies sent to rescue Lt. Shurly. Shurly had been assigned to command an escort which was to take an empty supply train from Fort C. F. Smith to Fort Phil Kearny and enroute exchange escort duties with a Wells Fargo supply train on its way to C. F. Smith. After making the exchange, Lieutenant Shurly began to retrace his steps to

---

[4]Barry J. Hagan, "More Light on the Adventures of Grant and Graham," *Journal of the Order of the Indian Wars* 2 (Fall 1981):32.

Fort C. F. Smith when, about twenty miles from Fort Phil Kearny, the supply train was attacked.

Two volunteers were sent back to Fort Phil Kearny for help and at daylight on November fifth, Col. John Green and Capt. David Gordon arrived with help. The wounded Lieutenant Shurly was taken back to Fort Phil Kearny and the Wells Fargo supply train proceeded on to Fort C. F. Smith, under the command of Captain Gordon.

On January 18, 1868, Captain Gordon's wife, Ann Hughes Gordon, gave birth to a son, Phil Kearny Gordon, "named by the officers of the garrison at a meeting called by the Commanding Officer, General John E. Smith, to perpetuate the name and memory of General Phil Kearny, and the post also named after him."[5]

Gordon remained at Fort Phil Kearny until its abandonment in July of 1868, when he "marched out leaving behind us over one hundred twenty dead comrades buried at the foot of Signal Hill in plain view of the old abandoned garrison."[6]

Captain Gordon went on leave in July of 1868 and then returned to his regiment in October of that year. He remained on frontier duty in Utah and Wyoming, being engaged with Indians at Popo Agie (September 1869) and Miner's Delight (May 1870), Wyoming (for which he was breveted lieutenant colonel for gallant services).[7] Captain Gordon is credited with selecting the site of Camp Stambaugh, Wyoming Territory, in June of 1870. The Camp

---

[5]Gordon to Bates, 2 March 1908.

[6]Ibid.

[7]David S. Gordon, Appointment, Commission and Personal File, Records of the Office of the Adjutant General, Record Group 94. Hagan Collection, Wyoming Room, Sheridan County Fulmer Public Library, Sheridan, Wyoming.

was to protect the South Pass mining towns from Sioux, Cheyenne and Arapaho raids.[8]

In June of 1877, Captain Gordon became Major Gordon and from August to September 1877 was a member of the Bannock expedition, and from June to August 1879, participated in the campaign against the Sioux, specifically engagements on Milk River and Poplar Creek in Montana.

Major Gordon commanded at Fort Ellis, Montana (1881-1884) and Fort Bidwell, California (1886-1890). Promoted to Lieutenant Colonel in November 1889, he was commander at Fort Huachuca, Arizona (1890-1892). In July of 1892 he was promoted to Colonel in the Sixth Cavalry. He commanded at Fort Niobrara, Nebraska (1892-July 1894) and went to command cavalry forces in the Chicago labor strikes in August of 1894. Gordon was at Fort Sheridan, Illinois, until October 1894 and then commanded his regiment and the post of Fort Myer, Virginia, retiring on May 23, 1896.[9]

Brigadier General David S. Gordon died on January 28, 1930, in Tacoma Park, Maryland. At that time he had achieved the second oldest age ever reached by a U.S. Army officer, 97 years, 8 months and 8 days.[10] One of the most remarkable if not unprecedented incidents in the military career of Colonel Gordon were his promotions and thirty-two years of continuous service in the same regiment, the Second United States Cavalry.[11]

DAENA HINKLEMAN, AUTHOR
CATHERINE CURTISS, CONTRIBUTOR

---

[8]John D. McDermott, "19th Century Military Sites in Fremont County: A Report," McDermott Associates, Sheridan, Wyoming, 1991.

[9]Gordon, ACP File.

[10]*New York Times*, 29 January 1930.

[11]Gordon, ACP File.

Samuel Miller Horton

When appointed an assistant surgeon in the United States Army on August 26, 1861, Samuel Miller Horton stated that he had been born in the state of Pennsylvania on May 6, 1838, and that his current residence was in Ithaca, New York. Horton's application to the army declared that he was a graduate of the Jefferson Medical College of Philadelphia, had been in the profession for five and a half years, and had been in practice for more than a year.

After beginning his army medical career in St. Louis, he was put in charge of the wharfboat *Nashville* for about a month, near Columbus, Kentucky. From there he went for a month to Benton Barracks in Missouri, moving with its command to Memphis, Tennessee, in December of 1862.

In March of 1863, Horton was made an inspector of Memphis hospitals, re-examining all patients due for discharge and investigating the credentials of any contract surgeon reported as incompetent.

In June 1863, he went to Vicksburg, Mississippi, with the First U.S. Infantry. Following the siege of Vicksburg, he received a twenty-five day leave of absence, his first since entering the service. It was during this leave that he married Sallie Knox Dunnica, for they were wed on August 6, 1863 in St. Louis, Missouri.

In August 1863, the First U.S. Infantry was ordered to Carrollton, Louisiana; Horton went with the unit. In September, he was sent to New Orleans and served in several hospitals. In June of 1864, he accompanied 450 sick and wounded men to St. Louis, then returned to New Orleans where he continued primarily administrative duties. During September and October he was president of the board examining all officers applying for either leave or resignation. He made his fourth trip with sick and wounded in November, from New Orleans to Natchez. In all, Horton helped transfer more than fifteen hundred incapacitated military men in about three years. On his return to New Orleans he was ordered to close the St. James General Hospital; in December he vaccinated all prisoners in the New Orleans vicinity.

Horton was transferred to Jefferson Barracks, Missouri, in January 1865, and on February sixteenth, he arrived at the general hospital in New Albany, Indiana, and was placed in charge of Hospital No. 8. In April 1865, he was placed in charge of Hospital No. 6 in New Albany, which he closed in May, transferring patients to Joe Holt General Hospital.

Between June and October, 1865, Horton was at Camp Thomas, Columbus, Ohio. When it was closed in October, he reported at Fort Leavenworth with the First Battalion, Eighteenth U.S. Infantry. There he was transferred to the Second Battalion, Eighteenth U. S. Infantry, and proceeded with Col. Henry Beebe Carrington to Fort Kearney, Nebraska Territory. On reaching Kearney he received notice that he had been breveted captain and major on March 13, 1865. He acknowledged receipt of the same on December 12, 1865. From Fort Kearney, Colonel Carrington wrote an endorsement on April 14, 1866, in which he stated,

> From knowledge of Dr. Horton's services with the 18th U.S. Inty and at this Post, I am prepared to say that I regard him as one of the best surgeons of his age with whom I ever had contact. He has *nerve, judgment, patience,* devotion to his books and profession; and, in habits and manners, is a gentleman. His treatment is successful and he inspires affection and respect from the men. He is no less officer-like as a soldier, then he is as a man, a gentleman.[1]

---

[1]Henry B. Carrington, Endorsement, 14 April 1866, Surgeon S. M. Horton's U.S.A. Medical Officer's File, Record Group 94, National Archives, Washington, D.C.

Samuel Horton's wife was with him at Fort Kearney and she would accompany him up the Bozeman Trail and remain at his side during their two years at Fort Phil Kearny. Leaving Fort Kearney, Nebraska, on May nineteenth, the great army column slowly advanced towards Fort Laramie and up the trail. Mrs. Margaret Carrington, Henry's wife, wrote about a happening at Clear Fort on July twelfth:

> With Mrs. Horton and Mrs. Bisbee the splendid sunset was watched with real pleasure. Our camp chairs were near the tents on the banks of the creek. A chance interruption of our meditations led to the agreeable information that we were sitting just over three valuable rattlesnakes, which an orderly was kind enough to find and mangle to death.[2]

On June twenty-fourth, near Fort Reno, Mrs. Horton had been given a special gift when trader "French Pete" Gazeau presented her with a young antelope. The Hortons retained the antelope and Margaret Carrington wrote,

> ...for months after we were well settled at Phil Kearny, this antelope, a spotted fawn, and two colts of Captain [Tenodor] Ten Eyck, had each evening a spirited scamper on the parade-ground, until the Indians stole the ponies and the antelope poisoned himself by the substitution of fresh paint for his usual treat of sweet milk.[3]

Mrs. Frances Grummond (later Carrington) recalled being often startled as she was sewing or reading by the antelope, who would poke its head into her tent; she would pet it and give it a treat.

---

[2]Margaret Carrington, *Ab-Sa-Ra-Ka, Home of the Crows: Being the Experience of an Officer's Wife on the Plains* (Philadelphia: J. B. Lippincott & Co., 1868), p. 101.

[3]Carrington, *Ab-Sa-Ra-Ka,* p. 87.

On August 30, 1866, Horton was assigned to Fort Phil Kearny as the post surgeon and immediately requested permission to supervise the building of an adequate hospital. There seems to have been little progress made on this structure when Horton wrote to Carrington on November twenty-first or twenty-second concerning the quality of workmen assigned for the duty. Post Adjutant William Bisbee disagreed and stated that there were twenty wagonloads of roofing near the structure, that Horton had no right to think idlers had been selected for the construction, and that argument and discussion were improper in endorsements. Doctor Horton was relieved from any further care of the construction of the post hospital.[4]

On December nineteenth, Carrington wrote, "I do decidedly wish that Dr. C. M. Hines remain...[here]. He is the best surgeon and physician I have, of far more experience than Dr. Horton..."[5] On December twenty-first, Horton would acquire experience in mass deaths, and on December twenty-sixth, he would request an appropriation of twenty dollars be made to pay "for assistance in washing 160 bloody sheets, which were taken from the Post Hospital to cover and put under our dead soldiers..."[6] These were the three officers, seventy-six enlisted men and two civilians killed in the Fetterman Massacre. Doctor Horton also prescribed sleeping draughts for the pregnant widow of Lt. George Grummond.

---

[4]Fort Phil Kearny, Endorsements Sent, 1866-1868, No. 63, "Records of the United States Continental Commands, 1821-1920," Record Group 393, National Archives, Washington, D.C.

[5]Henry Carrington, Letter, 19 December 1866, Fort Phil Kearny, Letters Sent, 1866-1868, Record Group 393, National Archives, Washington, D.C.

[6]Samuel Horton, Letter, 26 December 1866, Fort Phil Kearny, Letters Received, 1866-1868, Record Group 393, National Archives, Washington, D.C.

On January 13, 1867, Horton reported he had under his care 115 men suffering from scurvy, of whom eighty-five were soldiers; of these, six were crippled from the illness, four seriously so, and his supply of antiscorbutics was almost exhausted. He had no fresh vegetables for the men, only pickles, pickled onions and dried apples in insufficient amounts. Scurvy would remain a very serious problem for the garrisons of Fort Phil Kearny and Fort Reno (at the latter post, five men literally rotted to death by the end of March 1867), while the men stationed at Fort C. F. Smith were unaffected.

On August 2, 1867, Horton arrived with a relief party at the besieged Wagon Box site with whiskey for the survivors. He would have three death certificates to fill out, after treating the wounds of two of the men. Two days later, three more soldiers' bodies would be found at a nearby side camp

Doctor Horton sent various artifacts to the Surgeon General's Office on March 3, 1868. These included three arrows from the bodies of those who died in the Fetterman massacre and four arrows from the site of the Wagon Box Fight.

Captain George M. Templeton, while temporarily stationed at Fort Phil Kearny in 1868, recorded in his diary that the Hortons left the post on July fifteenth. In the next twenty-six years, this doctor and his wife would be at posts in Nebraska, New York, Texas, Maryland, Wyoming, Utah, Kansas, Rhode Island and California. Horton's sick leaves would total almost two years in time, including one for six months in 1888 and one for ten months in 1891. He retired from the service on June 6, 1894. In March of that year his examining physician stated,

> He was quite free from asthma at the time I saw him but he undoubtedly has frequent and severe attacks of asthma, which...incapacitates him for duty. He also has chronic bronchitis which at times is very troublesome....His appearance is that of age greater than his years warrant.

> Complexion pale and waxy, is on all occasions very nervous, and easily agitated...[7]

Samuel M. Horton died on November 23, 1918, in Albany, New York. His widow, Sallie K. Dunnica Horton, died October 14, 1923, at the home of her daughter in Boston, Massachusetts. The Hortons also left a son, Theodore.

FATHER BARRY HAGAN

---

[7]Dr. A. Hartsuff, Letter, 14 March 1894, Surgeon S. M. Horton's U.S.A. Medical Officer's File, Record Group 94, National Archives, Washington, D.C.

Margaret Sullivant Carrington

At Fort Kearny, Nebraska, in May of 1866, Gen. William Tecumseh Sherman suggested that the ladies accompanying Colonel Carrington and his Eighteenth regiment westward keep a daily record of their experiences. (Sherman and others apparently felt little or no reason for concern for the safety of women and children on the expedition.) The Commanding Officer's wife, Margaret, took Sherman's advice and thus has left to posterity one of the most complete and thoughtful accounts of the trip and events surrounding the dramatic story of Fort Phil Kearny. Published in 1868, her journal, entitled *Ab'Sa'Ra'Ka,* remains a "best-seller" among students of Indian wars and frontier history.

Margaret Irvin McDowell Sullivant Carrington was born to a distinguished family in Danville, Kentucky, on May 10, 1831. Her grandfather was the founder of Franklinton (now Columbus, Ohio). Her father, Joseph Sullivant, was the founder of Ohio State University and a cousin, Gen. Irvin McDowell, was one of the early commanders of the Union Army of the Potomac during the Civil War. Notable among her relations were Justice John Marshall, President James Madison, and Ephraim McDowell, who was the first surgeon to perform the operation of ovariotomy and was the founder of the McDowell Medical College of St. Louis.

Margaret married Henry Beebe Carrington in 1851. Of their six children, four died in childhood. The surviving children, Jimmy and Harry, accompanied the couple West.

Born a woman of privilege, Margaret and her husband were acquainted with most of the important people of their time, including Abraham Lincoln. But Margaret was first and foremost an Army wife; she was one of many whose personal creed it was to follow her husband wherever he was assigned, accepting without complaint whatever hardships were in store. In *Ab'Sa'Ra'Ka* she writes,

> It is indeed not always easy to adapt a carpet to dirt floors, or changing sizes of army habitation[1]....The triplet of "I never could, I never would, and I never will" became almost obsolete; and in their place was these other impulses, "I wouldn't but I must and I will" or "I could, I can, and I do!"[2]

Margaret's journals were comprehensive. She wrote of the trip to what was to become Fort Phil Kearny and of her high regard for her husband's trusted guide, interpreter, scout and advisor, mountain man Jim Bridger. Of him she says,

> To us, he was invariably straightforward, truthful, and reliable. His sagacity, knowledge of woodcrafts and of the Indian was wonderful, and his heart was warm and his feelings tender wherever he confided or made a friend.[3]

Of the buffalo encountered along the way she wrote,

> With tens of thousands in a herd, sweeping back and forth, filling the valleys as far as the eye can reach and adding their weight and numbers to the other substantial claims of the red man to entitle this same Absaraka, "their last and best hunting grounds."[4]

---

[1]Margaret Irvin Carrington, *Ab'Sa'Ra'Ka: Land of the Crows* (Philadelphia: J.B. Lippincott & Co., 1868; reprint ed., Lincoln: University of Nebraska Press, 1983), p. 176.

[2]Ibid., p. 174.

[3]Ibid., p. 114.

[4]Ibid., p. 33.

On arriving at the site of Fort Phil Kearny, Margaret wrote of the country's beauty: "The nights in Absaraka were peculiarly beautiful when cloudless...in the glory of the full moon the snow-clad mountains shone as silver."[5] And with her observant eye, taking in all around her, she describes the land and vegetation:

> Wild wheat and oats abound in all the main valleys... The grasses are heavy, so that in the summer of 1866 they were almost too resistant for easy use of machinery, and so thick that a horse could not be trotted rapidly in the bottom lands of Goose Creek and Tongue River. Grasshoppers now and then made a visit, coming in clouds, like the drifting smoke of a prairie fire. Of wild fruit there is a great variety. Raspberries, strawberries, gooseberries, red currents, plums, cherries and rock grapes are among the number.[6]

With her particularly broad scope of interests, she writes of dressmaking, history, soils and water, minerals, socializing, the winter's cold and summer's heat, and, later, of her tender sympathy for Frances Carrington (who lost her husband on Fetterman Ridge, and would become, on Margaret's death, the second wife of Henry Carrington).

Almost apologetically, she gives her view of the Indians: "Yes, even a woman...will draw conclusions for friends to consider, even if they only elicit a smile at her timidity, simplicity, or weakness."[7] She describes the warriors thus: "In ambush and decoy, splendid; in horsemanship, perfect; in strategy, cunning; in battle, wary and careful of life; in

---

[5]Ibid., p. 164.

[6]Ibid., pp. 29-30.

[7]Ibid., p. 181.

victory, jubilant; and in vengeance, fiendish and terrible."[8] With a unique depth of understanding and empathy for the plight of the Indian people, she writes,

> These same Indians have read the book of fate...when this end is reached and the great route through Absaraka is occupied and guarded, the game will flee the range of the white man's rifle, and the desperate Indian must abandon his home, fight himself to death, or yield to the white man's mercy....There comes the inevitable sentiment of pity, and even of sympathy with the bold warrior in his great struggle.[9]

When, on December 21, 1866, a small selected group of Indians decoyed Capt. William Fetterman and eighty men into ambush, to the death of all, Margaret writes,

> As if Nature herself were shocked by the enormity of the Indian torture there inflicted...as of the night of December 21st, the winter became unmitigated in its severity, driving officers, ladies and men to beaver, buffalo, or wolf skins for protection from the cold.[10]

The next day, as Margaret's husband led troops out to find the balance of the bodies and bring them back for burial, contingency plans were made to put all women and children into the magazine and blow them up if the fort were over-run by Indians.[11]

---

[8]Ibid., p. 182.

[9]Ibid., p. 184, 186.

[10]Ibid., p. 212.

[11]A number of accounts say that the women and children at the Fort were placed in the magazine with orders to blow up the magazine if Indians attacked and capture was imminent. However, Margaret does not

In early January, Carrington was relieved of command, and on January twenty-third, he and his family, accompanied by Frances Grummond, the body of her dead husband (Lt. George Grummond) and a contingency of troops, left the fort. Their trip to Fort Caspar was one of great suffering. Margaret describes it thus:

> At three o'clock the thermometer gave out entirely. The mercury settled in the bulb, froze itself stiff...FORTY BELOW ZERO!...Do or die was the impulse of all....With the dawn came the report of the sad work of the night. Assistant Surgeon Hines had the fingers of both hands frozen...while many teamsters and nearly half of the escort were more or less frozen, some of them requiring amputations as soon as we reached Fort Reno.
>
> If we claim no special credit for endurance, and have never questioned the necessity of such a march at such a season, certainly, like good wives, we followed wherever led, and we do not envy any officer's wife, of however long experience, her claim to have had a harder trip after such a summer. Perhaps some have. Ours was ample for us.[12]

Reflecting later, Margaret writes,

> Nor does a single sentiment of complaint or reflection upon the Indians, the weather, or anybody else, have its place in our recollections of the past. It was our impulse and duty to go and we went. No regrets are entertained; but sometimes it seems that we should have had more enjoyment and quiet had there been more men along, and that the Indians would have treated larger numbers with

---

mention this in *Ab'Sa'Ra'Ka*, leading some to believe that although contingency plans were made, the women were not told and were not placed in the magazine.

[12]Carrington, *Ab'Sa'Ra'Ka*, pp. 233-235.

> greater respect; and sometimes it seems very strange that that trip to Fort Caspar, just then, was such a matter of life or death to the nation, as to make it a question of life or death to us.[13]

Margaret Carrington died of tuberculosis on May 11, 1870, one day after her thirty-ninth birthday, and only three years after her return with her husband from Fort Phil Kearny.[14]

MARY ELLEN MCWILLIAMS

---

[13]Ibid., p. 236.

[14]Biographical data used in this article is obtained from the historical introduction to *Absaraka: Home of the Crows*, published by Lakeside Press in 1950 and written by M. M. Quaife. The Lakeside Press edition went back to the original 1868 version of *Absaraka* as written by Margaret Carrington. Quotes used in this biography, from the 1983 edition, match verbatim with those written in 1868.

James Beckwourth
Wyoming State Museum

Capt. William H. Bisbee
Wyoming State Museum

John Bozeman
Montana Historical Society

Mitch Boyer
Little Bighorn Battlefield National Monument

Max Littman
American Heritage Center, University of Wyoming

Davis Willson
Montana Historical Society

John Bratt

Jim Bridger
Wyoming State Museum

Frances Grummond Carrington
American Heritage Center, University of Wyoming

Sam Gibson
American Heritage Center, University of Wyoming

Lt. George W. Grummond
Wyoming State Museum

Dennis Driscoll
American Heritage Center, University of Wyoming

Nelson Story
Montana Historical Society

Lt. George Belden (self-portrait)
New York Bureau of Illustrations

Lt. John Jenness
Little Bighorn Battlefield National Monument

Fincelius "Finn" Burnett
American Heritage Center, University of Wyoming

Dr. Samuel Horton
National Archives

William Daley
Courtesy Bill & Carol Daley

Chiefs Little Wolf (standing) & Morning Star (Dull Knife)
Wyoming State Museum

Chaplain David White
Fort Larned National Historic Site

Chief Red Cloud
Wyoming State Museum

Capt. Tenodor Ten Eyck
Wyoming State Museum

Gen. Jonathan Smith
Wyoming State Museum

John "Portugee" Phillips (seated) & Capt. James Powell
Wyoming State Museum

Col. Henry B. Carrington
Courtesy Ted Maguder

Capt. Frederick H. Brown
Wyoming State Museum

Henry W. Wessells
National Archives

Edmund Richard Pitman Shurly
Chicago Historical Society

Capt. William J. Fetterman
Wyoming State Museum

Margaret Sullivant Carrington
American Heritage Center, University of Wyoming

American Horse
Wyoming State Museum

JAMES BEEBE CARRINGTON

James Beebe Carrington (1860-1929), son of Colonel Henry Beebe and Margaret Sullivant Carrington, was born on 23 October 1860, in Columbus, Ohio. As a young boy he accompanied his mother and father to the military posts commanded by his father in Nebraska, Colorado, and Dakota Territory. He was six years old and living at Fort Phil Kearny at the time of the Fetterman Disaster.

In "Across the Plains with Bridger as Guide," an article written by James Carrington for *Scribner's Magazine* in 1929, he remembers his days at Fort Kearney, Nebraska, before leaving for the soon-to-be-built Bozeman Trail post, Fort Phil Kearny:

> Not far from Fort Kearney there was a Pawnee reservation, where I had many friends among the Indians, some of whom would use my good offices to get by the sentinel in front of headquarters....I used to have a lot of fun with the Indian boys, shooting at a mark with bows and arrows, and when General Sherman visited the post we had a contest to see who could shoot the highest. My bow was boy's size, but I won by lying on my back and putting both feet against the bow to pull it.[1]

James continues:

> A few days before we left the old Fort Kearney, on the long and memorable march across the plains, our house burned down early in the morning, and I recall the terror

---

[1]James B. Carrington, "Across the Plains with Bridger as Guide," *Scribner's Magazine* 85 (1929):70.

of the scene, the mad scramble to save a few things, but especially the rapid popping of several big army revolvers that the fire set off.[2]

Of the trip to Fort Phil Kearny, he writes,

> Our home for weeks was to be an army ambulance of the old kind, bumpy, drawn by mules, as were all of the big covered wagons....There followed many weary days and nights, never free from the apprehension of a possible Indian attack....Nightly we heard the weird and mournful howling of wolves, sometimes the deep rumble of a stampeded herd of buffalo, that fairly shook the earth. And all through the dark, at regular intervals, the reassuring calls of the sentinels.[3]

One delightful memory was that of a calico pony:

> My brother and I had been given a small Indian pony that we called "Calico," and during the day we would take turns riding him around, to get relief from the monotony and cramped quarters of the ambulance. I can still remember passing prairie-dog villages where there were thousands of the funny little rodents running around, or sitting up to bark at us and then ducking down into their hole. Never a day without the sight of leaping antelopes, an occasional sneaking cayote, big jack rabbits, often herds of buffalo in the distance, and ever the monotonous expanse of sage covered plains, blinding dust, the big skies stretching to the blue horizon, distant mountains, gorgeous sunsets, and in the heat of some days a shimmering mirage that looked like a great sea.[4]

---

[2]Ibid.

[3]Ibid.

[4]Ibid.

Frances Courtney Grummond Carrington in her book *My Army Life*, writes: "Jimmy Carrington, my little favorite, whose loving disposition made him a welcome guest..."[5] According to Frances, James

> possessed a remarkably sweet voice, and together we sang familiar Sunday School hymns his mother had taught him, one of which I especially recall, "There is a light in the window for me," and his sweet childish tones sang the words deeply into my heart.[6]

James' and Henry's calico pony was killed when ridden by Capt. Fredrick H. Brown into the battle on Fetterman Ridge. It is interesting that James makes no mention of the death of his pony in the article but has a strong memory of the death of Gray Eagle:

> Father's magnificent horse that had been presented to him by old soldiers. He succumbed to bad weather and lack of proper food. His strength exhausted, he had to be shot, and we watched his poor body as long as we could, in silence, but, needless to say, not without blinding tears.[7]

James Carrington writes that many of the memories were "vague" but it is not surprising that the memory of December 21, 1866, is "one that comes foremost":

> How many times later I awoke in the dark in terror, to see again the tortured bodies and bloody arrows of that night. It was about noon of the day that out of the quiet came,

---

[5]Frances C. Carrington, *My Army Life and the Fort Phil Kearney Massacre* (Philadelphia: J. P. Lippincott Company, 1911), pp. 101-102.

[6]Ibid.

[7]Carrington, "Across the Plains," p. 70.

> with startling distinctness, and suddenness, the sound of volley-firing over the hills and out of sight of the fort. This was succeeded by shattering shots - then silence. That night, the wagons and ambulances that had gone out with a rescue party came back loaded with the horribly mutilated bodies of most of Captain Fetterman's command of eighty-one men, who had been ambushed and completely annihilated by an overwhelming body of Indians.[8]

The terror of that night faded from the mind of a six year old and was replaced in adulthood by more pleasant memories:

> Looking back over the many years that have gone, it seems to me that we children thought chiefly of the good times we were having; to us it was a wonderful and glorious adventure. Little did we appreciate the ever-present anxiety that filled the minds of our mothers, the downright hardships and privations they endured, the wearing responsibilities that bore so heavily upon the shoulders of the commander, his officers and men. To us it was mostly "wash-ta-la," good, but to our elders it was all "wau-nee-chee," very bad, if I am right in my recollection of the Indian words.[9]

James Carrington married Eva Josephine Doolittle of Springfield, Illinois, in 1878. He studied at Wabash College in Crawfordsville, Indiana, and Russel's Commercial and Collegiate Institute in New Haven, Connecticut. He received an honorary master's degree from Wabash College in 1898.

Carrington was recognized as an editor and author, especially in the fields of art, architecture and natural history. He established the Chicago office of *Scribner's Magazine* in

---

[8]Ibid., p. 71.

[9]Ibid.

1887 and eventually became an associate editor and the editor for architecture and art in the New York City headquarters.

His "Art of the American Wood-Engraver," (1884) was the first bibliography of wood-engraving in the United States. He was personally responsible for an art and architecture column entitled "Point of View" in *Scribner's Magazine* and also wrote on wood-engraving and art for "Johnson's Universal Cyclopedia" (1893-1895). In 1917, he became the editor of *Architecture*, a monthly magazine published by Scribner's.

Photography and sailing were his hobbies, and he was sought as a speaker because of his boyhood experiences on the frontier and his self-made lantern slides of art, sailing and nature. He was a member of the Salmagundi Club of New York City.

After retirement in 1926, James Beebe Carrington died at his home in Ridgefield, Connecticut, on July 14, 1929, and was buried in Wallingford, Connecticut.

CATHERINE CURTISS, AUTHOR
THEODORE L. MAGUDER, CONTRIBUTOR

SUSAN FITSGERALD

Susan Fitsgerald,[1] also known as "Black Susan," served as a maid for Capt. Tenodor Ten Eyck while he was stationed at Camp Cottonwood, near Fort Kearney, Nebraska, after his black manservant, Dick, was left at Leavenworth, Kansas. Susan became a laundress for Company H and bought a washing machine shortly after the arrival of the Eighteenth Infantry at Fort Phil Kearny. She also bought a cow the same day. She was illiterate and Ten Eyck wrote letters to her family and handled all her business accounts as long as she was with him. Once he sent twenty dollars to his wife to buy a wig for her, and there is also an account of a partition being placed in the hall of his quarters for a sleeping room for her.

Colonel Carrington issued a "strong order" to Ten Eyck with regard to "Susan selling pies & etc."[2] Some accounts state that she was using government flour and fruit to make the pies and selling them to the soldiers for "Half a Dollar." There were reports, too, that she was selling whiskey to the soldiers. Her redeeming feature, with respect to the officers' wives, was to "make sausage, and good sausage, out of almost every kind of meat, except impossible pork."[3]

---

[1]Susan Fitsgerald may also have been known as Susan Kirkpatrick or Susan Kilpatrick. There are notations on occasion of letters written to a Littleton Pettitt (unexplained) and a brother (no name given).

[2]Tenodor Ten Eyck, Diary, 24 November 1866, Special Collections Section, University of Arizona Library, Tucson, Arizona.

[3]Frances C. Carrington, *My Army Life and the Fort Phil Kearney Massacre* (Philadelphia: J. B. Lippincott, 1911), pp. 106-107.

Susan left Fort Phil Kearny with Ten Eyck when he was ordered to go to Fort Laramie in 1867. She was paid and left him. She returned to begin cooking for mess at Fort Fetterman in January 1868. She again left with him when he went to Chicago on leave, and then went home to Tennessee. He held $220 in Chicago for her. She returned a week later with her son and niece on their way to Omaha. She then went back to Chicago and he wrote to the Principal of Oberlin Academy for her, ostensibly to have her son admitted to that school. A reply was received but the contents are unknown.[4]

The last accounts of her activities were in December 1868 when she went back to Omaha and Ten Eyck bought her ticket (twenty two dollars) and paid fifty-five dollars for furniture at Sedgewicks. On December 21, 1868, Ten Eyck sent a list of Susan's account to Lieutenant Manley.

JEAN H. KIMBLE

---

[4]Her son's name may have been George, as Ten Eyck's diary entry on 7 November 1868, reads, "Susan and George arrived" while Ten Eyck was in Chicago. This was after the entries regarding the correspondence with Oberlin Academy when her son returned with her to Chicago from Tennessee.

ELISABETH A. WHEATLEY BREAKENRIDGE & GEORGE BREAKENRIDGE

Virtually everyone familiar with the story of Fort Phil Kearny has read about the death of the two civilian contractors in the Fetterman fight, one of whom was James Simpson Wheatley. Wheatley left behind a nineteen-year-old wife, Elisabeth, and two tiny sons, John William and Milton Henry. Finn Burnett described Elisabeth "as a beautiful girl, a fine woman...a brave and splendid little soldier."[1]

James Wheatley was originally from the Blue Springs area in Nebraska. In 1864, and for some time after, he was the contractor for hay and firewood at Fort Kearney, Nebraska. It is possible that it was here Wheatley learned of the potential for lucrative sub-contract work available at the posts to be built on the Bozeman Trail.

What is known about Elisabeth Wheatley Breakenridge comes from a Depredation Claim, number 1758, filed with the U.S. government on July 2, 1873. In the claim, Elisabeth states that the family was enroute westerly in 1866 and, when passing Fort Laramie,

> ...a treaty of peace and amity was being made and concluded between commissioners on the part of the United States and the confederated bands of the Sioux nation of Indians and that she and her husband were encouraged and

---

[1]Dee Brown, *The Fetterman Massacre*, formerly *Fort Phil Kearny: An American Saga* (Lincoln: University of Nebraska Press, 1971), p. 200.

> induced to believe that a lasting and permanent treaty of peace would be established.[2]

Believing that they would be safe, the Wheatleys traveled to Fort Phil Kearny, arriving on July 9, 1866. They then built and maintained a civilian mess and boarding house just outside the stockade, with ready access to the main gate. The claim states that during the months of November and December, the Wheatley's lost four large, well-broken mares, two cows, two mules and seven oxen to Indian raids.

On December 21, 1866, James made the fateful decision to volunteer to join Captain Fetterman. He carried with him a silver mounted Henry rifle, five hundred dollars in U.S. currency and some important personal papers.

Upon request, in February of 1867, Elisabeth gave her one good horse to carry the mail to Fort Reno. Enroute to Fort Reno, Indians attacked, killing the mail carrier and stealing the horse. An attack on the stock near the fort on August 2, 1867, resulted in the theft of her cow.

In June of 1867, Elisabeth married George Breakenridge, an army wheelwright and one of the higher paid civilian employees. Elisabeth also received permission to "build a better and more comfortable house for the accommodation of the mess and her boarders."[3] The new construction cost three thousand dollars and the house contained five rooms and was furnished with carpet, an iron bed, a walnut bed, a

---

[2]Department of the Interior Office of Indian Affairs, Washington, D.C., 22 December 1866; Depredation Claim 1758. The claim must be evaluated with special scrutiny as the document is what Elisabeth *claimed* were her losses from Indian raids and the government's decision to abandon Fort Phil Kearny. The value and number of possessions and livestock might be inflated. In addition, her reasons, as stated in the claim, for going to the post are no doubt colored by her desire to be fully compensated for her losses.

[3]Ibid.

wardrobe, cane chairs, two kitchen tables, cupboards, and various tin, glass and silver wares. Mention is also made of a "tin safe," perhaps a pie safe.

Fort Phil Kearny was abandoned in August of 1868, and on the fourth of that month, in pursuance of military orders, the Breakenridges left the Fort and traveled to Fort Laramie. Due to the difficulty of finding transportation, Elisabeth was compelled to leave her furniture and most of her housewares.

In the fall of 1868, George Breakenridge left government employ and contracted to the railroad to build a roadbed in Weber Canyon, south of Ogden, Utah. He also opened a livery stable in Ogden and ran freight to Bannack, Montana Territory.

In September of 1867, the Army had established quartermaster and commissary depots at Fort D. A. Russell, some ninety miles to the south of Fort Laramie. A military stage line linked the two posts and a great deal of travel by army personnel and trains of freight wagons traversed the route daily. In the fall of 1869, the Breakenridges moved back to Cheyenne and apparently set up a road ranch, six miles up the Chugwater from Fort Laramie, on the road to Cheyenne.

During these years, Elisabeth and the children remained at the road ranch where she ran the station while her husband went off to the most lucrative employment he could find. George ran freight from Cheyenne to Denver and contracted for grading work with the Kansas Pacific Railway, which was quickly approaching Denver.[4]

On July 2, 1873, Elisabeth Breakenridge made her Depredation Claim for $6,339.00, at Fort Laramie, stating she had been a resident of that county for seven years. In addition to noting the livestock and goods she lost, she said she was making the claim "because she had no adequate

---

[4]William Breakenridge, *Helldorado: Bringing the Law to Mesquite* (New York: Houghton Mifflin Company, 1928) pp. 54-56.

means with which to educate and prepare her children for a useful pursuit in life."

Elisabeth was never compensated. The claim states that her attorneys were notified on September 22, 1883, that they must file testimony as required by Department rules; the attorneys did not reply to the notification. Special Agent L. H. Poole, a field investigator, addressed a letter to Elisabeth at Fort Laramie, her last known place of residence, which was returned unopened. He made inquiries, without success, as to her whereabouts. Her case for claim, closed on December 22, 1886, noted that

> claimant has failed to substantiate the charges in her declaration against said Indians; and it also appears from the record that her application for relief was not made within the time prescribed by the law then in force and the claim is barred and should be disallowed.[5]

Sometime between 1875 and 1876 the Breakenridges moved to another road ranch, this time about 4.37 miles north of Fort Laramie on the Platte, where the new trail to the Black Hills broke away from the Oregon-California Trail. At that junction the family was settled by the time Army mapping parties visited the area in 1875-76. The days of this trail were numbered by the approach of railroads to the Black Hills from the Missouri River Country.

The family must have seen the handwriting on the wall and they set out for yet another frontier of opportunity. They found it in the new city of Billings, Montana. Billings was a railroad town on the new Northern Pacific Railroad, which reached that point in 1882. The very first Billings

---

[5]Department of the Interior, Depredation Claim 1758.

business directory of the mid-1880s carries an advertisement for a Livery Stable, operated by the Wheatley Brothers and George Breakenridge.

ROBERT MURRAY, AUTHOR
CATHERINE CURTISS, CONTRIBUTOR

Special thanks to John D. McDermott for making the Indian Depredation Claim available for study. McDermott discovered the document in the National Archives during a visit in March 1991.

EDMUND RICHARD PITMAN SHURLY

Edmund Richard Pitman Shurly, born in Cambridge, England, on January 27, 1829, to John and Clumley Shurly, was an experienced soldier by the time he was assigned duty on the Bozeman Trail. As a young man, Shurly lived in Buffalo, New York. He was six feet tall and had a fair complexion, blue eyes and brown hair. He married Charlotte Augusta Godwin in Rochester on November 25, 1856. The Shurlys were to have three children.[1]

Shurly was living in Illinois, working as an engineer, when he enlisted in the Twenty-sixth New York Infantry in May 1861. He was mustered into the service as first lieutenant and was commissioned captain three months later.[2] While leading his command in the Battle of Fredericksburg on December 13, 1862, he was severely wounded in the thigh. After recovering, he returned to duty as captain in the Invalid Corps in August 1863. He was appointed Post Adjutant at Camp Douglas, Chicago.

While at Camp Douglas, which was being used as a prison camp for captured Confederate soldiers, Shurly played a key role in uncovering and thwarting a massive prison

---

[1]Biographical information is from Shurly's pension file in the National Archives.

[2]Shurly's official record is in Francis B. Heitman, *Historical Register and Dictionary of the United States Army, 1789-1903,* 2 vols. (Washington, D.C.: Government Printing Office, 1903; reprint, Urbana: University of Illinois Press, 1965), 1:885. See also Frederick Phisterer, *New York in the War of Rebellion, 1861-1865,* 3rd edition (Albany: J. B. Lyons Co., 1912), p. 2,037.

escape. Known as the Camp Douglas conspiracy, the aim of the plot was to free the eight thousand prisoners, sack Chicago, and proclaim it as the capital of the Northwest Confederate States of America. Shurly learned of the conspiracy from a spy and alerted the commanding officer, thus averting what would have been a major disaster of the Civil War. Following the exchange of prisoners at the close of the war, there were several commanders of Camp Douglas in quick succession. Shurly was the seventh, next to the last commander of the post.[3]

In March of 1865, Shurly was brevetted major for gallant and meritorious service at Fredericksburg and lieutenant colonel for gallant and meritorious service during the war. He was honorably mustered out of the Volunteer Army in October of 1865. In May 1866, he enlisted in the Eighteenth Infantry as a second lieutenant. In September of that year he was transferred to the Twenty-seventh Infantry.

In the spring of 1867, Lieutenant Shurly was sent to Fort C. F. Smith, attached to the column of Col. John E. Smith, who left North Platte, Nebraska, with supply trains, 350 recruits, and newly reported officers for Fort Phil Kearny. The column arrived at Fort Phil Kearny on July 3, 1867, where Colonel Smith assumed command of the post. Lt. Alexander Wishart was also with this column, and he notes in his diary that while at Fort Phil Kearny, Shurly relieved him as Officer of the Day on July 14.[4]

Colonel Smith sent Lt. Col. Luther P. Bradley, with reinforcements, recruits, and supplies, to take command at Fort C. F. Smith. Shurly accompanied Bradley's column and

---

[3]Shurly's role in the Camp Douglas conspiracy is documented in the files of the Chicago Historical Society.

[4]Wishart's diary is published in *Books and Photographs of Elsa Spear* (Sheridan, Wyoming: Fort Phil Kearny/Bozeman Trail Association, 1987), pp. 26-34.

arrived at the post on July twenty-third, where he became Post Commissary and Quartermaster.[5] On August first, he participated in the renowned Hayfield Fight. Late in the afternoon, he was sent out of the fort with twenty mounted men to relieve the besieged men at the hayfield. His small command was surrounded by Indians and forced to turn back. It was not until Bradley sent more men and a howitzer to Shurly that the corralled men at the hayfield were rescued. Shurly received a slight wound in the hand in this engagement.

Although Shurly was not stationed at Fort Phil Kearny, his name is associated with the last major engagement near the fort, which has since become known as the Shurly Fight.[6] On October 28, 1867, he was assigned to command an escort detachment of five non-commissioned officers and thirty-five privates to accompany an empty supply train to Fort Phil Kearny. His orders were to meet and exchange escort duties with a Wells Fargo train which was enroute from Fort Phil Kearny to Fort C. F. Smith.

The Wells Fargo train consisted of sixteen ox-drawn wagons and was escorted by a detachment of Twenty-seventh Infantry with a mountain howitzer and a government ammunition wagon, both pulled by mules. Early on the morning of November second, six miles north of Fort Phil

---

[5]Shurly's presence at Fort C. F. Smith is documented in Lt. George Templeton's Diary, Graff 4099, Newberry Library, Chicago, Illinois.

[6]An excellent account of the Shurly fight is Barry J. Hagan, C.S.C., "'Save the Gun at all Hazzerds!'," *Journal of the Council on Abandoned Military Posts* 10 (Winter 1978-1979):35-47. In addition, two letters written by Shurly give his own version of the fight. The first was written a week after the fight, from Fort Phil Kearny, and is published in *Books and Photos of Elsa Spear,* pp. 40-41. The other, written in 1888 to Col. James S. Brisbin, is in "Skirmish at Goose Creek: Edmond R. P. Shurly's Bozeman Trail Reminiscence," ed. Brian Cockhill, *Montana, The Magazine of Western History* 33 (Spring 1983):60-63.

Kearny, the train was attacked by Indians and forced to corral. Later that day Shurly found the corralled Wells Fargo train, exchanged escort details, and on the morning of November third proceeded to retrace his route, with the Wells Fargo train, back to Fort C. F. Smith. However, a violent snow storm set in and they were compelled to camp after moving only a mile and a half.

On November fourth, the train proceeded down the old road to Fort C. F. Smith, following the bottom of Peno (now called Prairie Dog) Creek. About twenty miles north-east of Fort Phil Kearny, while making the steep descent to Goose Creek, the train was suddenly attacked by Indians. This place in the road was an ideal location for an ambush. The steepness, compounded by bad road conditions from the snow storm, made it necessary to fasten ropes to the wagons in order to let them down the hill. And to make matters worse, when the Indians attacked, the train was widely separated. Three supply wagons and the howitzer were still on the brow of the hill, two wagons were part of the way down, and the balance of the train was at the foot, about eight hundred yards away.

Shurly was with the rear wagons and when the attack began, he sent a man to the wagon master with orders to corral the wagons. The Indians closed in from both front and rear, but made the heaviest attack on the separated rear wagons. The howitzer was loaded and fired when the attack began, but perceiving that the Indians were trying to capture it, Shurly ordered it limbered and told the driver of the gun to "make for the corall, save the gun at all hazzerds."[7] He and the seven men who had been cut off in the rear with him also retreated towards the corral. His progress was excruciating, however, since he was wounded by an arrow that lodged in his left foot.

---

[7]"Cockhill, "Skirmish at Goose Creek," p. 62.

Shurly made it to the corral, but the soldier manning the howitzer died shortly after reaching it. The arrow in Shurly's foot had passed through so that the point protruded through the sole of his boot. He pushed the arrow through and bandaged his foot with his necktie. He was very weak but was still able to command the beleaguered force. Upon reaching the corral, he learned that the lead ammunition wagon had bolted straight into the hands of the Indians. He then assessed the strength of his remaining force as thirty-one soldiers with about forty rounds to each man left, twenty-six drivers with only a few revolvers, and one wagon master. He told the men that the Indians would know they were low on ammunition, and that the first man that fired without his order he would shoot.

The Indians immediately ransacked the three wagons left on the hill. Shurly later learned that those wagons contained sutler's goods, and that two of them were loaded with red blankets which were highly prized by the Indians. In fact, their importance was such that American Horse used this event to represent 1867-68 in his winter count.[8] Then the Indians renewed their attack on the corral. Before long, Shurly became so weakened from loss of blood that wagon master William Harwood took over the command. Several rounds from the howitzer drove the Indians back, and they were held off for the remainder of the day. After dark, two volunteers were sent to Fort Phil Kearny for assistance.

At daylight the attack resumed, but shortly afterwards soldiers were seen riding over the crest of the hill, from the

---

[8]American Horse's pictograph of this year is a wagon, with a blanket protruding from it representing the goods found in the wagons, which he labeled, "They captured a train of wagons near Tongue river. The men who were with it got away." See Garrick Mallery, *Picture-Writing of the American Indians,* Tenth Annual Report of the Bureau of American Ethnology, 1888-89 (Washington, D.C., 1893; reprinted in two volumes, New York: Dover, 1972), p. 570.

direction of the fort. The rescuers were Col. John Green with three companies of the Second Cavalry and Capt. David Gordon with his company. They brought with them a surgeon, ambulance, and a bale of blankets. Shurly was taken back to Fort Phil Kearny with the other wounded, and the Wells Fargo train proceeded onto Fort C. F. Smith under Captain Gordon. Three soldiers died in this engagement; Shurly, a soldier and a civilian were wounded; and the Indian casualties are unknown.[9]

Shurly remained at Fort Phil Kearny for several weeks, recuperating from his wound, returning to Fort C. F. Smith in the spring of 1868. The Bozeman Trail posts were abandoned that summer.

On July eighth, Shurly commanded a detachment of cavalry escorting army paymaster Maj. R. D. Clarke. Upon arriving at Fort D. A. Russell, he was joined by his wife, Charlotte.[10] From there they went to Ogallala Station, where Shurly retired from the army in December 1868.

Shurly and his wife returned to Chicago, where he entered business as a jeweler and watchmaker. He was a successful businessman and in his later years became well-

---

[9]Official records indicate the fight took place about twenty miles northeast of Fort Phil Kearny, near Goose Creek. The problem for historians is that there were two roads between Fort Phil Kearny and Fort C. F. Smith in 1867 and 1868. Shurly was on the old road, or Bozeman's original route, which went down Prairie Dog Creek, crossed the divide to Goose Creek, and crossed it somewhere near present day Sheridan. However, the new road is the one that has become known as the Bozeman Trail, and there are many local historians who believe that the fight took place near where that road crossed Big Goose Creek.

[10]Templeton Diary, 30 August 1868. Elizabeth Reynolds Burt also mentions meeting Mrs. Shurly at Fort D. A. Russell in her reminiscences. See Merrill J. Mattes, *Indians, Infants and Infantry, Andrew and Elizabeth Burt on the Frontier* (Denver: The Old West Publishing Company, 1960; reprint, Lincoln: University of Nebraska Press, 1989), p. 176.

known in Chicago as a Civil War veteran and Indian fighter. He remained plagued for the rest of his life by the wounds he had received at Fredericksburg and in the Shurly fight. Shurly died February 20, 1910, in Detroit and was buried in Rochester, New York.

CONNIE WILSON

FINCELIUS "FINN" BURNETT

Finn Burnett was born in 1843, in Lewis County, Missouri, the son of Washington J. and Eliza Burnett, who were early Missouri pioneer settlers. He received his early education in the public schools and for a short time attended Christian University at Canton, Missouri. He enlisted in the Monticello Grays at the outbreak of the Civil War and served most of his time on the Missouri border. When it appeared he would be conscripted into the Union Army, he and a friend, like many other young men in the border states, left Missouri and made the long trek to Omaha - a trek which was, at that time, not without its own perils.

Finn had always had a strong desire to see the frontier and in Omaha he was given an opportunity to do just that by one A. C. Leighton, a well-to-do Omaha storekeeper who provided sutlers' supplies for the various posts on the frontier. Leighton had just received appointment as sutler for the Powder River expedition into Dakota Territory under Gen. Patrick Connor. Finn signed on for sixty-five dollars a month and board and bed.

It took thirty days for the wagon train to make the trip from Omaha to Fort Laramie and it arrived in time for Finn to spend his twenty-first birthday at the post. He didn't have to wait long to see the wild west first hand. Shortly after arriving he witnessed the infamous hanging of the three chiefs which left an indelible impression on Finn. He could never forget the swaying forms that hung upon the gallows at Fort Laramie or the words of Jim Bridger, who Finn became acquainted with on the expedition and who prophesied, "this hanging [will] lead to dreadful consequences later on the trails."[1]

Finn inevitably became involved in those consequences as warfare on the western plains escalated as increasing numbers of whites penetrated Indian territory. The Powder River expedition had been organized as a punitive expedition against the Northern Plains Indians. Delays were numerous, but by the end of July 1865, final provisions were made and the column began its march.

Finn learned much and observed much during the expedition though the campaign itself fell far short of expectations. A late start, bad weather in August and poor coordination between the three columns of troops all exacerbated the difficulties. The Indians shrewdly conceived hit-and-run tactics, adding to the cavalry's woes. Consequently, the mission to chastise the Northern Plains Indians was thwarted and would not be accomplished for well over a decade.

Following the breakup of the Powder River expedition, Mr. Leighton placed Finn in charge of a wagon train and directed him to return to Omaha. After spending the winter at his home in Missouri, Finn's thoughts turned again to the West. He returned to Omaha in the spring of 1866 where Mr. Leighton was waiting for him with a job as wagon boss. Finn returned to Dakota Territory and spent time at Fort Phil Kearny, Fort Connor, and other military posts during the so-called "two bloody years on the plains." He was present at Fort Phil Kearny when the Fetterman disaster occurred in the winter of 1866. In fact, Finn participated in hauling the frozen bodies back into the fort the day after the fight. When "Portugee" Phillips made his remarkable ride to Fort Laramie for relief, Finn was among the depleted forces anxiously awaiting his safe delivery.

---

[1]Robert Beebe David, *Finn Burnett, Frontiersman* (Glendale: Arthur H. Clark Co., 1937) p. 43.

Finn continued supplying the beleaguered forts along the Bozeman Trail through the spring and summer of 1867 and in August, near Fort C. F. Smith, on the Big Horn River, he participated in one of the most significant battles in the trail's turbulent history, the Hay Field Fight. One Lieutenant Stromberg, with eight soldiers and nine teamsters, defended an open corral against the attack of approximately five hundred Cheyenne Indians. The group repulsed three attacks lasting well over four hours. A new shipment of Sharp's repeating rifles tipped the balance in favor of the defenders who were able to surprise the Indians with firepower equivalent to a much larger party.

The victory was of considerable importance. The Sioux and Cheyenne had divided their forces to attack the two hated forts, Phil Kearny and C. F. Smith. With the victory at the Wagon Box fight near Fort Phil Kearny and the Hay Field Fight, the possible destruction of the two posts was thwarted and the way paved for negotiations with the Sioux and Cheyenne. The forts along the trail were ultimately abandoned and Finn entered a new phase of his life.

In 1869, Finn purchased teams of oxen and mules and became a grader on the Union Pacific right-of-way. He worked in Wyoming, Nevada, and Utah during the race to join the rails of the first transcontinental railroad. On the day of the festivities at Promontory Point, Utah, Finn was there to watch the driving of the "golden spike."

Finn then went back to work for Leighton in his store in Atlantic City, Wyoming. Gold had been discovered there and Finn did a little prospecting on the side. It was there also that Finn met and married Eliza Ann McCarthy, a native of New York who had come west to work for a Mrs. Stewart who operated a boarding house.

On May 1, 1871, Finn was hired by Dr. James Irwain as "boss farmer" on the Shoshoni reservation in Wind River Valley. Finn and Eliza moved with their first son, Jim, to Camp Brown, where the city of Lander was later established.

The area became their home. They were blessed with eight children and Frank, their second son, was the first white child born in the valley.

Finn's days as "boss farmer" were filled with the challenges as well as the actual dangers of attempting to convert thousands of Shoshoni Indians from nomadic hunting to agriculture. The plan was fraught with difficulties from the start and there were also serious problems with the Sioux and the Arapaho who were not friendly toward the Shoshoni and were contemptuous of the white man's policies. Chief Washakie's leadership proved to be the key to a peaceful transition of his people and he and Finn developed a lasting friendship.

Finn took full advantage of the opportunity to learn the habits, customs and history of the Shoshoni tribe. Through the early years Finn worked hard with what he had, to help his Indian friends accommodate to often well-intended, but more frequently ill-conceived federal policies to promote acculturation. He lived among the tribe and identified with them. Some of his children intermarried and Finn became a dedicated advocate of Shoshoni tribal rights, sometimes in the face of federal mismanagement and outright corruption. At one point he was asked to resign, but he refused and despite the best efforts of his detractors was, after a hearing before his superiors, retained in his post.

In 1877, Finn ended his service with the government and took up cattle raising. He won a contract with the agency at Fort Washakie and drove five hundred head of cattle from Bozeman, Montana, to the reservation. This was the first cattle drive from Bozeman, over the Owl Creek Mountains, into the Wind River Valley. With proceeds from the sale of the cattle, Finn settled down to a life of ranching on Owl Creek. It was not long before Chief Washakie and ten of his chieftains came to ask Finn and his family to return to the Wind River, but he refused on the grounds that such a move might be misconstrued by the administration of the reservation and could create conflicts. Washakie then offered him land for a ranch wherever he wanted to settle. Finn chose the area near Crowheart Butte and he was deeded 750 acres in the shadow of that historic landmark for his ranching business. This was Washakie's way of showing his admiration and gratitude for Finn's service and efforts on behalf of the tribe.

Finn died in 1933 at the age of ninety. He left a legacy not just of early frontier adventure, but of compassion and forbearance during America's efforts to fashion an accommodation between the white and Indian cultures. Finn Burnett was a pioneer with a mission and his enlightened example helped improve white-Indian relations during that period.

PETER K. SIMPSON

GEORGE M. TEMPLETON

Of eighty infantry officers, including contract surgeons, only two men were stationed continuously on the Bozeman Trail during its two year military history: George M. Templeton and surgeon Samuel M. Horton (who served at Fort Phil Kearny). First Lieutenant Templeton arrived on the trail in July 1866, and reached Fort C. F. Smith on August 10, 1866, in time to approve the selection of the site for the post on August twelfth, and remained there until June 18, 1868. He left the Bozeman Trail in August, when the last contingent of the army closed Fort Reno.

Born in Cannonsburg, Pennsylvania, on November 3, 1841, George M. Templeton gave his occupation as "student" when he enlisted as a private on August 22, 1862, in the 149th Pennsylvania Volunteers. He was promoted to corporal in the autumn of 1862. March and April 1863 found him sick in the hospital, but he was well enough in July to be present at all of the battle of Gettysburg.

Templeton was discharged from the Volunteers on February 28, 1864, enabling him to accept a promotion to captain in the regular army. On March fourth, he began his new duties with the Thirty-second U.S. Regiment, Colored Troops. He served at Morris Island, Hilton Head, and Honey Hill, South Carolina. It was at Honey Hill on November 30, 1864, while serving as a field officer frequently exposed to attack, that he was severely wounded in the right thigh by gunshot. He recovered sufficiently to serve with Gen. E. E. Potter in the campaign from Georgetown to Camden, South Carolina, and was discharged on August 22, 1865.

Templeton returned to Cannonsburg and enrolled at Washington and Jefferson College, where he took advanced studies. The life of a student may have seemed dull after his war experience, for in December 1865, he applied for and later received an officer's appointment with the regular U.S. Army.

The officer who reported for duty at Fort Columbus on Governor's Island, New York, stood tall for his generation. Templeton was about six feet in height, and the two extant descriptions of him agree that he had black eyes, dark hair and a fair complexion. Ordered West on May 13, 1866, he reached Fort Leavenworth, Kansas, where he boarded at the Post Mess for one dollar a day. Learning of a baseball club in town, he played or umpired when duty or the spring rains allowed. On May twenty-second he heard that the *Army and Navy Journal* had carried an announcement of his promotion to first lieutenant, effective February twenty-third. He wrote in his diary, "Who says 'Republicans are ungrateful'?"[1]v

On June thirteenth, Templeton left Fort Leavenworth in command of a detachment of the Eighteenth U.S. Infantry. In commenting on the Indians seen in the vicinity of Scotts Bluff, he described them as dirty, wearing very "airy suits,"[2] but he found the Sioux at Horse Creek very well dressed and their chief, Standing Elk, dignified and aloof. He would later comment on the beauty of the children of the Crow Indians.

Templeton reached Fort Laramie on July tenth and on July thirteenth, leaving behind that famous post, he began the trip up the Bozeman Trail. About 2:00 a.m. on July fourteenth, Lt. Napoleon H. Daniels reached Bridger's Ferry, where Templeton, four other army officers, about nineteen enlisted men, three army wives, five children, a military chaplain, at least two civilians, nine wagons and two army ambulances had made camp. When, after a six day march,

---

[1]George M. Templeton, Diary, 22 May 1866, Everett Graff Collection, 4099, Newberry Library, Chicago, Illinois.

[2]Ibid., 7 July 1866.

this train reached Crazy Woman's Fork at noon on July twentieth, Templeton and Daniels rode ahead about one mile, searching for a suitable lunching spot. Daniels suddenly shouted, "Look there."[3] As the words were spoken, Templeton and Daniels were cut off by around fifty or sixty mounted Indians. Templeton saw that Daniels, now some two hundred yards ahead, had been shot in the back by an arrow and was falling from his horse. Not able to help, Templeton spurred his horse and headed for his train, where he commanded that the wagons be corralled. Later, when Daniels' corpse was found, it had been impaled by twenty-eight arrows, scalped, mutilated, and one finger chopped off. Daniels was the first officer killed on the Bozeman Trail.

On August tenth, Templeton reached Fort C. F. Smith and was soon deluged with paper work, serving as acting post adjutant, acting assistant quartermaster, and acting commissary of subsistence. Throughout the twenty-three months he was at Fort C. F. Smith, he was either in command of, or second in command of, Company D, Twenty-Seventh U.S. Infantry. Templeton had been keeping a diary for some time before his arrival in the West, and he continued this practice throughout his time on the Bozeman Trail. It is the sole extant source of continuity at any of the three posts.

What did he record? He wrote twenty-five times, often on a Sunday, "read in Bible" (he had a Greek Testament), and during periods when the Indians were not actively hostile, he recorded twelve hunting expeditions, extolling on several occasions the excitement of the buffalo hunt and rejoicing when he was lucky enough to make a kill. He also mentioned his sadness at the death, by poisoning, of his little dog and later, the killing of his cat by wolves.

Templeton noted morale was good in those early, cold months of 1868. In April, he was in command of a wagon

---

[3]Ibid., 20 July 1866.

train containing, among other items, potatoes and turnips purchased from farmers in Gallatin Valley, Montana Territory. These antiscorbutics reached Fort Phil Kearny on April fourth, after a four-day trip. Unhampered by wagons, Templeton and his men made the return trip to Fort C. F. Smith in the fastest time ever for that part of the trail, just two days. No one died of scurvy at Fort C. F. Smith because of the supplies Templeton was able to acquire.

Templeton, after the affair at Crazy Woman's Fork in 1866, recorded several brushes with Indians attempting to steal stock. He was one of the first to fire a newly issued army breech-loading gun at Indians on August 1, 1867, the day of the Hayfield Fight near Fort C. F. Smith. It was typical of Templeton that, on the day his company came to the aid of the post hunter (firing about one hundred rounds of ammunition), he did not mention that he himself was in charge of the relief; nor that, this same day, he rescued the family of the post commander, Andrew S. Burt (who, in his own official report of the incident, omitted any reference to his family; Mrs. Burt, in her autobiography, mentions her debt to Templeton).

The impression conveyed by his diary, as well as by several of his letters published in newspapers while he was at the post, is of an officer who was cool-headed, dispassionate, yet frequently kindly.

Upon leaving Fort C. F. Smith for the last time in June 1868, Templeton went to Fort Phil Kearny, which he reached on June twenty-second. He left that post on July thirtieth, reaching Fort Reno at noon on August first. He was that post's last commanding officer, leaving the fort upon its abandonment by the army on August 18, 1868. The next month, he was sent to the relief of Maj. George A. Forsythe and his column, attacked by Indians at Beecher's Island. Templeton arrived after the conflict had ceased. His last station was at Cheyenne where he was placed in command of the Ordnance Depot.

Templeton never alluded to his former war wounds causing problems, and only mentioned being "unwell for several days"[4] in January 1867. Several times he mentioned being tired on Sunday and glad of the time to rest and read. Nevertheless, he left Cheyenne with a certificate of disability in April 1870, and headed for his home in Cannonsburg, Pennsylvania. He never reached it. Arriving in Pittsburgh on April thirtieth, he was so weak that he was carried from the train to the carriage of his brother-in-law, George M. Reed, at whose home he died on May 4, 1870, aged twenty-eight. The cause of his death was attributed to diabetes.

FATHER BARRY HAGAN

---

[4]Ibid., 26 January 1867.

MITCH BOYER

The only known photograph of Mitch Boyer shows a square-faced, serious man of mature years. He wears a fur cap, decorated with small badges or ornaments, a single vertical feather, and the skins of two birds, one a jay. Feathers or skins dangle at the ears. He wears a neck scarf with a dotted pattern, and a leather vest over a white shirt, while over the left shoulder is thrown a fabric robe decorated with machine embroidery, fringe, and a linear design of buttons. His ornaments include a cloth or fur-wrapped braid or necklace, a two-strand hairpipe and bead necklace, and a circular medallion.[1] The photograph appears to have been taken in the early or mid-1870s, possibly in the vicinity of Bozeman or Fort Ellis, Montana Territory.

Mitch Boyer's name turns up with surprising frequency during the Plains Indian War period. Efforts have been made both to glorify him or depict him as the villain of the Custer massacre.[2] He was a man who lived in two worlds, valuing his American Indian heritage and experiencing its problems,

---

[1]While most citations of the Mitch Boyer photograph list the National Archives or Custer Battlefield/Little Bighorn National Monument, these views appear to be re-photographs of an original, due to the smaller view field and lack of detail. The clearest known large photograph is the one used in Thomas B. Marquis, *Memories of a White Crow Indian*, 1967 edition.

[2]While positive Boyer references are plentiful [i.e., Granville Stuart, *Pioneering in Montana* (reprint edition: University of Nebraska Press, 1977) p. 62n], the best example of a truly negative text is Everett E. McVey's 1952 pamphlet, "The Crow Scout Who Killed Custer," housed at Brigham Young University, Provo, Utah. Few of McVey's assertions are supported by facts.

and at the same time was respected for his accomplishments on the Euroamerican Plains frontier. This truth is expressed in his Indian name, "Two Bodies."

Boyer's father, John Baptiste Boyer, an engagé in the fur trade, took several wives among the Santee Sioux. Mitch was born in 1838 or 1839; two brothers, John and Antoine, are known. In the 1850s, the Boyer family settled in the vicinity of Deer Creek on the North Platte, finding employment in the Indian trade and the growing westward emigration. The majority of the trade was with the Sioux and Cheyennes. Although the Boyer family had Santee connections, there was apparently hostility with the western bands of Sioux, which affected Mitch Boyer throughout his life.

The traders along the Platte Road offered services including ferrying across the Platte River and providing guides. Many older fur trappers found employment in such enterprises. The Richard family operated ferries near the site of Fort Caspar, while the Jannisse and Bissonette families had a post at Deer Creek, near Fort Laramie.

In 1855, James Bridger guided the wealthy Irishman Sir George Gore on a hunting tour from the Platte to the Yellowstone. A young Mitch Boyer accompanied the party, which spent the fall along the Powder River, wintered near the mouth of the Tongue, and encountered a band of Crows along the Rosebud.[3] Boyer may have developed his deep appreciation for the Crow people at this time, but by 1859, he had returned to Deer Creek. That year, Margaret Wallace,

---

[3]Information on the Gore expedition comes from J. Cecil Alter's two books, *James Bridger, Trapper, Frontiersman, Scout and Guide: An Historical Narrative* (Salt Lake City, Utah: Shepherd Book Company, 1925) and *Jim Bridger* (Norman: University of Oklahoma Press, 1962); Mitch Boyer's involvement with the hunting party in 1855 was described in his obituary published in the *Helena Herald*, 15 July 1876, written by Lieutenant James H. Bradley, and summarized in John S. Gray, *Custer's Last Campaign: Mitch Boyer and the Little Bighorn Reconstructed* (Lincoln: University of Nebraska Press, 1991), pp. 11-22.

a half-Crow woman, married Fellows David Pease at Fort Union; she is remembered by her family as having been previously married to Mitch Boyer, and mother of a daughter by him.[4]

In the fall of 1859, the Raynolds' army survey and mapping expedition, guided by Bridger, wintered at Deer Creek after an exploration of the Powder River basin.[5] From October 19 to November 3, Boyer was engaged in guiding a detached party of topographers from Deer Creek to Pumpkin Buttes. On October twenty-seventh, they intersected the trail of a band of Oglalas, and Boyer "...could not conceal his joy at not meeting them."[6]

By 1862, when gold was discovered in southwestern Montana, a need was felt for northern routes to the Yellowstone and the gold mines at Bannack and Alder Gulch. In 1864, the Townsend train, using the route pioneered by John Bozeman, encountered hostile Indians just after crossing Powder River; although reminiscent accounts of the journey identify Mitch Boyer and John Richard, Jr. as guides, the actual guide was Raphael Gallegos, who was joined by Old

---

[4]Helen Pease Wolf, *Reaching Both Ways* (Laramie, Wyoming: Jelm Mountain Publications, 1989), ed. Barbara Ketcham. The author states that her grandmother, Margaret Wallace Pease, was a half Crow woman who was married to Mitch Boyer before her marriage to Fellows David Pease in 1859 in Fort Union.

[5]William Franklin Raynolds. "Report on the Exploration of the Yellowstone River," Senate Executive Document No. 77, 40th Cong., 1st (2nd) sess., 1878. This document contains the account of the 1859-1861 exploration of the Powder River area through to the vicinity of Three Forks.

[6]Snowdon, quoted in Raynolds, "Report on the Exploration of the Yellowstone River," p. 158.

John Boyer after the Indian attack.[7] The Richard family did, however, send a wagon to the Gallatin Valley that year, as in August, John Richard, Jr. was listed as one of the locators of the townsite of Bozeman, and his business affairs were of interest to the *Montana Post*.[8] The close association between John Richard, Jr. and Mitch Boyer is a source of information on Boyer's activities.

In 1864, Boyer was employed by the Richard interests at the Platte River crossing.[9] In 1865, Boyer is reported by several writers to have been involved in the development of the Big Horn ferry, near the site of Fort C. F. Smith. This crossing was the scene of several encounters with Sioux and Arapahos, and Boyer was seriously wounded in one engagement.[10] Boyer does not appear to have participated in either the Sawyers' Wagon Road Expedition, or in the military campaign in the Powder River area directed by General

---

[7]The reminiscent account is from E. O. Railsback, "The Townsend Trail," *Old Travois Trails,* Powder River Number, p. 84. The Townsend train encounter is discussed in John S. Gray, "Blazing the Bridger and Bozeman Trails," *Annals of Wyoming* 49 (No. 1):78. A secondary account, apparently derived from Railsback, is Burton S. Hill, "John Bozeman and the Bozeman Trail," *Annals of Wyoming* 36 (No. 2):205-34, which summarizes both the Townsend train and the Coffinbury train which followed a week later.

[8]E. Lina Houston, *Early History of Gallatin County* (Bozeman, Montana: Pioneers Society of Gallatin County, 1933), p. 17.

[9]Thomas B. Marquis, *Memoirs of a White Crow Indian: Thomas H. LeForge* (Lincoln: University of Nebraska Press, 1974).

[10]The usual source for material on the Bighorn ferry is E. S. Topping, *The Chronicles of the Yellowstone* (Minneapolis: Ross and Haines, 1968). The Palmer account (H. E. Palmer, "History of the Powder River Indian Expedition of 1865," Nebraska State Historical Society, 1887) contains inaccuracies for both 1865 and 1866, regarding the whereabouts of Boyer.

Patrick Connor in the summer of 1865.[11] The following year, one H. E. Palmer, a quartermaster from the Connor campaign, reportedly attempted to construct a trading structure at the confluence of French Creek and Clear Fork near present Buffalo, Wyoming; although Boyer and Louis Richard were said to be present, Cheyenne Indians forced Palmer to retreat to the Big Horn ferry.[12] There is reason to doubt this story, as other accounts place Boyer with the Richard family interests in Bozeman and at the Big Horn ferry during this time period.[13]

On July thirteenth, Colonel Henry B. Carrington's train reached the Clear Fork crossing; within the next few days, Fort Phil Kearny was established on the forks of the Piney, bringing permanent military presence to the Bozeman Trail. In August, construction began on Fort C. F. Smith, near the old ferry crossing. The northern fort was less subject to hostile Indian attacks, but suffered from lack of communication and shortages of supplies.[14] In February 1867, Boyer was hired at C. F. Smith to carry mail and supplies to Fort Phil Kearny. On February ninth, he escorted sergeants Grant and Graham; they were pursued by Indians, lost their horses and

---

[11]The account of the Sawyers Expedition is told in Leroy Hafen and Ann W. Hafen, *Powder River Campaigns and Sawyers Expedition of 1865* (Glendale, California: Arthur C. Clark Company, 1961).

[12]This incident is best described in Topping, *Chronicles of the Yellowstone*, p. 51.

[13]Gray, *Custer's Last Campaign*, pp. 32-33; discusses the chronology of Arapaho attacks on the trains approaching the Bighorn ferry, and identifies the Palmer account as a source of mistaken identity for placing Mitch Boyer with the Connor expedition the previous year.

[14]Margaret Irvin Carrington, *Absaraka, Home of the Crows* (Lincoln: University of Nebraska Press, 1983), p. 102n.

the mail, but arrived safely with the military dispatches.[15] According to Post Returns, Boyer returned to C. F. Smith on March thirteenth.

Lack of supplies plagued Fort C. F. Smith throughout the spring of 1867, but communication with the Gallatin Valley improved. Attracted by the potential for lucrative supply contracts, Tom Cover and John Bozeman ventured to the fort on the Bighorn. On April twenty-first, they spent the night at Nelson Story's cow camp at Benson's Landing, where several horses run off by Indians were reportedly recaptured by Mitch Boyer, apparently escorting a supply train.[16] The following day, Bozeman was killed by Blackfeet Indians and Cover was wounded.

Post Returns from Fort Phil Kearny indicated Boyer was employed there from April through July of 1868. His work apparently involved convoying trains between the Bozeman Trail forts and the newly established post near Bozeman, Fort Ellis. In August of 1868, the Bozeman Trail forts were abandoned by the army. Mitch Boyer apparently turned his attention to matters at Crow Agency, where he served as an assistant to the Indian agent at various times.

During this time, Thomas LeForge, who had previously met Boyer in 1864 at Platte Bridge, became reacquainted when he was adopted into the Crow tribe. LeForge's wife, Cherry, was close friends with Magpie Outside, or Mary, Boyer's wife. The Boyers had two children, a son and a daughter. The couples lived at Old Agency, near Mission

---

[15]Robert A. Murray, "The Long Walk of Sergeants Grant and Graham," in *The Army on the Powder River* (Fort Collins, Colorado: Old Army Press, 1972), p. 33n; summarizes this little known incident.

[16]This incident is reported by Granville Stuart in *Pioneering in Montana,* from a story told him by Cover after Bozeman's death. This is the only time Stuart mentions Mitch Boyer. Boyer is not mentioned by Bishop Tuttle, who recounts the same incident as told to him by Cover.

Creek, about thirty miles east of Bozeman.[17] In 1873, Boyer was involved in a scheme, apparently perpetrated by Nelson Story, to steal Crow annuity goods. Ultimately, what remained of the annuities was turned over to Mitch Boyer for the Crow tribe because of his reputation's integrity.[18]

In March, 1876, the army hired a number of Crow Indians as scouts, to assist with gathering intelligence about the Sioux. Boyer was hired as an interpreter and guide, joining Gibbon's column on April eighth. While the Montana column waited for General Terry's troops to meet them, Boyer was kept busy convoying supply trains between Gibbon's deployment and Fort Ellis. Terry arrived on the steamer Far West on June eighth, met with Gibbon, and secured Mitch Boyer's services as a guide, taking him downstream to his detachment in the vicinity of Glendive. LeForge, also employed with the Montana column, had suffered a broken bone, and remained behind.[19] Captain Reno, with Boyer and Charlie Reynolds as guides, reconnoitered the Powder River and Tongue River drainages, joining Gibbon at the Yellowstone on June eighteenth. Four days later, Custer's column marched up the Rosebud, crossing the divide to the little Bighorn on the morning of the twenty-fifth, to engage the combined Sioux and Cheyenne. Mitch Boyer, guide and interpreter for the Crow scouts, was assigned to Custer's troops. Once the village was sighted, the

---

[17]Marquis, *Memoirs of a White Crow Indian,* p. 28.

[18]The source of this information is a statement by Charles Hoffman, Appendix A, 9 December 1878, in "Brisbin's Report of Indian Frauds Made to General Sheridan," 21 December 1878. Typescript, Burlingame Collections, Montana State University, Bozeman, Montana.

[19]James H. Bradley, *The March of the Montana Column: A Prelude to the Custer Disaster* (Norman: University of Oklahoma Press, 1961), p. 7n. Bradley, an innovative and observant officer, was placed in command of the Crow scouts.

Crows were released from duty; Boyer, who could have gone with the Crow scouts, inexplicably remained with Custer.[20]

According to an agreement between Boyer and LeForge, LeForge, who shortly after his return was widowed, married Boyer's widow and adopted and raised his children. More than a century later on the Little Bighorn battlefield, bone fragments identifiable as those of a mixed-blood, mature male who had smoked a pipe, were found. A computer photo comparison clearly showed the match with Mitch Boyer's portrait.[21]

B. J. EARLE

---

[20]John S. Gray, *Centennial Campaign: The Sioux War of 1876* (Fort Collins, Colorado: Old Army Press, 1976), pp. 106-208. Reno's reconnaissance of the Powder River, Tongue, and lower Rosebud drainages produced valuable intelligence, but it was not correctly interpreted. Custer arrived after Reno had departed on his exploration and did not meet Boyer until the column started up the Rosebud. Several witnesses have reported on conversations between Boyer and Custer in the early morning of June twenty-fifth.

[21]Douglas Scott, Melissa Conner and Clyde Snow, *Nameless Faces of Custer Battlefield: Greasy Grass,* volume 4 (Custer Battlefield Historical and Museum Association, 1988); Lorna Thackery, "Experts Trace Facial Bones to Custer Interpreter," *Billings* (Montana) *Gazette,* 26 October 1986.

JOHN RICHARD, JR.

John Richard, Jr., was born about 1844, the son of John Richard, Sr., and Mary Gardiner, a Sioux woman.[1] He received some schooling at St. Charles, Missouri, when he was young, but lived most of his early life along the Platte River. In 1864, John Jr., moved to the Gallatin Valley in Montana Territory, and during his often extremely difficult supply expeditions along the Bozeman Trail during 1866-68, he was often accompanied by Baptiste "Big Bat" Pourier and Mitch Boyer.

John Richard, Jr., was described as being 5'8" or 5'10" tall, lean and "of good appearance." (In 1869, and perhaps earlier, he had a dark moustache.) It was Lt. George M. Templeton who noted Richard's first visit to Fort C. F. Smith on September 29, 1866, when Richard, Tom Cover, a business associate, and Jim Bridger arrived: Richard and Cover had three wagonloads of potatoes (6,540 pounds) which they sold at twenty-four cents a pound. Because he was among the few men outside the army frequenting the trail in 1867, Richard's comings and goings were often noted by Templeton.

At a time when the garrison was being threatened with the outbreak of scurvy, it was saved by the arrival on February 2, 1867, of John Richard, who arrived with a party of ten men and two wagons loaded with vegetables and butter. During their thirty day trip from Bozeman, begun on January first, they had had to leave two broken-down wagons at Clark's Fork. In the course of time Indians destroyed these.

---

[1]The name Richard was pronounced Ree-shard and was variously spelled Resha, Reshaw, Reichard, Rechard, Ruboud, Rechaud, etc.

At Richard's departure from Fort C. F. Smith on February ninth, Captain Kinney sent word through Richard to two dissident Sioux chiefs whom Richard thought he would see at Pryor's River. Richard also carried dispatches for the governor of the Montana Territory. He reached Virginia City about March fifteenth. The *Montana Post* of March thirtieth reported that Richard had been given permission to trade with the Indians, but was forbidden to sell alcohol and gun powder to them, and the newspaper was curious why two kegs of powder had been found among his goods. The same paper had earlier reported that when Richard had returned to the Gallatin Valley, he had no money; that the army had refused to pay for the potatoes it consumed, saying his prices were unreasonable. Yet, Richard wanted to get an order to supply flour to Fort C. F. Smith.

Richard arrived at the post on May sixth, coming in with three other men, to act as Tom Cover's agent for the sale of flour. They had made the trip in six days. Richard left on May seventh, saying he would return within sixteen days with eight wagons of flour. Somehow he and his companions made it to Bozeman City within three days, arriving there on May tenth. He and his supply train then left Bozeman on May twenty-second.

When Richard reached Fort C. F. Smith on June fourteenth with ten wagons of provisions, he was accompanied by the Montana Militia. The post commander forbade the militia's crossing the river to the post. Richard had been on the road for forty-one days, usually riding well in front of the train for frequent talks with the Sioux. The slow progress was largely due to late snow, high rivers and extremely muddy roads. When the supplies were eventually ferried across the Big Horn River on June sixteenth, Templeton, the acting commissary officer, purchased flour, beans, salt, pepper, and perhaps 150 bushels of potatoes. Richard left for Fort Phil Kearny on June seventeenth at 6:00 p.m. with two Indians, planning to arrive there the next day. (No details exist about this trip, neither the date of his arrival at Phil Kearny nor the date of his departure.)

Richard returned to Fort C. F. Smith on July third, according to Templeton, who added that Richard had been employed by the army to stay in the Crow camp and watch the movements of the Sioux among the Crows. On July sixth, Richard left for the Crow camp. On July eleventh, he returned, reporting that he had felt his life was in danger from the Sioux. Then on July fifteenth, after a consultation with the Crows, Richard passed on the information that the forts on the Bozeman would soon be attacked by the Sioux. This story was confirmed on July seventeenth by two Crow chiefs, Iron Bull and White Mouth.

When Lt. Col. Luther P. Bradley arrived to take command at Fort C. F. Smith in late July, he found that on July twelfth a contract had been let to Richard for 350 tons of hay at seventeen dollars a ton. Bradley planned to increase the amount by an additional two hundred tons. Then on August first, the Sioux attacked the men working in the hayfields near Fort C. F. Smith.

Richard returned to C. F. Smith on August eighth; this time his supply train had been attacked by Indians near the Rosebud. The Indians had chased the six wagons for six miles, but they had finally escaped. The next day, Richard went to work in the hayfields near the post. On August twenty-fourth he rode out with four men looking for more hay, when they spotted buffalo; they killed four.

Templeton heard a rumor on September twenty-fourth that Richard had been killed. Richard, however, was very much alive, arriving at the fort on September twenty-ninth, riding well in advance of another supply train from the Gallatin Valley; he was seeking assistance for his train of ten wagons and twenty-two men who were mistakenly under siege from the Montana Militia. A company of infantry was dispatched to aid the train, returning without firing a shot; the supply train came in safely on October fourth.

Templeton recorded on October seventh that Richard had ridden into the mountains seeking timber.

The next mention of Richard concerns his interpreting at Fort Laramie in behalf of the Crows at the peace conference held in late 1867. An observer commented that Richard's translation skills were minimal. The garrison at Fort C. F. Smith next saw Richard on December thirteenth, when he came up from Fort Phil Kearny to get a string of wagons to bring back gifts for the Crows from the peace commissioners. He left again on December sixteenth, only to return on December seventeenth, as snow had made the trail impassable.

All mention of Richard's name disappears until the middle of June 1868, when he visited his father near Fort Laramie. It was here that he received a letter from Nelson Story who, with a few other merchants, had purchased the surplus materials at Fort C. F. Smith prior to the closing down of that post. There was more left than their wagons could hold, so they instructed Richard to get his wagons ready to pick up the "junk" they had to leave behind. Reaching the fort on July twenty-ninth just as the last soldiers marched out, Richard, with the twenty men who accompanied him, loaded their wagons. The following day a large party of Sioux came, throwing most of the supplies in the river and setting the fort on fire. It was only due to the intervention of Red Cloud that Richard and his party were not harmed, but allowed to proceed. After delivering the goods to Story, Richard returned to the area near Fort Laramie.

Whether Richard had a drinking problem while he was on the Bozeman Trail supplying Fort C. F. Smith is unknown, but from 1869 until his violent death, liquor and women dominated his life. For a while he was in a prosperous business near Fort Laramie, which may have included a hog ranch. In November of 1869, he was ordered from a brothel by an armed corporal; the unarmed Richard promised revenge. But first someone stole goods worth some ten thousand dollars from his ranch. Shortly afterwards, Richard shot down an unarmed corporal, Francis Conrad of Company E, Fourth U.S. Infantry, near Fort Fetterman. Richard then fled north to Crow country in the company of Emily Janis, former wife of old Jim Beckwourth. While there he took as wives two or three sisters or daughters of the Sioux chief Yellow Bear, for whom he paid according to Indian custom.

When Richard's uncle, Red Cloud, went to Washington, D.C, in 1870, he insisted that his nephew be an official member of the Sioux delegation. In the nation's capitol, Richard received either a pardon or its equivalent for the murder of Corporal Conrad, a murder for which he had not been officially accused or tried. In 1871, he married the half-breed, Emily Janis.

On May 15, 1872, partially urged on by Emily's brother, Peter, and partially under the influence of alcohol, Richard went to the lodge of Chief Yellow Bear, near Fort Laramie. After a two hour visit with the chief, in the presence of many of the chief's friends, Yellow Bear agreed to Richard's taking back as his wife the younger sister or daughter. Then Richard, suddenly, without provocation, shot Yellow Bear, and was in turn knifed and shot to death by the other Indians in the lodge.

FATHER BARRY HAGAN

GEORGE B. DANDY

Even though Fort Phil Kearny existed for two years, the eighteen months after Col. Henry B. Carrington left the post are often overlooked. The story of George B. Dandy's service at Phil Kearny provides insights into this period of the fort's existence, and one soldier's contributions to its history.

By the time George Brown Dandy arrived at Fort Phil Kearny on December 27, 1866, his military career had spanned almost twenty years. Born in Macon, Georgia, on February 11, 1830, Dandy entered the army in 1847. After the Mexican War, he attended West Point for three years, then rejoined the ranks as an enlisted man. During the 1850s, Dandy campaigned against Indians in Washington Territory, eventually being promoted to first lieutenant. Wounded in combat during the Civil War, he rose to the rank of brevet brigadier general before that conflict ended in 1865. Reverting to his regular army rank of captain, Dandy served as Assistant Quartermaster of the Division of the Mississippi during the winter of 1865-66, and Chief Quartermaster of the Division of the Platte from May to December, 1866, when he left Fort Laramie to assume the Post Quartermaster position at Fort Phil Kearny.

Dandy's first impressions of the situation at this new post were not favorable. In his *Annual Report to the Quartermaster General* (June 30, 1867), he wrote,

> I found the garrison shut up in the stockade in a demoralized condition from fear, and half frozen for want of proper fuel. The extreme severity of winter had been allowed to approach and little or no provision had been made for supplies.

After assuming his duties on January 1, 1867, Dandy wrote a report (to Gen. William Myers, January 4, 1867) assessing the condition the fort was in:

> These Buildings [the Commissary and Quartermaster warehouses] are mere shells constructed on inch slabs and boards have not capacity sufficient for one fourth of the stores that are or should be at the post and have been burgulariously entered and the stores stolen. Sentinels are placed over them, but this does not remedy the evil.

The contractor in charge of the sawmills was "a drunken worthless fellow and knows nothing of his business, and the mills are nearly ruined, through his ignorance and neglect." Other descriptions outlined the poor condition of the Quartermaster wagons, harness and draft animals.

While not placing direct blame for the condition of the fort on specific individuals, Dandy attributed many of the problems to the "inexperience and ignorance of their duties" on the part of the previous quartermasters, and the fact that, "there are no records and the business has been managed without system." Reflecting an observation made by Gen. William B. Hazen in the fall of 1866, Dandy wrote,

> The machinery, material and labor of the post seem to have been confined mainly to two objects viz - building the stockade and erecting the quarters of the Commanding Officer.

Since combat engagements with Indians decreased for the winter after the Fetterman Battle, most of the problems faced by the garrison were Dandy's responsibilities. As Post Quartermaster and Chief of Commissary, he was responsible for building construction and maintenance, obtaining and distributing supplies, and providing transportation for military personnel. The lack of supplies and extreme weather conditions proved to be continuing challenges during the next four months, especially after the garrison was increased greatly in late January, without a corresponding influx of supplies. However, Dandy did achieve a notable success in transportation.

In January of 1867, Colonel Carrington was ordered to Fort Caspar, and several women and children were to travel with the escort. It was the quartermaster's duty to provide transportation for military dependents, and Dandy turned his attention to this task. In her book *Absaraka*, Margaret Carrington wrote,

> General Dandy, with discernment and courtesy, fitted up army wagons for the women and children, and deserves due thanks for our earthly salvation, as that preparation alone secured us a safe deliverance during the trip that ensued.

Describing the same event many years later in *My Army Life*, Frances C. Carrington observed, "General George B. Dandy who had accompanied the troops as quartermaster was just the man for the hour...." While the wisdom of the trip itself was questionable, the results of Dandy's efforts favorably reflected on his abilities.

Unfortunately for the garrison, the problems at Phil Kearny were not so quickly solved. Dandy was appointed Chief Quartermaster and Chief of Commissary for the Mountain District, thus making him also responsible for Forts Reno and C. F. Smith. There was little to be done about C. F. Smith since the road north was closed by snow, but the situation at Fort Phil Kearny continued to worsen, especially the lack of forage and fuel. According to Dandy, "The animals were reduced to such extremity that they ate their harness and the tongues and bodies of the wagons." Since most of the wood near the fort had been used, parties on foot carried fuel from distances of up to six and a half miles. Frostbite and scurvy were rampant, the hospital full, and rations limited to bacon and hardtack. Dandy observed in his *Annual Report*, "I have heard of no parallel since my service in the army to the sufferings endured by the garrison of this post last winter."

The supply situation improved in the spring of 1867, although the increase in Indian attacks continued to hamper supply trains coming up the Bozeman Trail and the contract parties cutting hay and wood for the posts. The Mountain District forts now had a reputation for danger, and Dandy could not secure enough skilled civilian labor for his building projects and supply efforts. In his *Annual Report* he expressed frustration that

> but for the complications resulting from the hostile attitude of the Indians and their great numbers, the question of procuring supplies would be an easy solution in this district.

Even with the handicaps of distance and continuing hostilities, supplies did reach Fort Phil Kearny on a regular basis and Dandy was able to continue constructing new buildings and improving existing ones, while improving the supply stockpiles and the transportation situation. When Maj. E. B. Grimes arrived to inspect the Quartermaster Records at Fort Phil Kearny in November 1867, the situation had changed considerably. Grimes reported that large amounts of building materials had been manufactured (606,000 feet of lumber, 260,000 shingles, 130,000 bricks, 4,000 lath), the Quartermaster draft animals were in good shape, and the supplies were adequately stored and distributed properly. The inspection report (December 2, 1867) stated that

> General Dandy deserves credit for the energetic and practical manner in which he conducted matters during the past fiscal year. Evidences of thrift and economy mark his administration.

The post was much better prepared for winter than it had been the previous year.

Dandy's period of service at Fort Phil Kearny ended in December of 1867. His military career would continue for another twenty-seven years, with assignments at forts in Arizona, the Dakotas and the Northwest. Eventually he rose to the rank of lieutenant colonel and Deputy Quartermaster General, retiring in 1894. George Brown Dandy died in New York City on January 14, 1911.

SONNY REISCH

Lt. Col. Henry Walton Wessells

Henry Walton Wessells was born in February 1809 in Connecticut, and died in January of 1889, having spent his entire career in military service. He served as Commander at Fort Reno for only seven weeks before being reassigned to Fort Phil Kearny, where he served from January 18 through July 4, 1867.

Wessells was often described as quiet, delicate, and a gentleman. George Templeton, after meeting Wessells at Fort Leavenworth, said, "Col. Wessels is apparently a very quiet, unassuming man."[1] Captain Burt's wife, Elizabeth, refers to him as having courtly manners and says, "His white hair and delicately built frame made me feel he ought not be required to make that march...,"[2] referring to a trip from Fort Saunders to Fort Fetterman. Margaret Carrington describes him as "a soldier with laurels and a gentleman without blemish."[3]

Wessells graduated from West Point in 1833, twenty-ninth in a class of forty-three. He fought Seminole Indians in Florida and served admirably in the Mexican War as Brevet Major. He did Indian frontier service from 1849 to 1861 in California, Kansas and the Dakotas, finally making

---

[1]George Templeton, Diary, May 1866, Everett Graff Collection, Newberry Library, Chicago, Illinois..

[2]Elizabeth Burt, Diary, p. 130. Excerpts in Hagan Collection, Sheridan County Fulmer Public Library, Sheridan, Wyoming.

[3]Margaret Irvin Carrington, *Absaraka, Home of the Crows: Being the Experience of an Officer's Wife on the Plains* (Philadelphia: J. B. Lippincott, 1868), p. 226.

Major in June of 1861. By that time, he had spent twenty-eight years in commissioned service.

Wessells saw considerable action as a Brigadier General of Volunteers during the Civil War. Near the end of the war he received commissions to Brevet Colonel and Brevet Brigadier General. Mustering out of the Volunteers, he returned to the regular army as Lieutenant Colonel of the Eighteenth Infantry, making him Carrington's Executive Officer. However, with the regiment scattered, the positions were seldom together.

In the post-Civil War army, the scramble for officer slots and grades was based as much on political influence as it was on the professional qualifications of the appointee. For example, Carrington came from zero to Colonel in a few short years. Wessells, by contrast, was out of the Military Academy in 1833, fought in many engagements, came out of the Civil War as a Brevet Brigadier General, yet after thirty-three years of service retired as only a Lieutenant Colonel. Only Phillip St. George Cooke, Department Commander of the Class of 1827, had more years of service.

The next block of principal players in the saga of Plains warfare were Grant, Sherman, Augur and Palmer, all from the Class of 1840. While not an Academy graduate, Colonel John E. Smith, Wessell's successor at Fort Phil Kearny, was of this age group, a member of the inner circle, and was accepted for exceptional leadership as shown in the Volunteers.

Then there were the young "chargers," graduates of the Military Academy: Ben Smith (1849), Van Voast (1852), Dandy (1853) and Hazen (1855). They represented a lot of talent and ambition, out to make their mark in the world.

The critical part of the Fort Phil Kearny building was finished in November 1866 and General Cooke, Commander of the Department of the Platte, was pressing Carrington for a little winter action against the Indians. To this end, Wessells was sent up the trail from Fort Kearny, Nebraska Territory, with additional troops and temporarily stationed at Fort Reno on December 1, 1866. It was further planned for Wessells to take over the Mountain District on the coming reorganization and the departure of Carrington for Fort Caspar.

Carrington's "winter campaign" didn't last long. It started with the December 6th fight and ended with the Fetterman Fight on the 21st of the same month. Fetterman really upset things in many ways: all concerned were scrambling to avoid any blame; Cooke made the ongoing reorganization transfer of Carrington look like a relief from command instead; General Grant, bypassing the Missouri Division Commander, General Sherman, reassigned Cooke and brought in the younger General Augur; the national uproar brought on a reassessment of military operations in the West and in overall Indian policy.

Wessells was elevated from Commander of Fort Reno to Commander of the Mountain District and Fort Phil Kearny, in his brevet grade of Brigadier General. This was fitting for the position but he now outranked Carrington.

Immediately following the Fetterman disaster, Portugese Phillips was hired to take Carrington's report of the Fetterman disaster to the telegraph station at Horse Creek, near present day Glendo, Wyoming. This message was sent directly to Carrington's Department Commander, General Cooke in Omaha. So why is Fort Laramie so closely linked to this famous ride? During Phillip's rest stop at Fort Reno, Wessells gave him a message to deliver to the Fort Laramie Commander, Colonel I. N. Palmer. The text of this message doesn't show up in the letter files of either post, and is not available to us, probably for good reason. The next day, December 26, 1866, Palmer sent a telegram to General Cooke discussing the Fetterman fight, Wessell's message, and possibilities for sending reinforcements. He said that Van Voast, the suggested relief commander, would go unwillingly if obliged to be under "Col. C."

With the assignment of Bvt. Brigadier General Wessells to the Mountain District, Cooke was expecting an active winter campaign. This was not to happen. The additional reinforcements brought the total troop strength to about 650 plus civilians. The reinforcements brought no supplies and the unusually severe winter precluded getting anything up the trail.

Wessells was a good man to have in this situation. He came with about all the background and experience that the Army had to offer. With him came some very good officers: Dandy, Van Voast and others. In reading through the orders and letter files of the period, it is noted that Wessells had four main areas of concern.

Most important was caring for the 650 men and all the stock under very difficult conditions...basic survival. Within a month the stock was starving and the men were eating flour and bacon left over from the Connor Expedition of 1865. Scurvy and cold weather injuries were serious problems countered by innovation and leadership.

Secondly, training and discipline were Wessells' area of greatest improvement. The order files show both officer and enlisted training programs, plus cold weather indoor training; the supply records show expenditure of ammunition for training. Garrison courts-martials supported discipline.

Thirdly, improvements were made to the post. Timber cutting operations were resumed, several barracks and a new quartermaster building were completed, and a new hospital was framed in. Because of Carrington's extensive building efforts, subsequent commanders were able to devote most of their energies to operations and training.

Finally, the Indians were inactive during the bad weather and trained troops and good leadership greatly limited their effect as the encounters resumed in the spring. Letters to the Department Commander and others indicate that Wessells had some concerns about keeping the Crows friendly and out of the fight. This may have had some influence on the assignment of Captain Andy Burt to Fort C. F. Smith later that year. Burt was noted for his ability to get along with the Indians and did become a favorite of the Crows during his assignment there.

General Sherman, commanding the Division of the Missouri, had planned a spring campaign, but weather and poor supply delayed it until summer. Besides, the Army had its hands full down along the railroad and in Kansas. In the meantime, Sherman was getting his Mountain District team in place.

Wessells was certainly beyond his prime for active field campaigning and though effective and efficient, he simply wasn't the dynamic figure required for such ventures. Colonel John E. Smith was just the fireball for this job, and he and his assistant, Major Benjamin F. Smith, rode into Fort Phil Kearny in early July of 1867. But before any action could be taken, a new Peace Commission was appointed with General Sherman as a member.

Colonel Wessells went back to doing what he did best. When this episode started he was at Fort Kearny on the Platte, tearing down old buildings and training troops. Later, from Fort Phil Kearny, he was sent to Fort McPherson to take over the Eighteenth while Carrington was on six months leave. But by September he was on the road again, this time to build and organize Fort Fetterman. In one year he had commanded five forts!

Henry Wessells went unassigned on March 15, 1869, and retired with thirty-seven years service on January 1, 1871. He died back near his old Connecticut home in January 1889 at age seventy-nine.

ALAN W. BOURNE

Col. Johnathan Eugene Smith

Ask any gathering of western history buffs if they have heard of Col. Johnathon or John E. Smith, and ninety-nine percent of them will give you a very blank look.

Colonel Henry B. Carrington commanded Fort Phil Kearny only three months and the Mountain District for only six months. Lieutenant Colonel (Brev. Brigadier General) Henry W. Wessells commanded there for a bit over five months. But Smith commanded the post and was senior officer in the region for fully thirteen months.

Smith entered the Army with a direct commission as a colonel in early summer of 1861, direct from civilian life (from Illinois). Smith quickly became a top combat leader of troops in the field. He served through the war as Colonel of the Forty-fifth Illinois Volunteer Infantry, receiving one brevet for gallant and meritorious service and for gallantry in action, another for his part in the assault on Vicksburg, Mississippi, and another for his role in the taking of Savannah, Georgia.

Smith was designated Colonel of the newly authorized Twenty-seventh U.S. Infantry of the Regular Army in the summer of 1866. He set about selecting a fine staff. The reorganization was made effective January 1, 1867, but Smith could not bring up his recruits or other men to build the new regiment around what had been the Second Battalion, Eighteenth Infantry until early summer of 1867. Then they came west on the Union Pacific to North Platte Station and set out up the old trails from there.

In addition to some first class officers, Col. Smith brought with him brand new Allen conversion 50-70-450

Springfield breechloading single shot rifles, enough for every man in his command, along with an initial issue of 250,000 rounds of ammunition.

Smith immediately began to build on the training instilled by Wessells in winter and spring, instituting new security measures and field procedures. His men won the Wagon Box Fight on August 2, 1867, and a handful of decreasing sized engagements in which the Indians learned Smith's men were better armed than earlier troops.

Smith disliked the Fort Phil Kearny location, but made do with it and improved the post considerably that year. When the time came for the (long-planned) withdrawal of forces, in keeping with the 1868 treaty, Smith moved on to other commands.

The Twenty-seventh was dissolved in the 1869 reorganization and reduction in force of the Army. Smith remained on full pay as an unassigned officer from March 15, 1869 to December 15, 1870, when he took command of the Fifteenth U.S. Infantry, but soon transferred to the Fourteenth Infantry, and led them on a march from the Texas settlements to Fort Concho.

He moved north again and swiftly settled an impending revolt of the Bannacks in Idaho. He moved on again to command Fort Laramie. In 1874, Oglala Sioux at Red Cloud Agency -- just newly relocated near present-day Crawford, Nebraska -- began to harass the agency staff, and Little Big Man chopped down the agency flagpole. This was going too far, and Smith marched off from Fort Laramie, with all the troops he could scrape up there or at nearby posts, on the "Sioux Expedition."

This massive show of force quieted the potential hostiles, and Smith methodically established Fort Robinson there and Camp Sheridan at Spotted Tail Agency for the Brules thirty miles to the northeast. His men kept the lid on the simmering agencies all through the great Indian war of 1876-77.

Smith remained as Colonel of the Fourteenth until his retirement at age sixty-two in May of 1881.

ROBERT A. MURRAY

CAPT. JAMES POWELL
HONOR TO WHOM HONOR IS DUE

On a hot August day in 1867, a small party of thirty-two men commanded by Capt. James Powell, a tough, disciplined old-Army soldier, held off repeated attacks by hundreds of inspired Sioux warriors for over three hours. Powell's small force -- twenty-six men and one officer of Company C, Twenty-Seventh Infantry and four civilians -- fought at a small wagon box corral five miles from Fort Phil Kearny. Company C was originally part of the Second Battalion, Eighteenth Infantry, garrisoned at the fort under Colonel Henry B. Carrington. Captain Powell was one of Carrington's most battle-experienced officers, seeing hard action throughout the Civil War.

Though his military career spanned almost twenty years, Powell might had been forgotten but for the steady, disciplined leadership under fire he displayed at the Wagon Box Fight on the morning of August second. The determination of the Indian warriors certainly would have inflicted total annihilation on a lesser officer.

James Powell was born May 12, 1831, at Ellicott's Mills, Maryland. Enlistment papers indicate he was 5'8" tall, with blue eyes, brown hair and fair complexion. Powell entered military service on February 11, 1848, three months prior to his seventeenth birthday. Enlisting in Maryland, he was a private assigned to Company H of the Eleventh U.S. Infantry. He was honorably discharged August 15, 1848, after a six-month enlistment. Little is known of his activities until he enlisted again on March 26, 1851, and was assigned to Troop I of the First U.S. Dragoons, later called Cavalry. He was honorably discharged after five years, as a private first class, on March 26, 1856.

Private First Class James Powell re-enlisted again on November 17, 1856, into Troop I of the newly formed First U.S. Cavalry Regiment and was promoted to corporal, sergeant and first sergeant of Cavalry. First Sergeant Powell was officially discharged from the First Cavalry on August 6, 1861, allowing him to accept a commission as a second lieutenant in the Eighteenth U.S. Infantry, effective May 14, 1861, just one month after the outbreak of the Civil War. Powell was promoted to first lieutenant on October 24, 1861, brevet captain on September 9, 1864, and brevet lieutenant colonel on August 2, 1867.[1]

After his commission with the Eighteenth Infantry, Lieutenant Powell was placed on detached service with the Fourth U.S. Cavalry in Missouri. The Fourth Cavalry was Powell's pre-war First Cavalry Regiment, redesignated the Fourth Cavalry by Congress on August 3, 1861. From August to October of 1861, while serving with the Fourth Cavalry, Lieutenant Powell participated in the battle of Wilson's Creek, Missouri, and in the Tennessee campaigns until July 1862. Between October 1861 and July 1862, newly promoted First Lieutenant Powell fought in the battles of Forts Henry and Donelson, Shiloh, and the siege at Corinth, Mississippi, which followed.

Lieutenant Powell left detached service with the Fourth Cavalry and joined the Eighteenth Infantry at Camp Thomas, Ohio, on July 15, 1862. While on leave from Camp Thomas on August 16, 1862, Powell married Annie M. Woodson at Pittsburgh, Pennsylvania (by Rev. David Jones). Powell returned to Camp Thomas and served with the regiment until March 1863, when he accompanied the Second Battalion of the Eighteenth Infantry into the field for action in Tennessee and Georgia. Lieutenant Powell remained with

---

[1]Brevet: a higher rank bestowing honor, generally for combat action, allowing use of the title and seniority.

his regiment until he was severely wounded at the Battle of Jonesboro, Georgia, on September 1, 1864.

From March 1863 until September 1, 1864, Lieutenant Powell saw some of the bloodiest actions of the War, including the battles at Hoover's Gap, Chickamauga, Chattanooga, Mission Ridge, Resaca, New Hope Church, Peach Tree Creek, Smyrna Church, Atlanta and Jonesboro. Powell received the brevet of captain on September 20, 1863, for "Gallant and Meritorious Conduct" in the Battle of Chickamauga, Georgia, and was breveted major on September 1, 1864, for "Gallant and Meritorious Service" during the Atlanta campaign and the battle of Jonesboro. Powell was promoted to captain on September ninth while recovering from the wounds received at Jonesboro, with two rifle balls remaining in his body.

In his report on Powell dated October 1, 1864, Surgeon Lew Slusser of the Sixty-ninth Ohio Volunteers stated,

> For several days after I regarded his condition as not only extremely critical, but his recovery doubtful...and however well Lt. Powell may feel in a state of quiescence, I would not think it proper for him to engage in field service, until sufficient time has elapsed to determine the question as to what he was able to endure.[2]

Powell would carry the two balls in his body the rest of his life. He remained in the hospital until January 5, 1865, when he was placed on mustering duty at St. Louis, Missouri, and on January twenty-sixth, assigned to Army Recruiting Service until October 1866. Powell was then returned to active field service and sent west to rejoin the Eighteenth Infantry Regiment, Second Battalion, at Fort Phil

---

[2]Lew Slusser, Medical Report, 1 October 1864, Atlanta, Georgia, Army Hospital, Record Group 94, National Archives, Washington, D.C.

Kearny, Dakota Territory, for service in the Mountain District under Col. Henry B. Carrington.

Powell arrived at Fort Phil Kearny on November 3, 1866, from Fort Laramie with Capt. William J. Fetterman, Lt. Horatio S. Bingham and Company C of the Second Cavalry. Powell was assigned command of Company C of the Second Battalion, now the twenty-seventh Infantry. He, like all the men at Fort Phil Kearny, would see hard service, death and frequent skirmishes with hostile Indians during the fort's existence. The near disaster of December 6, 1866, and the total annihilation which attended Captain Fetterman's command on December twenty-first, was carefully avoided by Captain Powell on December nineteenth when he commanded a relief force and returned to the fort without being decoyed into ambush.

The loss of Fetterman and his entire command in a fatal decoy action by the Indians resulted in the immediate removal of Colonel Carrington as District Commander and formation of a Special Commission to investigate the cause of the tragedy. Judge Fitch Kinney, one of the six commissioners, met with various officers at Fort Phil Kearny in July of 1867 to take relevant testimony. For reasons unknown, Captain Powell gave testimony regarding his actions at the fort and statements critical of those of Colonel Carrington which are totally inconsistent with the record and information supplied by the other officers. This testimony, given by Powell on July 24, 1867, just nine days before his command at the Wagon Box Fight, may represent signs of an emotional or mental disorder resulting from his earlier and persistent physical wounds.

Powell's testimony, critical of Carrington, was forwarded to General Grant by Commissioner Kinney outside of military channels but with the endorsement of Gen. St. George Cooke. This resulted in Grant considering Carrington for court-martial. Carrington met later with generals Grant and

Sherman, raising the question of pressing charges against Powell. Sherman advised against it; "'...time alone,' he said, 'could heal the wounds left by the massacre.'"[3] Long after both men were retired, Carrington visited Powell, finding him in poor health. When Carrington brought up the testimony to Judge Kinney, Powell said, "It is all so long ago that I do not recall anything about his [Kinney's] visit except that it was something about his sutler's account...." Carrington noted that

> Powell's manner was kindly and showed so plainly that he had forgotten all else with regard to his affidavit, that I parted with him with the conviction that his testimony furnished Judge Kinney was under a mental condition thoroughly unsound, and for which with his temperament, he was hardly responsible.[4]

Carrington's observation of Powell during this visit is confirmed by an army physician who later examined Powell at his home and declared him mentally incompetent and confined him to his home for the last fifteen years of his life.

Captain Powell was breveted Lieutenant Colonel for "Gallant Conduct in the fight with Indians near Fort Phil Kearny" on August 2, 1867, in the battle known to us as the Wagon Box Fight. In his report, Powell stated,

> I was surrounded by about eight hundred mounted Indians, but owing to the very effective fire of my small party, they were driven back with considerable loss....That

---

[3]Michael Straight, "The Strange Testimony of Major Powell," *The Westerners, New York Posse Brand Book* 7 (1960):8.

[4]Henry B. Carrington, Memorandum and notes presented to the Sheridan (Wyoming) Chamber of Commerce, 1908, at the dedication of the monument on Massacre Hill, Sheridan County Fulmer Public Library, Sheridan, Wyoming.

> we escaped with such a comparatively small loss...is due in a very great measure to the gallantry and coolness displayed by the men of my command together with their excellent marksmanship.[5]

This last brevet for his actions in the Wagon Box Fight, just five months before his retirement, was a reward for courage and endurance. On that August day, Powell was still suffering from painful wounds received in battle in September of 1864. On October 22, 1867, less than three months after the Wagon Box Fight, Powell was examined by Post Surgeon S. M. Horton at Fort Phil Kearny. Horton's medical certificate found Captain Powell "undergoing much suffering and inconvenience from gunshot wounds...both balls remaining in the body," further stating, "he is physically broken down and totally unfit for active service."

On November 29, 1867, Powell's medical certificate and request for orders to appear before the Retiring Board were forwarded to Washington and approved by General Grant on December 5, 1867. Captain Powell reported to the Retiring Board in New York City on December 18, 1867, and was found to be "incapacitated for active service as the result of gunshot wounds received in the line of duty."

Powell was thirty-six years old, had served twenty years in the army, and was retired on January 8, 1868, as a result of wounds received in the Civil War. James Powell, Lieutenant Colonel, United States Army, died at Peoria, Illinois, on April 16, 1903. Annie Powell, his wife of forty years, never remarried and received government pension checks of twenty dollars per month until her death on January 3, 1916.

Of all the officers at Fort Phil Kearny during that early and difficult time when the fort was under almost constant

---

[5]James Powell, Battle Report, 4 August 1867, Fort Phil Kearny, Letters Received, A.G.O., Record Group 94, National Archives, Washington, D.C.

siege, Captain James Powell may have possessed the most battle-disciplined experience, judgement and respect for Indian fighting prowess of the entire office corps.

H. STERLING FENN

Samuel L. Gibson

Born in Nottingham, England, about 1849, Sam Gibson emigrated to the U.S. with his family in 1865. He was an apprentice shoemaker by trade but chose a military career, enlisting in the army at Cleveland, Ohio, in April 1866.

Assigned to the Eighteenth U.S. Infantry, Gibson later served in the Twenty-Seventh Infantry and was stationed at Fort Phil Kearny, Dakota Territory, from the time the post was founded in 1866 until its abandonment in 1868. He later served at a number of posts, including Camp Proctor on the Yellowstone and the arsenal at Augusta, Georgia.

Five feet seven inches tall, with blue eyes, Sam Gibson was known to his comrades as "Whitey" because of his blond hair. As a member of Capt. James Powell's Company C, Twenty-Seventh Infantry, Gibson participated in the famous Wagon Box Fight on August 2, 1867, an event that was to eclipse all others in his life.

On the day of the Wagon Box Fight, eighteen-year-old Private Gibson was appointed lance corporal and placed in charge of a three-man picket post some four hundred yards south of the wagon box corral. The assignment proved to be one of those chances of fate that place individuals in situations where their mark on the fabric of history is indelibly etched.

When the Indians first appeared, Gibson, using a breastwork of rocks, took aim with his new Springfield-Allen breechloader and fired at one of the lead warriors. He later claimed that the bullet glanced off a rock and struck the Indian's pony, dislodging its rider. Whether it actually did or not is pure conjecture. More meaningful, young Sam Gibson may well have had the honor of firing the first shot of the Wagon Box Fight for the defenders.

Once the Indians struck, events moved swiftly. Gibson and his two comrades, privates Nolan Deming and John Garrett, suddenly found themselves in a race for their lives to reach the safety of the wagon box corral before the Indians cut them off. Gibson remembered that Indians "seemed to rise out of the ground like a flock of birds....We kept on running and shooting, expecting every minute to feel a bullet or an arrow in our backs."[1]

But make it safely to the corral they did, albeit breathless and frightened, aided in their race for safety by the cool marksmanship of another young immigrant soldier, Max Littman, who darted outside the corral, knelt down, and began delivering an effective covering fire.

During the course of the next several hours, the Indians launched several attacks against the corral. Some of the attackers were mounted and some were on foot; nevertheless, they were repulsed each time. Through it all, young Whitey Gibson conducted himself like a veteran. On one occasion, he and another soldier dashed out of the corral to cut down one of the officers' tents that was obscuring the defenders' field of vision. Later, in the brassy heat of the sweltering August day, Gibson and his comrade, Johnny Grady, ventured forth from the corral again, this time to retrieve some cooking kettles filled with precious water.

When a relief column from Fort Phil Kearny arrived several hours later, the defensive perimeter of the wagon box corral remained intact. The defenders had successfully turned back a determined Indian effort to overrun their position. When help finally arrived, Sam Gibson remembered,

---

[1]Grace Raymond Hebard and E. A. Brininstool, *The Bozeman Trail: Historical Accounts of the Blazing of the Overland Routes into the Northwest, and the Fights with Red Cloud's Warriors*, 2 vols. (Cleveland: Arthur H. Clark Co., 1922), 2:48-49.

> We all jumped to our feet and yelled. We threw our caps in the air. We hugged each other in the ecstasy of our joy. We laughed, cried and fairly sobbed like little children in the delirium of our delight. The awful strain was over.[2]

Sam Gibson retired from the army as a sergeant in 1904 after thirty-eight years of active service, including time in the Philippines. During his retirement years he was an active and enthusiastic veteran, always ready to discuss the frontier army and especially his days at Fort Phil Kearny. In 1908, he returned to Sheridan along with General and Mrs. Carrington and several others, to dedicate the new Fetterman memorial. Several years later he returned once more, this time to assist in locating the site of the wagon box corral. At the conclusion of his military career, Gibson returned to Bellevue, Nebraska, where he died about 1927.

JERRY KEENAN

---

[2]Ibid., p. 68.

Lt. John C. Jenness
A Gallant & Promising Young Officer

No more than a skirmish in military terms, the famed Wagon Box Fight of August 2, 1867, is legend in the annals of the American West. Only three of the thirty-two defenders of the Wagon Box corral died in that fight; one of whom was First Lieutenant John Claud Jenness. Being the only commissioned officer to die in the fight, he earned a permanent footnote in history, yet we know little of John Jenness the man.

When the guns sounded at Fort Sumter, John, like thousands of other young men, stepped forward to defend the Union. On November 25, 1862, at age nineteen, he donned the army blue as a private in Company A, Seventeenth New Hampshire Volunteer Infantry. After serving as Quartermaster Sergeant and later as a clerk in the Office of the Military Commander for the State of New Hampshire at Concord, Jenness was eventually commissioned as a first lieutenant in the First New Hampshire Heavy Artillery.[1] Soon afterwards his regiment was posted along a portion of the defenses surrounding Washington, D.C. For the remainder of the war, Jenness served in the dual capacity of regimental and brigade adjutant until his muster out on June 15, 1865.

When the regular army was expanded to embrace forty-five regiments of infantry a year later, he seized the opportunity to return to the service. Jenness immediately applied for a commission, while at the same time mustering an impressive array of political influence. His efforts paid off with an

---

[1] *Revised Register*, First Regiment New Hampshire Heavy Artillery, p. 941.

appointment as second lieutenant in the newly-organized Twenty-seventh U.S. Infantry, which was to be activated on January 1, 1867.

This unit happened to be stationed at Fort Phil Kearny, unquestionably the hottest arena of Indian activity west of the Mississippi. After a long and uneventful overland journey, Jenness arrived at the fort on February 16, 1867, whereupon he was informed that there was no permanent vacancy for him. Until some of the new unit's administrative details could be sorted out, Jenness was detailed as a "general assistant" to Captain Tenodor Ten Eyck, commanding H Company.[2]

In July, Jenness received word that he had been promoted to the rank of first lieutenant and was to join Capt. James Powell's Company C. He could hardly have drawn a better superior, for Powell was an experienced and twice-wounded veteran of the Civil War. His company's first assignment was to serve as guard for the woodcutters at the pinery about five miles west of the fort. Armed with new .50-caliber breech-loading Springfield rifles, Powell, Jenness and the fifty-one men of the company marched out of the fort for the short trek to the wagon box corral up Little Piney Creek.

Just two days later, on the morning of August 2, 1867, a large number of Sioux assembled on the hills and plains around their exposed position. While the tiny garrison quietly prepared for what everyone felt would be certain death, Lieutenant Jenness stood outside the corral among a

---

[2]Ten Eyck Diary 1866-67, Fort Phil Kearny Collection, Wyoming Room, Sheridan County Fulmer Public Library, Sheridan, Wyoming (hereafter cited as Ten Eyck Diary); Post Returns, Fort Philip Kearny, D.T., March 1867; Ten Eyck Diary; Jenness was promoted when 1st Lt. Alpheus H. Bowman was detailed as the regimental adjutant. Letter, Secretary of War U. S. Grant (interim) to 1st Lt. John C. Jenness, 27th U.S. Infantry, 7 October 1867; Heitman, *Historical Register*, p. 234.

small group of soldiers. Minutes later the Sioux launched a furious attack against the corral.

Following this first assault, there was a lull as the Indians regrouped out of range of the soldiers' rifles. The soldiers inside the corral breathed a little easier, not only surprised that they were still alive, but they had not suffered a single casualty. Jenness, standing behind a wagon bed at the west end of the corral, watched intently as a group of warriors assembled for a new thrust. Suddenly, these warriors loosed a fusillade on the corral at a range of about seventy-five yards and charged. The soldiers returned a galling fire at the mass of warriors running headlong toward the corral. Bracing for the onslaught, Jenness calmly told his men, "Boys there are a good many Indians coming, but there may not be very much danger."[3] Just then another volley of Indian bullets ripped through the corral, one of them striking the lieutenant squarely in the head.[4] After the assault was repulsed, a

---

[3]Max Littmann to W. M. Camp, 8 March 1916, Walter M. Camp Collection, Little Bighorn Battlefield National Monument, Crow Agency, Montana. In a 1920 letter to Grace Raymond Hebard, Littmann stated that Jenness was in mid-sentence when killed. Although this may be as valid as the quotation used, the author prefers to use the earlier account. Hebard and Brininstool, *Bozeman Trail*, 2:78. Former private Frederick Claus also stated that Jenness had just boasted that he did not need to take cover because "he knew how to fight redskins as well as anyone." This statement is discounted, however, because Claus was positioned at the opposite end of the corral and therefore was not close enough to have heard such a statement. Moreover, Gibson casts considerable doubt as to Claus's veracity and accuses him of cowardice during the fight. Gibson to Pitman, 19 September 1924, Gibson-Pitman Letters, Little Bighorn Battlefield National Monument.

[4]While all those who witnessed Jenness's death agree that he was shot through the head, some remembered that he also received a simultaneous wound in the chest. Gibson, for instance, recalled that Jenness was shot through the temples, but also told Grace Raymond Hebard that he was "shot through the head and heart." Littmann states that Jenness was shot in the left breast. Letter, Gibson to Pitman, 19 February 1924, Gibson-

soldier, perhaps William Black, shouted to Captain Powell that Jenness was hit. The captain ordered the body to be covered.[5]

Sergeant Max Littmann, giving a slightly different version, said that just after Jenness fell, a mule tied at the end of the same wagon bed was shot down. Littmann attempted to drag the mule's carcass closer to the dead officer in order to protect his body from further incoming fire. He gave up, however, because the mule was too heavy for one man to move. Gibson recalled that during the next lull in the firing he saw Cpl. Francis Robertson crawl across the interior of the corral and place a wagon sheet over Jenness's body.[6] Although Jenness was beyond any aid, these acts nevertheless reflected the soldierly respect the men held for their dead officer.

At about 12:30 p.m., after some three and a half hours of fighting, a relief column from the fort arrived on the scene. The appearance of these reinforcements, and a shot from a mountain howitzer fired in their direction, caused the Lakota to break off the engagement.

Two days later John Jenness was laid to rest with military honors in the post cemetery. It would be another twenty years before the army would reclaim its dead from the nearly forgotten post on the Little Piney. In October 1888, a company of the Seventh Infantry came to the site to collect the remains from the long-neglected cemetery for reinter-

---

Pitman Letters, Little Bighorn Battlefield National Monument; Littman in Hebard and Brininstool, *Bozeman Trail,* 2:78, states "a bullet struck him in the head," while Claus (Hebard and Brininstool, *Bozeman Trail,* 2:84) says Jenness caught "a bullet through the brain."

[5]Littmann to Camp, 8 March 1916, Walter Camp Collection, Little Bighorn Battlefield National Monument. Littmann was wrong about Black being a corporal; he was a private.

[6]Hebard and Brininstool, *Bozeman Trail,* 2:62.

ment at the new National Cemetery at the Little Bighorn Battlefield.

In his official report of the Wagon Box Fight, Captain Powell paid high tribute to the young lieutenant when he wrote,

> In the death of Lieutenant Jenness the service has lost a gallant and promising young officer -- one who had endeared himself to his comrades and who on the morning of his death fell while setting a noble example of coolness and daring to those who were serving with him.[7]

DOUGLAS C. MCCHRISTIAN

The author wishes to express his appreciation to Earl N. Dunn, descendant of Lieutenant Jenness, who so graciously shared his large collection of reference materials with the author. Thanks also to Sonny Reisch, Site Superintendent at Fort Phil Kearny State Historic Site, for the loan of microfilm.

---

[7]Letter, Capt. James Powell to 1st Lt. A. H. Bowman, Post Adjutant, Fort Philip Kearny, D. T., 4 August 1867. Fort Phil Kearny Collection, Wagon Box Fight File, Wyoming Room, Sheridan County Fulmer Public Library.

MAX LITTMAN

Like his comrade-in-arms Sam Gibson, five foot, four inch, blue-eyed Max Littman[1] was yet another of the many immigrant soldiers who served in the U.S. Army during the last half of the nineteenth century.

Born in Berlin in what was then the state of Prussia about 1845, Littman learned the cigar-maker's trade. As a young man, he emigrated to the U. S. and enlisted in the army in March 1866. Assigned to the Eighteenth Infantry, Littman accompanied the regiment on its cross-country march to a new station in Dakota Territory during the summer of 1866.

One of thirty-two who later participated in the defense of the Wagon Box corral in August 1867, participation in that event would also prove to be the highlight of Max Littman's military career, just as it was for Sam Gibson.

Although unable to speak English, Littman -- being eager to do well in his adopted country -- learned quickly and became a good soldier, memorizing the English words he needed to know. As a tribute to his hard work and perseverance, he was promoted to sergeant within seven months after enlisting.

When the Wagon Box Fight began, young Max Littman demonstrated his coolness and courage under fire when, on his own, he left the security of the wagon box corral to provide covering fire for Sam Gibson and his comrades in their flight from the picket post to the corral.

On that memorable day, "I kept my gun pretty well heated up," Littman said, recalling that,

---

[1]Although the name is spelled with one "n" on the enlistment papers, the current spelling of the name is Littmann.

> When we saw the hundreds upon hundreds of savage warriors pressing forward against our little improvised fort, not a man in the entire command expected to come out of that fight alive.[2]

Littman particularly remembered that there was one large Indian who seemed to have selected Littman as his special target. The Indian, armed only with bow and arrow, would approach the corral and leap high into the air, releasing his arrow at the apex of his leap. It took several shots, but Littman eventually won the duel.

The perspective of time did nothing but increase Littman's appreciation of the significance of the Wagon Box Fight. "The more one goes into the details of the fight," he later recalled, "the more deeply is one impressed that it was the greatest Indian battle of the world."[3]

When his enlistment expired in 1869, Littman settled in St. Louis where he became an eminently successful businessman, eventually becoming president of the Nixdorff-Krein Manufacturing Company and a founder of Temple Israel. He was also instrumental in the development of the Mt. Sinai Cemetery in St. Louis.[4]

After learning of the plans to dedicate a Fetterman memorial, Littman contacted both Carrington and Gibson and experienced an awakening of old memories. In 1912 and again in 1916, he returned to the Fort Phil Kearny area to revisit the scene of his army experiences, and to help locate the correct site of the wagon box corral.

---

[2]Grace Raymond Hebard and E. A. Brininstool, *The Bozeman Trail: Historical Accounts of the Blazing of the Overland Routes into the Northwest, and the Fights with Red Cloud's Warriors*, 2 vols (Cleveland: Arthur H. Clark Co., 1922), 2:75-77.

[3]Ibid., p. 80.

[4]Lewis Littmann to Norton Stern, 30 May 1972.

Max Littman died in August 1921, while vacationing in Europe.

JERRY KEENAN

Dennis Driscoll

Dennis Driscoll was born May 30, 1846, in Liverpool, England, of Catholic Irish parents. He was recruited into the Queen's army sometime between 1862 and 1864, and served in a regiment of the foot guards whose duty it was to patrol the Queen's property in London. Because of the persecution of the Irish, Dennis deserted and most likely stowed away on a ship bound for America, working his way across the Atlantic as a seaman.

On arriving in New York, he found that he could become an American citizen by joining the United States Army and he enlisted on July 24, 1866. He was assigned to the Eighteenth Infantry Regiment. He gave his age as twenty-one, his place of birth as Liverpool, and his occupation as basketmaker. He was assigned to Fort Phil Kearny and was one of the detachment sent to support Fetterman's command on December twenty-first.

Later, under the command of Captain Thompson, Driscoll was sent to Fort C. F. Smith with supplies; they were joined by Company A for the return trip on June 2, 1867. The two companies camped at Trout Creek. Here they were surrounded by a large party of Sioux. As supplies and ammunition were running low, it was apparent that they would be annihilated.

Realizing that to attempt to get through the Indians would likely be suicide, Captain Thompson was hesitant to order anyone to go for help, and he called for a volunteer to carry a dispatch to Fort C. F. Smith, forty miles away. On Captain Thompson's third call, Dennis stepped forward and volunteered. When the captain asked him if he was sure he could make it and not turn back he replied that he'd make the trip or die on the way. Jack Reshaw rushed forward and gave him his field glasses and a brace of Colt revolvers. They also gave him two hundred rounds of their dwindling ammunition, and he had a Springfield rifle.

The Indians had stampeded the stock and the only mount left was a mule blind in one eye. It fortunately began to rain and thunder that night. Dennis buttoned his shirt over the dispatches and took to the hills as he knew to follow the trail would be folly. By sticking to the rough ground, he managed to travel all night without being seen. He was able to progress by occasional star sightings; his time at sea stood him in good stead.

According to the stories Driscoll told his children and grandchildren, when morning came he made his way to a high spot. Sweeping the plain with Reshaw's glasses, he saw a herd of buffalo but no Indians. He thought he might rest then but looked again at the animals and discovered that they were an Indian party with buffalo hides thrown over themselves and their mounts, and were coming for him.

An Indian bullet went through his right foot and killed his mule. The bullet severed an artery but he stopped the holes with chewing tobacco. He knew it would be impossible to outrun them without a mount, so he lay down among the rocks. He later told his family,

> If I should live to be a hundred years old I shall never forget the sensations of that moment as one by one those Indians approached my hiding spot and began to circle around me as was their custom.[1]

---

[1]I have prepared this sketch of Dennis Driscoll's life based on *Montana High, Wide and Handsome* by Eric Thane; "Dare Devils of Destiny" in the
Great Falls Tribune; My Army Life by Frances Carrington; National Archives Records; articles in the *Glacier County Chief, Montana Standard, Anaconda Standard* newspapers; and accounts told to me by my father, Earl Keyes and my uncle, James Keyes, as they heard it from Dennis Driscoll, their maternal grandfather.

According to Driscoll's account, he used the body of the dead mule to protect himself and to steady his aim. The rocks protected him from the rear and the mule from the front. The Indians must have decided not to risk any more braves for they decided to try to burn him out. Because of the heavy rain of the night before, there soon was a very dense smoke. He wriggled away from the rocks and into the middle of the smoke.

When he got through the smoke it was night and he was at the edge of a stream. Knowing that it was now thirty-six hours since he left his companions, Dennis walked in the icy water most of the night. He almost stumbled into an Indian camp. He lay behind some rocks and began to shoot. He told his grandchildren,

> I began to lose all sense of fear and wanted to kill every Indian I could; every shot seemed to tell and they could not know they were fighting only one soldier.

He then started out to reach Backbone Mountain from which he knew he should be able to see the fort. However, it was after retreat and the flag was down so he could not locate the fort. Dennis knew that he was near C. F. Smith, so he circled around until he found the wagon road that was used to go for wood. Here he fainted from loss of blood and exhaustion. He had been without sleep for sixty hours, approximately fifty of those had been spent fighting Indians and traveling.

It is officially stated by his commanding officer and quoted by Frances Carrington in her book, *My Army Life*,

> Shortly afterward a wood party from Fort C. F. Smith found his apparently lifeless body in the road, and recognized Corporal Driscoll at once. He was searched and his dispatches were found, and he was taken to the hospital. Upon return to consciousness, his first inquiry was whether Major Burt, then commanding the Post, had

> received his dispatches, and then he asked, "Where am I? Has the relief party gone?" Being assured that Burt himself had already started, he exclaimed, "Then I wasn't too late, thank God!" and again relapsed into unconsciousness. After six weeks in the hospital he reached Fort Phil Kearny, was welcomed by the whole command, and borne into the fort itself upon the shoulders of his comrades.[2]

Great-grandfather had a varied life after this: two more enlistments in the Army, serving at Fort Laramie and Fort Custer, Montana, July 1870 to July 1875.

During his Army career he had two court martials, one for failure to answer on guard duty, and one for desertion, reportedly as the result of the pursuit of a woman. Dennis served his adopted country over a span of eighteen years and was discharged all three times with honorable discharges.

Records show he was a private at the start and finish of his career and had been a corporal and sergeant. Dennis came as an illiterate to this country; his wife taught him to read and write after their marriage when he was thirty-six and she was sixteen.

Later, he was coal miner, bar owner and organizer in the first labor union in Montana. According to family knowledge, he was also a moonshiner. He married Mary Finneran and they had four children: my grandmother Margaret, Beatrice, Irving and Florence.

On July 13, 1908, the survivors of the Eighteenth U.S. Infantry held a reunion at the site of old Phil Kearny at which were present General and Mrs. Carrington, William Daley, Sam Gibson, William Murphy, S. S. Peters, J. Strawn and Dennis Driscoll.

Through the efforts of General Andrew Burt, Dennis was awarded a pension of twenty-four dollars by an act of

---

[2]Frances C. Carrington, *My Army Life: A Soldier's Life at Fort Phil Kearny* (Boulder, Colorado: Pruett Publishing Company, 1990), p. 306.

Congress in 1909. Among the veteran's most prized possessions was an autographed portrait of General Burt on which the General had written,

> To my old friend and comrade, Dennis Driscoll, late corporal Company C., Twenty Seventh U. S. Infantry, a good soldier and a very brave man. Driscoll's daring ride for help to save his comrades who were surrounded by hostile Sioux Indians, is one of the memorable deeds of our frontier history. Comrade Driscoll may all the pleasure in life by yours, is the wish of your friend, Andrew S. Burt, Brigadier General U. S. Army, retired...[3]

Driscoll's last years were spent in the Soldiers' Home at Columbia Falls, Montana, and at the National Veterans' Home in Sawtelle, California. He died October 19, 1922, at the age of seventy-six from complications of pneumonia and tuberculosis. He is buried at the Sawtelle Veterans Cemetery, Los Angeles, California.

PATRICIA KEYES BEER

---

[3]This photograph is in the hands of Driscoll's descendants.

LT. GEORGE P. BELDEN

On July 4, 1870, Gen. James S. Brisbin, U.S. Army, wrote to Mr. C. F. Vent, Publishers, Cincinnati, Ohio, as follows:

> The Belden manuscripts have abruptly terminated. Mr. Belden has quit the army and returned to the wild life of a mountaineer. I doubt if I shall be able to secure from him any more manuscript for several months, and I have determined not to wait, but forward you what I have for publication....It is only fair to Mr. Belden to say that his career has been more varied and remarkable than that of any pale-face west of the Missouri; and in taking leave of him I cannot refrain from expressing the wish, in which I am sure all the readers of his narrative will join me, that he may long live to pursue the wild life he seems to enjoy so much.[1]

General Brisbin's wish for a long life for his friend was not to be. On September 20 and 21, 1871, two news articles in the *Omaha Weekly Herald* tell of his death. It was reported that he was shot and killed about thirteen miles from the Whetstone Agency, while traveling along, by an Indian from a hostile camp.[2]

---

[1]George P. Belden, *Belden, The White-Chief; or Twelve Years Among the Wild Indians of the Plains*, ed. General James S. Brisbin (Cincinnati: W. E. Starr, 1875), pp. 512-513.

[2]Jack Matthews, introduction to *Belden, The White Chief; or Twelve Years Among the Wild Indians of the Plains*, by George P. Belden (Athens: Ohio University Press, 1974), pp. xxiv-xxv.

Years later, Luther North wrote to his uncle, Frank North,

> Did I ever ask you if you ever knew George Belden? He was a lieutenant in the 5th Cavalry I think. Major Brisbane wrote and published his life under the title of *Belden, The White Chief*. He was dismissed from the army about 1869, I think, and afterwards went back to live with the Sioux and was killed by a halfbreed up at the Standing Rock Agency on the Missouri River.[3]

By virtue of his journals, notes and drawings (fleshed out by the New York Bureau of Illustrations), Belden's book left a record unsurpassed of life with the Plains Indians of the time.

Belden was born in 1844 in Tuscarawas County, Ohio. At the age of thirteen he ran away from home to seek his fortune in the West. His family moved West also, to Brownville, Nebraska, where his father started a newspaper. George stayed a short while working for his father, then ran away again.

Belden met up with a French trapper, La Frombe, who lived with the Sioux, and Belden joined him. Here, he writes that he was taken into the tribe and given a wife, Washtella. With a keen curiosity, desire to learn, and insight belying his youth, Belden kept extensive notes on all aspects of Indian life. He recorded in great detail ceremonies, customs, Indian lore and legends, beliefs, and much more about how they made their arrows, moccasins and items they used for daily living.[4]

At only seventeen years of age, hearing of the Civil War, Belden felt honor bound to join the fight, and enlisted in the

---

[3]Luther North, letter, 1923, MSS H75, 190, South Dakota Historical Society (courtesy of Jack McDermott, Sheridan, Wyoming).

[4]Belden, Belden, *The White Chief*, p. 31.

First Regiment of the Nebraska Infantry Volunteers as a drummer. He was the only musician in the regiment to carry a musket during the siege at Fort Donelson. He was commended for heroism at the battle of Shiloh and then discharged due to ill health from contracting malaria. After recuperating, he joined General Sully and fought the Sioux and Cheyenne at White Stone Hills.

On July 10, 1867, he was appointed second lieutenant in the regular army. He was sent to Fort Laramie and on to Forts Fetterman and Reno and then to Fort Phil Kearny. Here, from September 1867 through June 1868, he kept notes with the same care as he had during his life with the Indians, recording minute details of life at the Fort; a view of the Fetterman Battlefield the summer after the fight; descriptions of a number of encounters with the Indians not generally known; and his difficulty adjusting to Army life.

He did a lot of hunting during quiet times and often gave wild game to the officers. He traded with the Indians for buffalo robes and other items and kept records of items traded, costs, and from which tribe the trade took place. While at the fort, he took part in the christening of an Indian child.

Despite Belden's formative years with the Indians, he displays some inconsistencies in attitudes towards them. In speaking of Chief Washakie and his people, he writes,

> The face of the white man, like an insatiable fiend, presents itself constantly before the Indian, and a voice cries, "Back, back, to the setting sun. I want your land, your game, your home, even the graves of your people; and I will have all! All!"[5]

Yet, when writing of the abandonment of Fort Phil Kearny and the Bozeman Trail, he says,

---

[5]Ibid., p. 435.

> The policy of surrendering this territory to the Indians, after occupying it with a military force for years, has often been questioned...and produced sharp criticisms for the conduct of officials who advised and secured the abandonment of a rich fertile and beautiful country to a few thousand savages, who can make no use of it but to chase the lessening herds of buffalo and deer, and fit out from distant camps their yearly raids on the peaceful settlement of border States and Territories....Those interested in the West will naturally wonder that the Government should withdraw its outposts built for the protection of the border, and restore to the savage tribes what had been claimed for civilization, and it is a question that interests all of us; how long fifteen or twenty thousand Indians, less than the population of a farming county, shall hold for their exclusive use a valuable country as large as three or four States the size of Illinois?[6]

Belden saw no other solution but that Indians be placed on reservations and compelled to stay. Otherwise, he said:

> They will all the time be growing poorer in men and the means of living for it is well known that large game is growing scarcer every year, and before another generation has come on the ground, the buffalo, the Indian's meat and bread, will have become as scarce on the Powder, the Big Horn, and the Yellowstone, as it is now on the Platte. ...the verdict of the higher law will condemn us, unless we save and hand down to posterity at least a remnant of the race which we have driven across the continent, and to whom our example has been evil and not good for over two hundred years.[7]

---

[6]Ibid., p. 438.

[7]Ibid., pp. 439-440.

Belden did not have an easy time while serving in the military. His writings reflect this:

> I did not get along very smoothly in the army, the wild life I had led having in a great measure unfitted me for the duties of a soldier. Thus, one day, after finishing my nice new buckskin suit, I put it on and went out to show it to my friends, when the Adjutant of the post placed me under arrest for not wearing the United States uniform. ...Those who think an officer has an easy time of it are most woefully mistaken, for I certainly know of no harder or more thankless labor than serving in the army of the United States.[8]

George Belden was cashiered out of the Army by General Court Martial in November 1869 for violation of the Fourteenth Article of War and Disobedience of Orders for what seems a rather complicated incident regarding the sale of a horse which he did not fully own, "defection on payment of debts, and borrowing money on his salary beyond the legal limit."[9] Attempts to have him reinstated, including one by U.S. Congressman J. A. Bingham of Ohio, at Belden's mother's request, were unsuccessful, as the law did not allow it.[10]

Shortly after, Belden wrote to General Brisbin:

> I am out of the army, and once more a free man. My ponies are packed and I am about to be off for the trapping and hunting-grounds. If you can make a book out

---

[8]Ibid., p. 408.

[9]Matthews, p. xxi.

[10]Courtmartial records of 4 November 1869, and related correspondence are from the files of Jack McDermott, Sheridan, Wyoming, and Father Barry Hagan, Fort Phil Kearny/Bozeman Trail Association, Sheridan, Wyoming.

of the diaries and manuscripts I have sent you, do so, but I shall hardly be able to add anything to them. Good-by, and ho for the mountains![11]

The life of George P. Belden had come full circle.

MARY ELLEN MCWILLIAMS, AUTHOR
DIANE MARSDEN, CONTRIBUTOR

---

[11]Belden, *Belden, The White Chief*, p. 512.

Fred Newcomer

Frederick F. Newcomer was a private at Fort Phil Kearny. He later became a homesteader in the area, worked as a stone mason, and with his wife raised four children in the area. They have many descendants still living here today.[1]

Fred Newcomer was born 17 March 1849 in Hagesstown, Maryland. His father was Joseph Newcomer, a merchant, and his mother was Susan Armour. When Fred was in his early teens, his country fell into civil war. On 20 June 1864, Newcomer enlisted to serve for one hundred days for the Union. He served as a drummer boy in the Eleventh Regiment of Infantry until he was discharged 1 October 1864. He had received a leg wound at the Battle of Antietam.[2]

He re-enlisted in the U.S. Army 27 November 1865 and served for three years in the CY Infantry. In the summer of 1866 he accompanied General Carrington to the foot of the Big Horn Mountains and helped build Fort Phil Kearny.

In the winter of the same year, Newcomer was sent with a detachment back to Fort Bridger for supplies. Four days after he departed, on 21 December 1866, his company went out with Captain Fetterman to protect the wood train after many Indians had been sighted on the wood road. These men were diverted by the Indians, coaxed over Lodge Trail Ridge by them, and massacred. Had he not been sent to Fort Bridger four days earlier, Fred Newcomer would have been with them and his story would end here. As it was, he lived

---

[1]From oral history interview with Elva Carroll, great-grand-daughter of Frederick F. Newcomer, 24 February 1989.

[2]H. A. Coffeen, "July 6, 1864 Affair at the Antietam, Maryland," *War of the Rebellion: Records of Union and Confederate Armies.*

to help bury his comrades. At the end of his military term he received an honorable discharge on 27 November 1868.

To receive his honorable discharge, Newcomer went to Fort Douglas, Salt Lake City, Utah. While in Salt Lake he witnessed two historic events. He was present at the laying of the cornerstone of the Mormon Temple and he heard Brigham Young preach his first sermon in the Mormon Tabernacle.

Fred Newcomer went back to Missouri. There, in Savannah, he married Mary Frances McGuire 25 December 1869. They had five children, four of whom were raised in Wyoming near the Big Horn mountains where he had served as a soldier in his youth.

When Newcomer brought his wife and children back to the Big Horns, he only intended to pass through the area and keep going west. A crisis in the family, however, caused them to stop and stay in the area. The children's pet rooster got lost. They didn't want to go on without him. The Newcomers stayed. While the children looked for the rooster, Fred talked to several people in the area and found that there were homestead sites to be filed on. And so in 1883 the Newcomer family began homesteading on Prairie Dog Creek. Newcomer was also a stone mason. Much of the earliest stone work in this area was done by him. He built the stone wall around the courthouse in Buffalo. In the early 1880s he kept a diary in which he tells about building the Piney schoolhouse.

Newcomer never forgot his days as a soldier at Fort Phil Kearny. He longed to bring General and Mrs. Carrington back to the area for a reunion. This he accomplished and he and his wife had a picnic at Piney Crossing for the survivors on 3 July 1908, forty years after the closing of the fort.

JUDY PRADERE

LT. WILLIAM HENRY BISBEE

Four years of battle-hardened service; months of experience under the Carrington command at Fort Phil Kearny; the Fetterman disaster; and devotion to Captain Fetterman which lasted throughout his lifetime; all created in William H. Bisbee perhaps the most severe and certainly the longest lasting of all the critics of Col. Henry Carrington.

William Henry Bisbee was born in 1840 at Woonsocket, Rhode Island. He was one of a number of children and named for then President, William Henry Harrison. After a limited amount of schooling, he left for Ohio at age seventeen to work as a clerk in a dry goods store. The merchant career he seemed destined for ended at age twenty-one, when he enlisted as a private in the United States Army at the outbreak of the Civil War. There followed four years of distinguished service in some of the hardest fought battles.

Bisbee served in the Army of the West in the Mill Spring campaign and in June of 1962, after participating in the Siege of Corinth, he was appointed second lieutenant. In December of 1862, Bisbee attained the rank of brevet first lieutenant for gallant and meritorious services in the Battle of Murfreesboro, and brevet captain in September of 1864 for service in the Battle of Chattanooga. Bisbee was wounded during the battle of Hoover's Gap and again during Sherman's Atlanta campaign in 1864. He completed his Civil War duties between October 1864 and September 1865 at Lookout Mountain, Georgia.

Impressive as his war record was, perhaps the most important aspect of it lay in the comradeship he developed with fellow officers of his regiment. These were no ordinary friendships, but rather special types formed during life and death situations. The friendship Bisbee shared with William Fetterman was among the strongest and would last throughout his lifetime. Equally important, and on a different note, was the unfavorable opinion Bisbee (and other officers) developed about the commander of their regiment, Colonel Carrington. It was an opinion based on the fact that the Colonel had never once accompanied the regiment into battle during the entire Civil War. Whatever the reasons for Carrington's not doing so, the result was that it prejudiced Lieutenant Bisbee's opinion of him as commanding officer. Bisbee would confirm his opinion as to Carrington's unfitness for command during the months travelling to, building, and serving at Fort Phil Kearny.

Bisbee's tenure at Fort Phil Kearny was fortunate: beginning at its establishment in July 1866 and lasting long enough (five months) for him to gain some Indian fighting knowledge, and ending just before the Fetterman disaster, a battle he might otherwise have been a participant in. His time at the post, where he served as adjutant and E Company commander, can best be described as a steady education in the dangers and realities of Indian warfare. While his respect for the Indians as opponents did change, his opinion of Carrington as commander did not.

Certainly by the time William Fetterman arrived at the Fort in early November 1866, Bisbee's opinion of Carrington's leadership qualities seems to have been made up. From later testimony and statements he made, he considered Carrington totally unable to maintain the discipline, authority, or confidence of his men; a dress parade officer who should never have commanded in hostile territory.

On the other hand, it must have been easy for him to give his support to Fetterman, an officer he saw as having all the real fighting spirit and leadership qualities that the regiment had once possessed and now again needed. This all led to his becoming, along with Brown and Grummond, a key member of the pro-Fetterman group at the fort. In this now-festering situation concerning divided loyalties, he became involved in perhaps the most serious incident of the whole matter.

One Sunday morning, Sergeant Bowers, in full view of several officers and their wives, attacked Private Burke, verbally and physically abusing him. When a guard was summoned to put the combatants under arrest, Captain Fetterman interceded and also resorted to violent profanity when he endorsed the actions of the sergeant. Carrington, who had witnessed the incident, was horrified, not only at the officer's conduct but because it occurred on a Sunday in front of ladies. He issued an order condemning profanity, swearing, verbal abuse, kicks and blows. While most of the order was directed toward non-commissioned officers, one paragraph was surely aimed at Fetterman:[1]

> Officers at this post will communicate and carefully enforce this order seeking to inspire among non-commissioned officers, by precept and example, that calm and steady habit of command which will surely secure implicit obedience, and no less augment respect for authority requiring obedience.[2]

Although the order was signed by Bisbee as post adjutant, Bisbee recognized the reprimand for what it was and quickly sided with Fetterman and others in their contempt for it, calling it the "bully order" and making it the subject of many a profane joke amongst themselves. Bisbee and others openly showed their preference for Fetterman over Carrington.

In December of 1866, Bisbee left Fort Phil Kearny for a new assignment at department headquarters in Omaha. When he learned of the fate of Fetterman and his command, he had

---

[1]Dee Brown, *The Fetterman Massacre* (Lincoln: University of Nebraska Press, 1970), pp. 152-153.

[2]Ibid., p. 153.

no doubt where the real blame for the catastrophe lay and did not keep it secret; Bisbee conveyed his opinion, daily, to Departmental Commander Cooke. From that time on, right up to his death, William Bisbee would never forgive Carrington for what in Bisbee's mind was the truth of the matter: Carrington had caused the defeat of Fetterman and then had escaped blame by slandering the dead Fetterman with charges of disobedience.

In the following years Bisbee would become an enduring champion of his friend Fetterman's name and reputation, working continuously to restore and protect them by collecting testimony contradicting Carrington's and laying the responsibility for the disaster back onto the Colonel. He firmly believed that Carrington never issued the order

> Support the wood train, relieve it, and report to me. Do not engage or pursue Indians at its expense; under no circumstances pursue over the Ridge, namely Lodge Trail Ridge, as per map in your possession.[3]

Bisbee challenged the accepted fact that Fetterman had disobeyed orders and stated "that the files of the Order of the Indian Wars in Washington, D.C., contained evidence by witnesses that disproved the ex-parte statements made by Carrington after Fetterman lay dead and unable to defend himself."[4] In defense of Fetterman Bisbee concluded, "Col-

---

[3]Henry B. Carrington, Official Report of the Philip Kearny Massacre, 3 January 1867, Letters Received, Department of the Platte, Records of the United States Army Commands, Record Group 393, National Archives. Please see John D. McDermott, "Price of Arrogance: The Short and Controversial Life of William Judd Fetterman," *Annals of Wyoming* 63 (Spring 1991).

[4]John D. McDermott, "Price of Arrogance: The Short and Controversial Life of William Judd Fetterman," *Annals of Wyoming 63* (Spring 1991):52.

onel Fetterman was my friend....He was of military heritage, intelligently disciplined; incapable of willfully disobeying a positive order or disregarding its importance."[5] Bisbee also identified F. M. Fessendon as one of those who had witnessed the exchange between Carrington and Fetterman and had denied any mention of where not to go."[6]

Although recent historical evidence shows conclusively that Carrington did indeed tell Fetterman not to pursue the Indians over Lodge Trail Ridge, Bisbee spent his life supporting the honor of his life-long friend Fetterman.[7] A fact that helped Bisbee's task considerably was his own subsequently very successful military career. He was appointed Captain, Judge Advocate, Department of the Platte and subsequently served at forts in Wyoming, Kentucky, Arkansas, Nebraska, Utah and Idaho. In May of 1897, Bisbee was promoted to Lieutenant Colonel First U.S. Infantry and from 1898 to 1899 commanded a regiment during the Spanish-American War. On June 16, 1899, he was appointed Colonel Thirteenth Infantry and from August 1899 to December 1900, served in the Philippines.

On the second of October 1901, he was appointed Brigadier General by President Theodore Roosevelt. In 1902, he retired after forty-one years of service. Bisbee's remarkable life did not end there, as he lived on another forty years.

An officer whose career had begun in frontier times and lasted to the dawn of the atomic age, William Bisbee does

---

[5]William H. Bisbee, *Through Four American Wars* (Boston: Meador Publishing Co., 1931), p. 175.

[6]McDermott, "Price of Arrogance," p. 52. Later scholarship proves that Fetterman did in fact disobey orders. For a full account, please see McDermott, "Price of Arrogance" (endnote 3).

[7]For a full discussion of the Fetterman Disaster, see: John D. McDermott, "Price of Arrogance: The Short and Controversial Life of William Judd Fetterman," *Annals of Wyoming 63* (Spring 1991):42-53.

not belong to one particular time or place. At a remote outpost deep in Indian Territory, a friend made a stand at a place called Fetterman Ridge and stayed there forever; in his own way, William Bisbee stayed there forever as well.

DALE TREMAINE

Morning Star
(Chief Dull Knife)

I am going to share with you stories as I heard them from people that were living in those days. It is not necessarily a story that has dates and hours or number of people. It is like a story that you tell one another in your family.

It was probably in the 1820s when a Cheyenne war party was formed. This particular war party went into the Pawnee country and they came upon three Pawnee. There were two men and a young girl. The war party attacked. They killed the two men and were also going to kill the girl.

Morning Star, who later became Dull Knife, intervened and said, "Will you permit me to take the girl to replace a member of my family that was lost to the Pawnee previously?" This was allowed and Dull Knife took the girl home to his family. Later, when Morning Star became Chief, the Pawnee woman became one of his wives.

Out of the union of the Pawnee woman with Morning Star were born four daughters. They were Traveling Woman, Pure Woman, Broken Foot Woman and Holding Woman. Broken Foot Woman was my grandmother.

Morning Star also had a Cheyenne wife named Short Woman. She had three sons that I know of: Medicine Club, Standing Bull and the oldest was Buffalo Hump.

Later when Dull Knife became a Chief he fought in many battles. But in 1866 Dull Knife signed the peace treaty at Fort Laramie. I think he did so in good faith and preferred not to fight after that. Partly because of Dull Knife's commitment to peace, and because of his age at the time, I do not believe he took part in the Fetterman battle. He was probably well into his 50s at the time and in his mid-60s at the time of the Battle of the Little Big Horn.

About five months after Custer's defeat at the Little Big Horn, Dull Knife's camp on the Red Fork of the Powder River was attacked by the troops of Gen. Ranald Mackenzie. According to Risingsun, the Cheyennes escaped but their camp and winter supplies were captured. Risingsun says:

This was the beginning of the thought of surrender, largely because of concern with the women and children. Most major decisions are based on what is going to happen to the children; they are the Cheyenne of tomorrow. Because of their concern with their young, they chose to suffer defeat, to accept humiliation of a defeated people.

So in the spring of 1877 the Cheyenne decided to surrender at Fort Keogh, to General Miles, one of the few officers that they knew that they could trust.

Dull Knife and Little Wolf decided to take their people to Fort Robinson instead, intending to ask that they be permitted to live with their longtime allies and relatives, the Oglala Sioux. Permission was denied, and they were informed they would have to go to Oklahoma to live with their Southern Cheyenne relatives.

They went down under protest, but they were told if they did not like it, they could come home in a year. So reluctantly they agreed. There was never enough food, and beside that the climate was foreign to them, and they began to fall prey to the sickness and diseases of the Southland and they began to die.

And like any people anywhere in this world, they began to pressure the leaders. "Take us home. We want to go home." More Cheyenne got sick and more Cheyenne died. The pressure mounted. "Are you to take us home or are you going to let us starve to death like dogs down here?"

Finally the two Chiefs said, "All right, we will go home, but we will ask permission." The agent told them to give him a year, and he'd write to Washington, D.C., to see if they could be permitted to return to their homeland. Little Wolf said, "Within a year there might not be any Cheyenne to move, to travel north...if you are going to send soldiers after us, let us get a little ways from the agency because we do not want to bloody the ground upon which some of our people are going to live."

Three hundred of them left: old men, women and children with less than one hundred fighting men. My grandmother was thirteen years old. The troops caught up with them. The eighty men swarmed out and held the troops off while the rest of the people kept moving. My grandmother used to say, "There were more of them, and there were so few of us; yet we came through." Tears would run down her face. "We were not going to hurt anybody. We just wanted to go home."

They fought through five lines of defenses. The U.S. Army mobilized 213,000 troops to stop this handful of Cheyennes. But this was more than just personal concern to the Cheyenne. It was the survival of a people.

In the Sand Hills of Nebraska, they decided to split. Some would go with Dull Knife, the others with Little Wolf. Most of the old people went with Dull Knife.

The band under Dull Knife was captured in a snowstorm and was taken to Fort Robinson and put in an old cavalry barracks to await word from Washington, D.C. They were permitted freedom to hunt, to move around at the fort. And then word came from Washington to return the Indians to Oklahoma, that they must be taught a lesson, the leaders were informed. The leaders said, "We are dying in Oklahoma. No, we will not return. We will die up here on our own ground."

Food was cut off. Heat was cut off. Water was cut off. For four days they stayed in the barracks. Some of the better weapons amongst them had been taken apart and hid on their women.

On January ninth, one of the sentries was shot down and the people came out of the windows, out of the doors. Traveling Woman was carrying Holding Woman on her back. Holding Woman was about four years old. Traveling Woman was shot down a little ways from the barracks. She did not die right away. She took the little girl and said, "You saw the way they went, follow them." There was snow on the ground. It was thirty degrees below zero that night. My grandmother, as she fled across this little open path, was shot, wounded in the head. She used to show us her scalp wound.

The stories began to fade out here, the stories of what happened to Dull Knife. There are stories that he died hating the white man until the last. Those stories are not true. Dull Knife died on the present day Northern Cheyenne Reservation on his son Buffalo Hump's place. He was buried there on the hill.

In his old age Dull Knife would say, "We can no longer live the way we have been living. We are going to learn a new way of life. Let us ask for schools so that our little children can go to these schools and learn this new way of life." The tragedy of the story is that none of this got to the authorities. Fear on both sides, the fear of each other, prevented understanding, coming together to negotiate.

TED RISINGSUN

Risingsun's oral history does not include the years from 1864 through 1875. Historian George Bird Grinnell, however, places Dull Knife in action along the North Platte and in the attack on Platte Bridge Station in 1865.

Shortly after Col. Henry Carrington arrived at what was to become Fort Phil Kearny, Dull Knife and Black Horse rode in with about forty Cheyenne and met with Carrington. The Indians tried to persuade him not to build the fort, and to leave the Powder River Country, as the Sioux would fight them if they did not, and the Sioux would want the Cheyenne to join them. That evening, a confrontation with angry Sioux, at the camp of trader "French Pete" Gazzous, resulted later that night in the violent death of "French Pete" and others at the hands of the Sioux.

After the break-out at Fort Robinson in 1879, Dull Knife and some of his family escaped into the hills; they and others finally made their way to the Red Cloud Agency at Pine Ridge. At the request of Col. Nelson Miles, Dull Knife's group was allowed to reside near Fort Keogh, rather than be returned south, and shortly after, to live in his beloved homeland in Tongue River Country.

Grinnell, in Fighting Cheyennes *(New York: Charles Scribner's Sons, 1965), says Dull Knife died in about 1883. According to Peter J. Powell in* Sweet Medicine *(Norman: University of Oklahoma, 1969), it was Grinnell who had the bodies of both Dull Knife and Little Wolf reinterred side by side in the cemetery at Lame Deer, Montana, near where the Dull Knife Memorial College is now.*

MARY ELLEN MCWILLIAMS

AUTHORS & CONTRIBUTORS

PATRICIA KEYES BEER Great Falls, Montana. Pat, the great-granddaughter of Corporal Dennis Driscoll, has collected information on Driscoll and his courageous ride for help. She was a featured banquet speaker at the Fort Phil Kearny/Bozeman Trail Association's Bozeman Trail Days event in 1991.

ELBERT D. BELISH Ranchester, Wyoming. Elbert holds a master's degree in American Studies from the University of Wyoming. His more extensive version of the biography of American Horse appeared in the Spring 1991 edition of *Annals of Wyoming.*

ALAN W. BOURNE Sheridan, Wyoming. Colonel Alan Bourne (ret.) is a graduate of Northwestern University and of the U.S. Army Command and General Staff College at Fort Leavenworth. His attention has focused primarily on military aspects of western history. Alan is a member of the board of the Fort Phil Kearny/Bozeman Trail Association. He designed and built the metal sculptures on the hills above Fort Phil Kearny and the Fetterman battle sites.

CATHERINE CURTISS Sheridan, Wyoming. Catherine is project director for *Portraits of Fort Phil Kearny,* is a member of the board of the Fort Phil Kearny/Bozeman Trail Association, and serves on the Bozeman Trail Days committee. She served as the Association's first administrator, as director of several speaker's programs, and as coordinator for the 1992 and '93 archaeology projects at Fort Phil Kearny and the Wagon Box sites. Katie holds a master's degree and is a history instructor at Sheridan College.

BILL & CAROL DALEY Laramie, Wyoming. Bill is the great-grandson of the Bill Daley who helped build the flagpole at Fort Phil Kearny. He and his wife, Carol, have attended every Bozeman Trail Days event at the sites, and Bill participated in the 1993 archaeology dig at the Wagon Box

Fight site. Most material used in the William Daley biography is from their collection.

SUSAN BADGER DOYLE Albuquerque, New Mexico. Susan recently received her doctorate degree with her dissertation on the Bozeman Trail and is working on a two-volume edition of Bozeman Trail diaries to be published by the Montana Historical Society. She has done extensive work for the Fort Phil Kearny/Bozeman Trail Association in the filing of collections, as a symposium speaker, tour guide and member of the Association's Advisory Board.

B. J. EARLE Buffalo, Wyoming. B. J. is an archaeologist for the Buffalo Resource Area of the Bureau of Land Management, where she has worked the past seven years. She has done extensive work at sites along the Bozeman Trail and was a Bozeman Trail Days guide on the Fort Reno tours in 1988 and 1993.

H. STERLING FENN Redding, California. Dr. Fenn is a veterinarian and co-author of two books on antique firearms. He is presently writing a book on Fort Phil Kearny and the Fetterman Fight. Sterling has done years of research on Civil War and Indian Wars battlesites, and has participated in archaeology digs on a number of sites. His tour of Fetterman Ridge in conjunction with Indian guides Bill Tall Bull and Joe Marshall is a popular Bozeman Trail Days event. Sterling has been a member of the Association's Advisory Board since its inception and is one of four recipients of the FPK/BTA Spur award for outstanding service.

CYNDE GEORGEN Sheridan, Wyoming. As typographer, compiler of the bibliographies and proofreader, Cynde also did considerable editing for *Portraits of Fort Phil Kearny.* Cynde is Curator and Assistant Superintendent at Trail End State Historic Site in Sheridan and is Wyoming representative to the Colorado-Wyoming Association of Museums and Mountain-Plains Museum Association. She holds a degree in history from the University of Wyoming and is the author of *Centennial Minutes: 366 Events in Sheridan County History.*

BARRY HAGAN Portland, Oregon. Father Barry Hagan, CSC, archivist at the University of Portland, is recognized as one of the nation's foremost Indian Wars and Bozeman Trail archivists. He recently donated to the Association his Bozeman Trail collection of papers, microfilm and card files, housed in the Sheridan County Fulmer Public Library. Hagan is a founding member of the Association's Advisory Board and is a recipient of the FPK/BTA Spur Award for outstanding service.

DAENA HINKLEMAN Darien, Illinois. Daena is a free-lance writer with a strong interest in western history. She has published a number of articles on forts of the West. Daena is a professional member of the National Writers Club.

JERRY KEENAN Boulder, Colorado. Jerry is owner/manager of Lightning Tree Press. He is the recipient of the Wrangler Award from the National Cowboy Hall of Fame for his biography of Luther "Yellowstone" Kelly, published in *Montana: The Magazine of Western History.* Jerry is author of *The Wagon Box Fight,* and has conducted numerous tours of that site. He wrote and narrated the video *Fort Phil Kearny: Hated Post on the Little Piney* for Old Army Press of Fort Collins, Colorado. He is a member of the Association's Advisory Board.

ANN KILPATRICK Sheridan, Wyoming. Ann is a registered nurse who has served as a volunteer for the Association for several years. She has worked on family genealogy for many years, a hobby which helped with her biography of Chaplain David White. This is Ann's first experience with research and writing.

JEAN KIMBLE Banner, Wyoming. Jean is Vice President and membership chair for the Fort Phil Kearny/Bozeman Trail Association, and serves on the Bozeman Trail Days committee. She has done extensive research on Captain Ten Eyck and has transcribed years of his diaries, on file at the library in Tucson, Arizona. The family ranch, owned by Jean, her husband Cliff, and two children, was cited as one of Wyoming's 100 year old ranches during the state's centennial in 1990.

DEANNA UMBACH KORDIK Lincoln, Nebraska. Deanna is a free-lance writer who has been researching the life of Frances Grummond Carrington for a number of years. Deanna plans a full-length book on Frances and welcomes information from readers. The Kordik family has spent numerous vacations in the Fort Phil Kearny region.

THEODORE L. MAGUDER Windsor, Connecticut. Doctor Magruder is an associate professor of biology at the University of Hartford in West Hartford, Connecticut. Since discovering collections of Henry B. Carrington at his boyhood home, now Choate-Rosemary Hall, a prep school in Wallingford, Connecticut, Ted has done extensive research on

Carrington and his family. Ted, with Bill Tall Bull, conducted a "Walk on Little Piney," examining the plant life there, and also gave a program on Colonel Carrington during Bozeman Trail days in 1988.

DIANE MARSDEN Sheridan, Wyoming. Diane works for the State Parks and Historic Sites section of the Department of Commerce at the Trail End State Historic Site in Sheridan. She attended Chadron State College in Chadron, Nebraska, and has been involved as a volunteer in the 1991 and 1992 archaeology digs at Fort Phil Kearny.

JOSEPH M. MARSHALL Casper, Wyoming. Joe is a member of the Lakota (Sioux) tribe, serves on the Association's Advisory Board, and gives the joint Indian/White interpretive tour of Fetterman Ridge with Sterling Fenn. He holds a master's degree in education, is featured in numerous national television documentaries, has written columns and articles, and is co-author of *Soldiers Falling Into Camp.* Joe has been involved in the production of movies and videos as well, including *Hunter/Warrior Tradition of the High Plains Indians.*

MICHAEL MASSIE Laramie, Wyoming. The author of the Introduction to *Portraits of Fort Phil Kearny,* Mike is Assistant Director of the Wyoming Council for the Humanities. He holds a master's degree in American History with the American Indian and Western history as his major field of study. He is an adjunct professor of history at the University of Wyoming and a director of the City of Greeley Museums. Mike served as curator at South Pass City State Historic Site and as historian at the State Historic Preservation Office. He has written numerous articles for historical publications.

DOUGLAS C. MCCHRISTIAN Hardin, Montana. Doug is a long-time employee of the National Park Service and presently serves as Chief Historian at the Little Bighorn National Monument. He is the author of *An Army of Marksmen* and numerous articles and papers on frontier military history. Doug is a member of the Association's Advisory Board and is an active participant in Association planning and activities.

JOHN D. MCDERMOTT Sheridan, Wyoming. Jack is an independent historical consultant, having retired in 1986 from government service in Washington, D.C., where he served as Director of Policy for the President's Advisory Council on Historic Preservation. He is a former National Park Service Chief Historian at Fort Laramie. As a writer of development plans for a number of museums and sites, he co-authored the Master Plan for the Fort Phil Kearny site, and is author of *Forlorn Hope,* the story of Chief Joseph and the Nez Perce.

MARY ELLEN MCWILLIAMS Sheridan, Wyoming. Mary Ellen is one of the founders of the Fort Phil Kearny/Bozeman Trail Association, is a member of their Board of Directors, and has served primarily as coordinator for the organization. She is the originator of Bozeman Trail Days, writer and editor of several Association books, chief publicist, and editor of the Association's newsletter, *The Lookout*. She is a member of the FPK/BTA Endowment Foundation Board.

ROBERT A. MURRAY Sheridan, Wyoming. Bob Murray has published over thirty books and fifty articles, primarily on western history and archaeology. He holds a master's degree from Kansas State and spent several years as a historian for the National Park Service. Bob founded and operated Western Interpretive Services from 1968-1983, and serves now primarily as a historical consultant. He is the author of the classic study of the forts of this area, *Military Posts of the Powder River Country of Wyoming.*

PATTY MYERS Buffalo, Wyoming. Patty is a librarian at the Johnson County Library and a free-lance writer. She serves as Secretary of the Fort Phil Kearny/Bozeman Trail Association and Chair of the Bozeman Trail Days Committee. Patty has won a number of awards from the State Historical Society, particularly for work with oral history and with children. She is also on the joint powers board for the proposed Mountain Plains Heritage Center at Buffalo and on the FPK/BTA Endowment Foundation Board.

KEVIN O'DELL Sheridan, Wyoming. Kevin was recipient of the Wyoming Historical Society's Lola Holmshire $1,000 scholarship to a Wyoming college of his choice. He graduated from Sheridan College and presently attends Southeast Missouri University at Cape Girardeau, Missouri, working towards a degree in Historic Preservation, with special training in historic site administration. Kevin has donated many hours as a volunteer, especially with living history programs.

JUDY PRADERE Sheridan, Wyoming. Judy is a local artist with a special interest in history. Her enrollment in a Sheridan College course on "How to Research Fort Phil Kearny," prepared and taught by Jack McDermott and Sonny Reisch, resulted in the work she has done for this book.

SONNY REISCH Sheridan, Wyoming. Sonny is Site Superintendent at the Fort Phil Kearny State Historic Site, with jurisdiction extending to Fort Fetterman State Historic Site near Douglas, Fort Reno, Crazy Woman and other related sites along the Bozeman Trail near Kaycee, and Connor Battlefield State Park in Ranchester, Wyoming. He is an ex-officio member of the board of the Fort Phil Kearny/Bozeman Trail Association and serves on the Bozeman Trail Days committee. He has conducted a number of tours for the events and has prepared and taught a course on "How to Research Fort Phil Kearny," in cooperation with Jack McDermott.

TED RISINGSUN Busby, Montana. Ted is the great-grandson of Northern Cheyenne Chief Morning Star (Dull Knife) and has done considerable research on his life. He has appeared in several national television documentaries, including *How the West Was Lost,* and has given programs on Dull Knife at Bozeman Trail Days. Ted was awarded a Silver Star with President's Citation for service with the U.S. Army in World War II and Korea. In 1992 he was honored by the National Indian Education Association for outstanding work in education.

RICHARD SCHMIDT Sheridan, Wyoming. Rick has been camera man and pressroom foreman for many years at the *Sheridan Press.* He has done considerable camera work for the Association newsletter, *The Lookout,* and has designed the cover for *Portraits of Fort Phil Kearny.*

PETER K. SIMPSON Laramie, Wyoming. Peter is Vice President for Institutional Advancement with the University of Wyoming and holds a doctorate in History. He is the great-grandson of Wyoming pioneer "Finn" Burnett. A former State Representative from Sheridan County, he comes from one of Wyoming's most well-known political families: his late father, Milward Simpson, was both Governor of Wyoming and a U.S. Senator; his brother, Alan, is currently a U.S. Senator from Wyoming. Peter, a longtime educator, narrated the FPK/BTA video, *Along the Bozeman Trail.*

BILL TALL BULL Busby, Montana. Bill is Northern Cheyenne Tribal Historian, an instructor of Indian culture and history, as well as traditional and medicinal uses of native plants at Dull Knife Memorial College in Lame Deer, Montana. He is the grandson of Blue Feather, a Northern Cheyenne participant in the Fetterman fight, and conducted the initial tours of Fetterman Ridge with Sterling Fenn. He is the author of several books, and is a national consultant for a number of Indian concerns. He is a member of the Association's Advisory Board and developed the themes for the Indian Memorial at Fort Phil Kearny.

DALE TREMAINE Sydney, Australia. Dale developed an interest in the western frontier as a child which led him to pursue training in library science. He works in the library in Sydney. Dale has done years of research on the Fort Phil Kearny era and the American West.

KAREN WHITE EYES Kyle, South Dakota. Karen is Director of the Lakota Studies Program at Oglala Lakota College in South Dakota, and instructs courses in Lakota history and language. She was a participant in the Battle of the Rosebud Symposium during Bozeman Trail Days in 1990 and annually gives tours of Fort Phil Kearny to her students.

RICHARD WILLIAMS Boulder, Colorado. Rick is both Lakota (Sioux) and Cheyenne, is a member of the Lakota tribe, and is a blood relative of Chief Red Cloud. He is Director of the Learning Center at the University of Colorado at Boulder. Rick also serves on the Association's Advisory Board and has given the Indian interpretation in tours of the Wagon Box Fight and Rosebud Battle sites. He holds a master's degree in education from the University of Wyoming and has appeared in several national television documentaries, including *How the West Was Lost.*

CONNIE WILSON Sheridan, Wyoming. Connie worked for Reynolds Mining Company and was involved with the research done by that company in the early 1960's on the Fort Phil Kearny sites. She has been a volunteer for the Association and is a member of the Sheridan Genealogical Society.

ROBERT C. WILSON Banner, Wyoming. Bob is Curator and Assistant Superintendent at the Fort Phil Kearny State Historic Site. He researched, designed and did most of the construction on the model/diorama of the fort site as well as other models, displays, and interpretive maps and signage in the Visitors' Center, on the fort grounds, at Fetterman Ridge and at Fort Fetterman. Bob designed the map for *Portraits of Fort Phil Kearny.*

Selected Bibliography

Abbott, Teddy "Blue" and Smith, Helena Huntington. *We Pointed Them North.* New York: Farrar and Rinehart, 1939.

Alter, J. Cecil. *James Bridger, Trapper, Frontiersman, Scout and Guide: An Historical Narrative.* Salt Lake City, Utah: Shepherd Book Company, 1975.

_______. *Jim Bridger.* Norman: University of Oklahoma Press, 1962.

Appleman, Roy E. "Great Western Indian Fights: The Wagon Box Fight." In *Westerners Brand Book.* Lincoln, Nebraska: Potomac Corral of the Westerners, 1966.

Appointments, Commission and Personal Branch files. Records of the Adjutant General's Office, 1780s-1917. Record Group 94. National Archives, Washington, D.C.

Arizona (Prescott) *Weekly Miner,* 14 January 1871.

Army Navy Journal, 1865-70.

Baalon, Herman. Correspondence, 18 July 1866. Fort Phil Kearny Letters Received. Department of the Platte. Record Group 393. National Archives, Washington, D.C.

Bancroft, Hubert Howe. *History of Nevada, Colorado and Wyoming, 1540-1888.* San Francisco: The History Company, 1890.

_______. *History of Utah, 1540-1886.* San Francisco: The History Company, 1890.

Beck, Peggy V., and Walters, Anna Lee. *The Sacred Ways of Knowledge: Sources of Life.* Tsaile, Arizona: Navajo Community College, 1977.

Belden, George P. Belden, *The White Chief; or Twelve Years Among the Wild Indians of the Plains.* Edited by General James S. Brisbin. Cincinnati: W. E. Starr, 1875; reprint edition (Introduction by Jack Matthews), Athens: Ohio State University, 1974.

Bibliographical Directory of the U.S. Congress, 1774-1989. Washington, D.C.: Government Printing Office, 1989.

Bingham, David. Correspondence, 8 April 1989. O'Dell Collection, Sheridan, Wyoming.

Bisbee, William H. "Items of Indian Service." *In Proceedings of the Annual Meeting and Dinner of the Order of the Indian Wars of the United States. 19 January 1928;* reprinted in *Papers of the Order of the Indian Wars* (Introduction by John Carroll), Fort Collins, Colorado: Old Army Press, 1975.

_______. *Through Four American Wars.* Boston: Meador Publishing Company, 1931.

Boatner, Mark M. *The Civil War Dictionary.* New York: David McKay Company, 1959.

Bonner, Thomas D. *The Life and Adventures of James P. Beckwourth: Mountaineer, Scout and Pioneer, and Chief of the Crow Nation of Indians.* New York: Harper and Brothers, 1856.

Brackett, William S. "Bonneville and Bridger." *Contributions of the Montana Historical Society* 3 (1900).

Bradley, James H. *The March of the Montana Column: A Prelude to the Custer Disaster.* Norman: University of Oklahoma Press, 1961.

Bradley, Luther. Correspondence, 30 July 1867. Fort C. F. Smith Letters Received. Records of the United States Continental Commands, 1821-1920. Record Group 393. National Archives, Washington, D.C.

Brady, Cyrus T. *Indian Fights and Fighters: The Thirty-Two Against the Three Thousand.* Lincoln, Nebraska: 1971.

Bratt, John. Correspondence, 2 July 1908. Nebraska Historical Society, Lincoln, Nebraska.

_______. *Trails of Yesterday.* Chicago: University Publishing, 1921.

Breakenridge, Elizabeth. Depredation Claim 1728, 22 December 1866. Office of Indian Affairs, U.S. Department of the Interior. National Archives, Washington, D.C.

Breakenridge, William. *Helldorado: Bringing the Law to Mesquite.* New York: Houghton Mifflin Company, 1928.

Bronson, Edgar Beecher. *Reminiscences of a Ranchman.* New York: McClure, 1908; reprint edition, Lincoln: University of Nebraska, 1962.

Brown, Dee. *The Fetterman Massacre: An American Saga.* Lincoln: University of Nebraska Press, 1961; reprint edition, 1970.

Brown, Frederick H. Commission Branch File. Records of the Adjutant General's Office. Record Group 94. National Archives, Washington, D.C.

Burgess, Perry A. "From Illinois to Montana in 1866." Edited by Robert G. Athearn. *Pacific Northwest Quarterly* 41 (January 1950):43-65.

Burlingame, Merrill G. "John M. Bozeman, Montana Trailmaker." *Mississippi Valley Historical Review* 27 (March 1941):541-68; reprint edition, *John M. Bozeman: Montana Trailmaker,* Bozeman, Montana: Montana State University Museum of the Rockies, 1971.

Burrowes, Thomas. Correspondence, 16 July 1867. Fort C. F. Smith Letters Received. Department of the Platte. Record Group 393. National Archives, Washington, D.C.

Burt, Elizabeth J. Reynolds. "An Army Wife's Forty Years in the Service, 1862 - 1902." Library of Congress Manuscript Division, Washington, D.C.

Byron, Elsa Spear. *Bozeman Trail Scrapbook.* Published by the author. Sheridan, Wyoming: Mills Company, 1967; republished in *Books and Photographs of Elsa Spear,* Sheridan, Wyoming: Fort Phil Kearny/ Bozeman Trail Association, 1987.

________. *Fort Phil Kearny, Dakota Territory, 1866-1868.* Published by the author. Sheridan, Wyoming: Quick Printing Company, 1939; republished in *Books and Photographs of Elsa Spear,* Sheridan, Wyoming: Fort Phil Kearny/Bozeman Trail Association, 1987.

"Camp Verde, Arizona Territory, February 1871-October 1872." *Southern Arizona Genealogical Society Bulletin* 3 (December 1967).

Carrington Family Papers. Sterling Memorial Library, Manuscripts and Archives, Yale University, New Haven, Connecticut.

Carrington, Frances C. *My Army Life and the Fort Phil Kearny Massacre.* Philadelphia: J. B. Lippincott Company, 1910; reprint edition, retitled *My Army Life: A Soldier's Wife at Fort Phil Kearny* (Introduction by John D. McDermott), Boulder, Colorado: Pruett Publishing Company, 1990.

Carrington, Henry Beebe. Correspondence, 30 July, 6 November, 19 December 1866. Fort Phil Kearny Letters Sent, 1866-68. Record Group 393. National Archives, Washington, D.C.

________. Endorsement, 14 April 1866. Surgeon S. Horton's Medical Officer's File. Record Group 94. National Archives, Washington, D.C.

________. *The Indian Question.* Boston: DeWolfe and Fiske, 1909.

_______. Memorandum and notes, 1908. Wyoming Room, Sheridan County Fulmer Public Library, Sheridan, Wyoming.

_______. "Official Report of the Philip Kearny Massacre," 3 January 1867. Department of the Platte. Records of the United States Army Commands. Record Group 393. National Archives, Washington, D.C.

_______. Testimony. In "Records of the Special Commission to Investigate the Fetterman Massacre and the State of Indian Affairs, 1867." Bureau of Indian Affairs. Record Group 75. National Archives, Washington, D.C.

Carrington, James B. "Across the Plains With Bridger as Guide." *Scribner's Magazine* 85 (1929):66-71.

Carrington, Margaret Irvin. *Absaraka, Home of the Crows: Being the Experiences of an Officer's Wife on the Plains.* Philadelphia: J. B. Lippincott, 1868; reprint edition (edited by Milo Milton Quaife, Lakeside Classics Series, Number 48), Chicago: The Lakeside Press, R. R. Donnelly & Sons Company, 1950; reprint edition, Lincoln: University of Nebraska Press, 1983.

Carroll, Elva. Interview, 24 February 1989. Pradere Collection, Sheridan, Wyoming

Chicago Republican, 6 February 1867.

Clokey, Richard M. *William H. Ashley: Enterprise and Politics in the Trans-Mississippi West.* Norman: University of Oklahoma Press, 1972.

Clough, Wilson D. "Mni Aku, Daughter of Spotted Tail." *Annals of Wyoming* 39 (1967):187-216.

Cockhill, Brian, editor. "Skirmishes at Goosecreek: Edmond R. P. Shurley's Bozeman Trail Reminiscence." *Montana: The Magazine of Western History* 33 (Spring 1983):60-63.

Coffeen, H. A. "July 6, 1864 Affair at the Antietam, Maryland." In *War of the Rebellion: Records of Union and Confederate Armies.* Fort Phil Kearny/Bozeman Trail Association Collection, Wyoming Room, Sheridan County Fulmer Public Library, Sheridan, Wyoming.

Collister, Oscar. "Life of Oscar Collister, Wyoming Pioneer." *Annals of Wyoming* 7 (July and October 1930).

Cook, James H. *Fifty Years on the Old Frontier.* Norman: University of Oklahoma Press, 1957.

Curtis, Edward. *The North American Indian: Being a Series of Volumes Picturing and Describing the Indians of the United States and Alaska.* Volume 3. Cambridge: University Press, 1908.

Daily Leavenworth (Kansas) *Times,* 20 October 1866.

Daily (St. Louis) *Missouri Republican,* 22 November 1867.

Daily (Salt Lake City, Utah) *Union Vedette,* 15 October 1866.

Daley, William. Correspondence. Wyoming State Historical Society, Cheyenne, Wyoming.

Dandy, George B. "Annual Report to the Quartermaster General," 30 June 1867. Department of the Platte. Record Group 92. National Archives, Washington, D.C.

________. Personnel File. National Archives, Washington, D.C.

________. "Report to the Chief Quartermaster," 4 January 1867. Department of the Platte. Record Group 92. National Archives, Washington, D.C

Danker, Donald. "The Violent Deaths of Yellow Bear and John Richard, Jr." *Nebraska History* 63 (Summer 1982).

"Daredevils of Destiny." *Great Falls* (Montana) *Tribune,* n.d.

David, Robert Beebe. *Finn Burnett, Frontiersman.* Glendale, California: Arthur H. Clarke Company, 1937.

"Descriptive Books of the 27th U.S. Infantry." Records of the U.S. Regular Army Mobile Units, 1821-1942. Record Group 391. National Archives, Washington, D.C.

Dictionary of American Biography. Volume 2. New York: Charles Scribner's Sons, 1929.

Dockstader, Frederick J. *Great North American Indians.* New York: Van Nostrand Reinhold Company, 1977.

Dodge, Grenville M. "Biographical Sketch of James Bridger." *Annals of Wyoming* 33 (October 1961).

Driver, Harold E. "Girls' Puberty Rites in Western North America." Publications in *Anthropological Records* 6 (1941-42):21-90.

Eggenhofer, Nick. *Wagons, Mules and Men: How the Frontier Moved West.* New York: Hastings House, 1961.

"Elbridge Gerry Account Books." Typescript from Wyoming State Department of History and Archives, Cheyenne, Wyoming.

Encyclopedia of Frontier Biography. Glendale, California: Arthur H. Clark Company, 1988. S.v. "American Horse (Wasechun-tashunka)."

Ewers, John C. "Deadlier than the Male." *American Heritage* 16 (1965):10-13.

________. "Mothers of the Mixed-Bloods: The Marginal Woman in the History of the Upper Missouri." In *Probing the American West,* pp. 62-70. Edited by Kenneth Ross Toole. Santa Fe: Museum of New Mexico, 1962.

Fast, Howard. *The Last Frontier.* New York: Duell, Sloane and Pearce, 1941.

Finerty, John F. *Warpath and Bivouac.* Chicago: A. M. Donoghue, 1880; reprint edition, Norman: University of Oklahoma Press, 1961.

Fleming, Paula Richardson, and Luskey, Judith. *The North American Indians in Early Photographs.* New York: Dorset Press, 1986.

Fort C. F. Smith. Post Returns. Microfilm Publications. National Archives, Washington, D.C.

Fort Laramie. Post Records. Record Group 393. National Archives, Washington, D.C.

Fort Phil Kearny. Endorsements, 1866-68. Records of the United States Continental Commands, 1821-1920. Record Group 393. National Archives, Washington, D.C.

Fort Phil Kearny. Post Records. Record Group 393. National Archives, Washington, D.C.

Fort Phil Kearny/Bozeman Trail Association. *The Dull Knife Symposium.* Sheridan, Wyoming: Fort Phil Kearny/Bozeman Trail Association, 1990.

Fort Phil Kearny State Historic Site Collection. Story, Wyoming.

Fort Reno. Post Returns. Microfilm Publications. National Archives, Washington, D.C.

Gibson, Samuel L. Correspondence, 19 February, 19 September 1924. Gibson-Pitman Letters. Little Bighorn Battlefield National Monument, Crow Agency, Montana.

Gilbert, Hila. *"Big Bat" Pourier.* Sheridan, Wyoming: Mills Company, 1968.

Gilmore, Melvin R. "Notes on Gynecology and Obstetrics of the Arikara Tribe." Michigan Academy of Science, Arts and Letters, *Papers* 14 (1930):71-81.

Glover, Ridgway. Letters to the Editor. *Philadelphia Photographer* 3 (1866); reprinted by Ames: Iowa State University of Science and Technology.

Gordon, David S. Appointment, Commission and Personal File. Records of the Office of the Adjutant General. Record Group 94. National Archives, Washington, D.C.

_______. Correspondence, 2 March 1908. Fort Phil Kearny/Bozeman Trail Association Collection. Wyoming Room, Sheridan County Fulmer Public Library, Sheridan, Wyoming.

Gray, John S. "Blazing the Bridger and Bozeman Trails." *Annals of Wyoming* 49 (Spring 1977):23-51.

_______. *Centennial Campaign: The Sioux War of 1876.* Fort Collins, Colorado: Old Army Press, 1976.

_______. *Custer's Last Campaign: Mitch Boyer and the Little Bighorn Reconstructed.* Lincoln: University of Nebraska Press, 1991.

_______. "A Triple Play." In *The Westerners Brand Book.* Chicago: Westerners Chicago Corral, 1969.

Green, Norma Kidd. *Iron Eyes Family: The Children of Joseph LaFlesche.* Lincoln: Johnson Publishing, 1969.

Greene, Jerome A. *The Hayfield Fight: A Reappraisal of Neglected Action.* Fort Phil Kearny/Bozeman Trail Association Collection, Wyoming Room, Sheridan County Fulmer Public Library, Sheridan, Wyoming.

_______. *Slim Buttes, 1876.* Norman: University of Oklahoma Press, 1982.

Gridley, Marion E. *American Indian Women.* New York: Hawthorne Books, 1974.

Grimes, E. B. "Inspection Report to Chief Quartermaster," 2 December 1867. Department of the Platte. Record Group 98. National Archives, Washington, D.C.

Grinnell, George Bird. "Cheyenne Woman Customs." *American Anthropologist* 4 (January-March 1902):13-16.

_______. *The Fighting Cheyennes.* New York: Charles Scribner's Sons, 1915; reprint edition, Norman: University of Oklahoma Press, 1956.

Grummond, George W. Pension File. Records of the Veterans' Administration. Record Group 15. National Archives, Washington, D.C.

Guthrie, John. "Fetterman Massacre." *Annals of Wyoming* 9 (October 1932):714-718.

Hafen, LeRoy R., editor. *The Mountain Men and the Fur Trade of the Far West: Biographical Sketches of the Participants by Scholars of the Subject and With Introductions by the Editor.* Volume 4. Glendale, California: Arthur H. Clark Company, 1968.

Hafen, Leroy and Hafen, Ann W. *Powder River Campaigns and Sawyers Expedition of 1865.* Glendale, California: Arthur H. Clark Company, 1961.

Hagan, Barry J. "I Never Before Thought Death So Near." *Journal of the Council on Abandoned Military Posts* 10 (Spring 1978).

_______. "More Light on the Adventures of Grant and Graham." *Journal of the Order of the Indian Wars* 2 (Fall 1981).

_______. "Save the Gun at All Hazzerds." *Journal of the Council on Abandoned Military Posts* 10 (Winter 1978-79).

Hagan, Barry J. Collection of Fort Phil Kearny/Bozeman Trail era papers, Wyoming Room, Sheridan County Fulmer Public Library, Sheridan, Wyoming.

Hamersley, Thomas H. S. *Complete Regular Army Register of the United States: For One Hundred Years, 1779-1879.* Baltimore: William K. Boyle, 1880.

Hammond, Dorothy, and Jablow, Alta. *Women: Their Economic Roles in Traditional Societies.* Module in Anthropology, Number 35. Reading, Massachusetts: Addison-Wesley Publishing, 1973.

Handbook of American Indians. Totowa, New Jersey: Rowman and Littlefield, 1975. S.v. "American Horse."

Hartsuff, A. Correspondence, 14 March 1894. Surgeon S. M. Horton's Medical Officer's File. Record Group 94. National Archives, Washington, D.C.

Haymond, Henry. Correspondence, 20 July 1866. Fort Phil Kearny Letters Received. Department of the Platte. Record Group 393. National Archives, Washington, D.C.

Hazen, William B. "Report to Adjutant General," 29 August 1866. Department of the Platte. Record Group 98. National Archives, Washington, D.C.

Hebard, Grace Raymond, and Brininstool, E. A. *The Bozeman Trail: Historical Accounts of the Blazing of the Overland Routes Into the Northwest, and the Fights with Red Cloud's Warriors.* Cleveland: Arthur H. Clark Company, 1922.

Heitman, Francis B. *Historical Register and Dictionary of the United States Army, From its Organization, September 29, 1789 to March 2, 1903.* Washington, D.C.: Government Printing Office, 1903; reprint edition, Urbana: University of Illinois Press, 1965.

Helena (Montana) *Herald,* 15 July 1876.

History of Nebraska. Volume 2. Chicago: Western Historical Company, 1882.

Hoffman, Charles A. In "Brisbin's Report of Indian Frauds Made to General Sheridan." 21 December 1878. Burlingame Collection, Montana State University, Bozeman, Montana.

Hooker, William Francis. *The Bullwhacker: Adventures of a Frontier Freighter.* Lincoln: University of Nebraska Press, 1988.

Horn Cloud, Nancy Red Cloud. Interview, 30 May 1991. Williams Collection, Boulder, Colorado..

Horton, John B. Correspondence, 6 December 1991; 11 February 1992. McDermott Collection, Sheridan, Wyoming.

Horton, Samuel. Correspondence, 26 December 1866; 13 January 1867; 26 March 1867. Fort Phil Kearny Letters Received 1866-68. Department of the Platte. Record Group 393. National Archives, Washington, D.C.

_______. Medical Officer's File. Records of the Adjutant General's Office. Record Group 94. National Archives, Washington, D.C.

_______. Testimony. In "Records of the Special Commission to Investigate the Fetterman Massacre and the State of Indian Affairs, 1867." Bureau of Indian Affairs. Record Group 75. National Archives, Washington, D.C.

Houston, E. Lina. *Early History of Gallatin County.* Bozeman, Montana: Pioneers Society of Gallatin County, 1933.

Howes, Wright. *U.S. IANA (1650-1950): A Selective Bibliography in Which are Described 11,620 Uncommon and Significant Books Relating to the Continental Portion of the United States.* New York: R. R. Bowker for Newberry Library, 1962.

Hyde, George E. *A Sioux Chronicle.* Norman: University of Oklahoma Press, 1956.

_______. *Red Cloud's Folk: A History of the Oglala Sioux Indians.* Norman: University of Oklahoma Press, 1930; reprint edition, Norman: University of Oklahoma Press, 1937.

"Indian Curiosities." Army Medical Museum Catalogue. Records of the Adjutant General's Office, 17802-1917. Record Group 94. National Archives, Washington, D.C.

Irving, Washington. *The Adventures of Captain Bonneville, U.S.A. in the Rocky Mountains and the Far West.* Edited by Edgerly W. Todd. Norman: University of Oklahoma Press, 1961.

Johnson, Dorothy M. *The Bloody Bozeman.* New York: McGraw, 1971.

Jones, Brian. "John Richard, Jr. and the Killing at Fetterman." *Annals of Wyoming* 43 (Fall 1971).

_______. "Those Wild Reshaw Boys." In *Sidelights of the Sioux Wars.* London: The English Westerners Society, 1969.

Keenan, Jerry. *The Wagon Box Fight.* Sheridan, Wyoming: Fort Phil Kearny/Bozeman Trail Association, 1990.

Kinney, John Fitch. Papers. Nebraska State Historical Society, Lincoln, Nebraska.

Knight, Oliver. "Frontier Army-Navy Chaplains." Wyoming Room, Sheridan County Fulmer Public Library, Sheridan, Wyoming.

LaMar, Howard, general editor. *Reader's Encyclopedia of the American West.* New York: Thomas Y. Crowell Company, 1977.

Lawrence (Kansas) *Daily Journal,* 28 October 1901. David White Obituary.

Leeson, Michael A. *Montana Personal History and Reminiscences.* House and Mill, 1885.

Leonard, Elizabeth J. *Buffalo Bill, King of the Old West.* New York: Library Publishers, 1955.

Littmann, Lewis. Correspondence, 30 May 1972. Keenan Collection, Boulder, Colorado.

Littmann, Max. Correspondence, 8 March 1916. Walter M. Camp Collection. Little Bighorn Battlefield National Monument, Crow Agency, Montana.

Lockwood, James D. *Life and Adventures of a Drummer Boy; or Seven Years a Soldier.* Albany, New York: John Skinner, 1893.

Lone Hill, Ethel. Interview, 22 April 1992. White Eyes Collection, Kyle, South Dakota.

McDermott, John D. "Nineteenth Century Military Sites in Fremont County: A Report." Sheridan, Wyoming: John D. McDermott Associates, 1991.

_______. "Price of Arrogance: The Short and Controversial Life of William Judd Fetterman." *Annals of Wyoming* 63 (Spring 1881):42-53.

McFann, Mildred. "The History of Pine Bluffs and Vicinity." Speech for Laramie County Historical Society, Pine Bluffs, Wyoming, November 1965. Hagan Collection. Sheridan County Fulmer Public Library, Sheridan, Wyoming.

McVey, Everett E. *The Crow Scout Who Killed Custer.* Privately printed in Billings, Montana: Reporter Printing and Supply, 1952. Brigham Young University Library, Provo, Utah.

Mallery, Garrick. *Picture-Writing of the American Indians: Tenth Annual Report of the Bureau of American Ethnology, 1888-89.* Washington, D.C.: Government Printing Office; reprint edition, New York: Dover Press, 1972.

Marquis, Thomas B. *Memories of a White Crow Indian: Thomas H. LeForge.* Lincoln: University of Nebraska Press, 1974.

Martin, Charles. "Hernson House Register, 1865-1866." *Nebraska History* 48 (Spring 1967).

Mattes, Merrill J. *Indians, Infants and Infantry: Andrew and Elizabeth Burt on the Frontier.* Denver: Old West Publishing Company, 1960; reprint edition, Lincoln: University of Nebraska Press, 1988.

Millard, C. M. S. Correspondence, 4 September 1866. In the *Leavenworth* (Kansas) *Times,* 20 October 1866.

Miller, David H. *Ghost Dance.* New York: Duell, Sloan and Pearce, 1959.

Montana (Helena) *Post,* March-August, 1867.

Morgan, Dale L., editor. *The West of William H. Ashley: The International Struggle for the Fur Trade of the Missouri, the Rocky Mountains, and the Columbia, with Explorations Beyond the Continental Divide, Recorded in the Diaries and Letters of William H. Ashley and his Contemporaries, 1822-1838.* Denver: Old West Publishing Company, 1964.

Mumey, Nolie. *Wyoming Bullwhacker: Episodes in the Life of James Milton Sherrod.* Denver: Range Press, 1976.

Murphy, William. "The Forgotten Battalion." *Winners of the West,* 30 July 1928.

Murray, Robert A. *The Army on the Powder River.* Bellevue, Nebraska: Old Army Press, 1969; reprint, Fort Collins, Colorado: Old Army Press, 1972.

________. *The Bozeman Trail: Highway of History.* Boulder, Colorado: Pruett Publishing Company, 1988.

________. *Military Posts in the Powder River Country of Wyoming, 1865-1894.* Lincoln: University of Nebraska Press, 1968; reprint edition, Buffalo, Wyoming: The Office, 1990.

National Cyclopedia of American Biography. Ann Arbor, Michigan: University Microfilms, 1967.

New York Times, 16 July 1929; 29 January 1930.

North, Luther. Correspondence, 1923. South Dakota Historical Society, Pierre, South Dakota.

Northrop, Henry Davenport. *Indian Horrors; or Massacres by the Red Men.* Philadelphia: n.d.

Olson, James C. *History of Nebraska.* Lincoln: University of Nebraska Press, 1955.

________. *Red Cloud and the Sioux Problem.* Lincoln: University of Nebraska Press, 1965.

Omaha (Nebraska) *Weekly Herald,* 18 January 1867.

O'Meara, Walters. *Daughters of the Country: The Women of the Fur Traders and Mountain Men.* New York: Harcourt, Brace and World, 1968.

Order of the Indian Wars 1 (Fall 1980).

Ostrander, Alson B. *An Army Boy of the Sixties.* Yonkers, New York: World Book Company, 1924.

________. *The Bozeman Trail Forts Under General Philip St. George Cooke.* Privately published. Casper, Wyoming: Commercial Print Company, 1937.

Palmer, H. E. "History of the Powder River Indian Expedition of 1865." *Nebraska State Historical Society,* 1887.

Parkman, Francis. *The Oregon Trail.* Madison: University of Wisconsin, 1969.

Peterson, Harold L. *Remington Historical Treasury of American Guns.* New York: Thomas Nelson and Sons, n.d.

Phillips, John. Correspondence, 16 May 1867. Records of the Mountain District. Record Group 393. National Archives, Washington, D.C.

Phisterer, Frederick. *New York in the War of the Rebellion, 1861-1865.* Third edition. Albany, New York: J. B. Lyon Company, 1912.

Powell, James. Battle Report, 4 August 1867. Fort Phil Kearny Letters Received. Record Group 94. National Archives, Washington, D.C.

_______. Correspondence, 4 August 1867. Fort Phil Kearny Collection. Wyoming Room, Sheridan County Fulmer Public Library, Sheridan, Wyoming.

_______. Military Records File. National Archives, Washington, D.C.

_______. Pension File. Record Group 15. National Archives, Washington, D.C.

Powell, Peter J. *Sweet Medicine.* Volume 1. Norman: University of Oklahoma, 1969.

Prescott Arizona Courier, 8 April 1973.

Quartermaster Employee Lists, Fort Phil Kearny, 1867.

Railsback, E. O. "The Townsend Trail," *Old Travois Trails,* Powder River Number.

Rawlins (Wyoming) *Times,* December 1922; 17 August 1968.

Raynolds, William Franklin. "Report on the Exploration of the Yellowstone River." Senate Executive Document 77, 40th Cong., 1st (2nd) sess., 1878.

"Records of Events and History of the Eighteenth Regiment of Infantry, 1861 - 1865." Record Group 391. National Archives, Washington, D.C.

"Records of the Special Commission to Investigate the Fetterman Massacre and the State of Indian Affairs, 1867." Bureau of Indian Affairs. Record Group 75. National Archives, Washington, D.C.

"Register of Licenses for the Indian Trade, 1847-73." Bureau of Indian Affairs. Record Group 75. National Archives, Washington D.C.

"Report of the Chief Engineer for 1877." Map accompanying Appendix EE. Report of the Chief of Engineers. Department of the Platte. National Archives, Washington, D.C.

"Report of the Surgical Cases Treated in the Army of the United States from 1865 to 1871." Surgeon General's Office. War Department. Washington, D.C.: Government Printing Office, 1871.

Richard, John. Biographical information. Fort Laramie National Historic Site, Fort Laramie, Wyoming.

Ricker, Eli Seavey. Papers. Nebraska State Historical Society, Lincoln, Nebraska.

Rosa, Joseph G., and Rosa, Robin May. *Buffalo Bill and His Wild West.* Lawrence: University Press of Kansas, 1989.

Sand Creek Massacre: A Documentary History. New York: Sol Lewis, 1973.

Sandoz, Mari. *Cheyenne Autumn.* New York: McGraw-Hill, 1952.

Schmitt, Martin F., editor. *General George Crook, His Autobiography.* Norman: University of Oklahoma Press, 1946.

Scott, Douglas; Conner, Melissa; and Snow, Clyde. *Nameless Faces of Custer Battlefield: Greasy Grass.* Custer Battlefield Historical and Museum Association, 1988.

Scott, Leslee M. "Indian Women as Food Providers and Tribal Counselors." *Oregon Historical Quarterly* 42 (1941):208-19.

Secrest, William B. "I Buried Hickock." Hagan Collection. Wyoming Room, Sheridan County Fulmer Public Library, Sheridan, Wyoming.

Seymour, Flora Warren. *Women of Trail and Wigwam.* New York: Woman's Press, 1930.

Sheridan (Wyoming) *Post,* 22 April 1923.

Sheridan (Wyoming) *Press,* 1985."Post Return Wrappers."

Simonen, Louis Laurent. *The Rocky Mountain West in 1867.* Lincoln: University of Nebraska Press, 1966.

Slusser, Lew. Medical Report, 1 October 1864. Record Group 94. National Archives, Washington, D.C.

Sneve, Virginia Driving Hawk. *They Led a Nation.* Sioux Falls, South Dakota: Brevet Press, 1975.

Stands-In-Timber, John, and Liberty, Margot. *Cheyenne Memories.* Norman: University of Oklahoma Press, 1967.

Story, Malcolm. Correspondence, 27 January 1986. Fort Phil Kearny/ Bozeman Trail Association Collection. Wyoming Room, Sheridan County Fulmer Public Library, Sheridan, Wyoming.

Story, Peter. Correspondence, 5 February 1991. Fort Phil Kearny/ Bozeman Trail Association Collection. Wyoming Room, Sheridan County Fulmer Public Library, Sheridan, Wyoming.

Stover, Earl F. *Up From Handy Men: The United States Army Chaplaincy, 1865-1920.* Volume 3. Washington, D.C.: Office of Chief Chaplain, Department of the Army, 1977.

Straight, Michael. *Carrington.* New York: Knopf, 1960.

_______. "The Strange Testimony of Major Powell." In *The Westerners New York Posse Brand Book.* Volume 7. Westerners New York Posse, 1960.

Stuart, Granville. *Forty Years on the Frontier, as Seen in the Journals and Reminiscences of Granville Stuart: Gold-miner, Trader, Merchant, Rancher and Politician.* Edited by Paul C. Phillips. Cleveland: Arthur H. Clark Company, 1925; reprint edition, 1957.

_______. "The Yellowstone Expedition of 1863." *Contributions to the Montana Historical Society* 1 (1976):186-88.

_______. *Pioneering in Montana.* Lincoln: University of Nebraska Press, 1977.

Taft, Robert. *Photography and the American Scene.* New York: Dover Publications, 1938.

Templeton, George M. Appointment, Commission and Personal File. Records of the Adjutant General's Office. Record Group 94. National Archives, Washington, D.C.

_______. Diaries. Everett Graff Collection. Newberry Library, Chicago, Illinois.

Ten Eyck, Martha. Pension Records. National Archives, Washington, D.C.

Ten Eyck, Tenodor. Diaries. Special Collections Library, University of Arizona, Tucson, Arizona.

_______. Court Martial Case Files, Records of the Judge Advocate General. Record Group 153. National Archives, Washington, D.C.

Thackery, Lorna. "Experts Trace Facial Bones to Custer Interpreter." *Billings* (Montana) *Gazette,* 26 October 1986.

Thane, Eric. *Montana High, Wide and Handsome.* New Haven, Connecticut: Yale University Press, 1959; reprint edition, Lincoln: University of Nebraska Press, 1983.

Thomas, W. W. Diary. Printed in *Daily Leavenworth Times*, 20 October 1866.

Thrapp, Dan L. *Encyclopedia of Frontier Biography.* Volume 1. Glendale, California: Arthur H. Clark Company, 1988.

________. *Vengeance! The Saga of Poor Tom Cover.* El Segundo, California: Upton & Sons, 1989.

Time-Life Books. *The Indians.* Time Life Series on The Old West. New York: Time-Life Books, 1973.

Toledo (Ohio) *Blade,* 31 December 1866.

Topping, E. S. *The Chronicles of the Yellowstone.* Minneapolis: Ross and Haines, 1968.

"Trails of Yesterday." *Nebraska History,* July-September 1921.

U.S. Bureau of Ethnology. "Pictographs of North American Indians." In *Fourth Annual Report.* Washington, D.C.: Government Printing Office, 1886.

U.S. Congress. "Inspection by Generals Rusling and Hazen." Executive Document 45, 39th Cong., 2nd sess., 1866.

________, Senate. *Annual Report of the Commissioner of Indian Affairs.* Executive Document 5, 51st Cong., 1st sess., 1890.

________, Senate. *Indian Operations on the Plains.* Executive Document 33, 50th Cong., 1st sess., 1887.

U.S. Weather Bureau. *Climatological Records, 1819-1892.* National Archives, Washington, D.C.

Utley, Robert M. *Frontier Regulars: The United States Army and the Indian, 1866-1890.* New York: Macmillan, 1973.

Vaugh, J. W., and Bishop, L. C. "The Heck Reel Wagon Burning." *Lingle* (Wyoming) *Guide Review,* 3 and 10 April 1958.

Vaughan, J. W. *Indian Fights: New Facts on Seven Encounters.* Norman: University of Oklahoma Press, 1966.

Vestal, Stanley. *Jim Bridger, Mountain Man.* Lincoln: University of Nebraska Press, 1970.

Viola, Herman J. *Exploring the West.* Washington, D.C.: Smithsonian Books, 1987.

Wagner, Henry R., and Camp, Charles L. *The Plains and the Rockies: A Critical Bibliography of Exploration, Adventure and Travel in the American West, 1800-1865.* San Francisco: John Howell Books, 1982.

Walker, Henry Pickering. *The Wagonmasters: High Plains Freighting to 1880.* Norman: University of Oklahoma, 1966.

Warner, Ezra J. *Generals in Blue.* Baton Rouge: Louisiana State University, 1964.

Washington (Pennsylvania) *Reporter,* 11 May 1870.

Watson, Elmo Scott. "The Bravery of Our Bugler is Much Spoken Of." *Old Travois Trails* 1 (1941).

_______. "The Indian Wars and the Press, 1866-1867." *Journalism Quarterly* 17 (December 1940).

_______. "Photographing the Frontier." In *The English Westerners Brand Book.* Volume 8. London: English Westerners, 1966.

_______. "Shadow-Catchers of the Red Man." In *The Westerners 1950 Brand Book.* Volume 6. Denver, Colorado: The University of Denver Press, 1951.

Weist, Katherine M. "Plains Indian Women: An Assessment." In *Anthropology on the Great Plains,* pp. 255-71. Edited by W. Raymond Wood and Margot Liberty. Lincoln: University of Nebraska Press, 1980.

Weist, Tom. *A History of the Cheyenne People.* Billings: Eastern Montana College, n.d.

Werner, Fred H. *The Dull Knife Battle: Doomsday for the Northern Cheyenne.* Greeley, Colorado: Werner Publications, 1981.

White, David. Correspondence. Fort Phil Kearny/Bozeman Trail Association Collection. Sheridan County Fulmer Public Library, Sheridan, Wyoming.

_______. Diary. Verde State Park, Camp Verde, Arizona.

_______. "In Memorium." Military Order of the Loyal Legion of the United States. National Archives, Washington, D.C.

_______. Personnel File. Records of the Office of the Adjutant General. Record Group 98. National Archives, Washington, D.C.

Willson, Davis. Diary, 1866. Special Collections Library, Montana State University, Bozeman, Montana.

Wilson, Elinor. *Jim Beckwourth: Black Mountain Man and War Chief of the Crows.* Norman: University of Oklahoma Press, 1972.

Wolf, Helen Pease. *Reaching Both Ways.* Laramie, Wyoming: Jelm Mountain Publications, 1989.

Dec 21, 1866

12-21-1866

Fetterman
Massacre

~1876 Little Big Horn

/

Wagon Box Fight

Hayfield Fight

/ Slimly Fight

Brevet?